THE HORROR OF POLICE

THE HORROR OF POLICE

TRAVIS LINNEMANN

University of Minnesota Press
Minneapolis | London

Portions of chapter 1 were originally published as "Bad Cops and True Detectives: The Horror of Police and the Unthinkable World," *Theoretical Criminology* 23, no. 3 (2019): 355–74. DOI: 10.1177/1362480617737761.

Published by the University of Minnesota Press
111 Third Avenue South, Suite 290
Minneapolis, MN 55401-2520
http://www.upress.umn.edu

ISBN 978-1-5179-0591-0 (hc)
ISBN 978-1-5179-0592-7 (pb)

Library of Congress record available at https://lccn.loc.gov/2021062904

Printed in the United States of America on acid-free paper

The University of Minnesota is an equal-opportunity educator and employer.

28 27 26 25 24 23 22   10 9 8 7 6 5 4 3 2 1

Any real change implies the breakup of the world as one has always known it, the loss of all that gave one an identity, the end of safety. And at such a moment, unable to see and not daring to imagine what the future will now bring forth, one clings to what one knew, or thought one knew; to what one possessed or dreamed that one possessed.

—James Baldwin (1956)

CONTENTS

Introduction: Police Story, Horror Story   1

CHAPTER 1
Bad Cops and True Detectives   33

CHAPTER 2
The Police at the End of the World,   61
or The Political Theology of the Thin Blue Line

CHAPTER 3
RoboCop, or Modern Prometheus   109

CHAPTER 4
Monsters Are Real   155

CHAPTER 5
The Unthinkable World   195

Acknowledgments   221
Notes   223
Index   263

INTRODUCTION

Police Story, Horror Story

Hell is truth seen too late.

—Unknown

The Haunting of Hill House, one of Shirley Jackson's best-known and most beloved works, begins with a sentence placed by some among horror fiction's finest: "No live organism can continue for long to exist sanely under conditions of absolute reality; even larks and katydids are supposed, by some, to dream."[1] With this simple, foreboding line Jackson breezes past the schlock of blood and gore, nudging her readers toward the edge of an unthinkable abyss. Without the sheltering provisions of dreams, illusions, and self-spun fictions, she warns, the actual conditions of this world would surely deliver all living things to madness.

Dread and menace sitting just behind the familiar: this is the place from which horror fiction begins. Bloodcurdling revelation, the genre's remuneration. Who could have known that the missing and murdered were taken by a man turned wolf by moonlight? Who would have admitted the peculiar lord fed on the actual blood of the poor? A black screen on which to project our innermost fears, the genre, like the impenetrable night, is home to monsters of all kinds. But the cause of our dread, as Jackson's exquisite sentence reminds, is not only the monsters that inhabit the unknown night but the unknown itself, the creeping suspicion that the world and our place within it are not as certain as they seem. In this space between *what appears* and *what is*, as Tariq Goddard and Eugene Thacker caution, lies horror.[2] While this book is no work of fiction, a step into this strange liminality initiates it as well.

In 1988, the prolific American director John Carpenter released his eleventh theatrical film, *They Live*. Part science fiction, part horror, the film imagines a dystopian future Los Angeles—not unlike the present one—where obscene inequality and class division are managed by a twinning of ideology and open violence. Wandering into town looking for work, the film's protagonist, a Joadian drifter named John Nada, passes a street preacher who casts a menacing tone:

> They use their tongues to deceive you.
> Venom is on their lips.
> Their mouths are full of bitterness and curses.
> The fear of God is not before their eyes.
> They have taken the hearts and minds of our leaders.
> They have blinded us to the truth.
> Our human spirit is corrupted.
> Why do we worship greed?
> Outside the limit of our sight they're feeding off us.
> Perched on top of us from birth to death are our owners.
> They have us. They control us.
> They are our masters.
> Wake up.
> They're all around you.

Joining a band of rebels wise to the sinister workings beneath the city's slick veneer, Nada does indeed wake up. He dons glasses that interrupt a mesmerizing signal and sees for the first time the enemy who has enslaved humankind with the skill and precision of Madison Avenue. Like the subliminal ads that urge moviegoers to "Drink Coca-Cola" and "Eat Popcorn," the glasses reveal commands to "Obey" and "Consume" behind the ordinary texts of billboards and commercials. On the street, Nada confronts the grotesque faces of alien invaders cloaked behind the figment humanity of cops and the business class.

As is the wont of Hollywood films, Nada and the rebels win out and, by unmasking the monsters that surround them, move their kind nearer to a truer, albeit horrifying, reality. Decades on, the

LAPD officer in *They Live.*

film's satirical take on the gross self-interest of the Reagan era re-mains a popular device with which to illustrate the critique of ideol-ogy, showing as it does the shackles of false consciousness slipped by revolutionary ideas and action.

We begin here not only to prefigure the thematic horror evi-dent in the book's title but to introduce its central premise. Taking Jackson's and Carpenter's cues, from the whimsical and even puerile pages and films of popular horror we draw a dead-serious question:

What is hidden from view—or rather, what provisions have we made to shelter our own minds from that which is too terrifying to confront? Fit to the perennial problems of police, this question hints at horrifying answers indeed. What horrifying reality have we placed beyond the limits of our own sight? From what terrible truth do we retreat?

Peering through this refracted motif, *The Horror of Police* purposely misreads our vernacular police stories—television, film, literature, news media reportage, government reports, academic literature, the words and deeds of police themselves—not as comforting tales of innocence avenged and order restored but as *horror*. And from that, dear reader, I begin by asking you to consider the menace hiding behind this familiar world of ours. If we are able to make this great leap together, it becomes possible, perhaps certain, that we will find monsters in our midst.

Cook 'em, Danno

In late October 2012, a six-year veteran of the New York City Police Department, Gilberto Valle, was arrested by the FBI and later charged in New York's Southern District Court with conspiracy to kidnap and improper access of the National Crime Information Center database. While the charges were serious, what gave this previously anonymous cop his proverbial fifteen minutes was prosecutors also alleging he had shared plans to kidnap, rape, torture, kill, cook, and eat women with members of several online fetish communities. Officer Valle came to the attention of the FBI after his young wife, suspecting an affair, installed spyware on their shared computer and uncovered a trove of shocking material, including images of sexual torture; chat logs from the website Darkfetishnet.com detailing his plans; online searches for "how to tie someone up," "how to make chloroform," and "how to prepare human meat"; profiles of nearly one hundred potential victims; and a veritable blueprint mapping the machinations of the self-described aspiring "professional kidnapper."[3] In one of the many conversations discovered by his wife, Officer Valle, writing under the handle *girlmeathunter*—note Valle is a self-described hunter, which, as we will soon see, is an identity and power essential to police—delighted in an unsuspecting target's fate:

I was thinking of tying her body onto some kind of apparatus . . . cook her over low heat, keep her alive as long as possible . . . I love that she is asleep right now not having the slightest clue of what we have planned. Her days are numbered. I'm glad you're on board. She does look tasty doesn't she?[4]

Unsurprisingly the U.S. news media, particularly the shameless outfits like the *New York Post* and *NY Daily News*, seized on the story, naming Valle the "Cannibal Cop" under real headlines like "Meat mom says son is no cannibal" and parody ones like "Cook 'em, Danno."[5] At his criminal trial, Valle's attorney, Julia Gatto, took his alleged crimes head-on, telling jurors that she couldn't blame them for being horrified that "what turns Gil Valle on is the idea of a woman oiled, bound, laid out on a platter with an apple in her mouth" and admitting that his fantasies were, indeed, "the stuff that horror movies are made of."[6] Gatto was, however, also quick to add that Valle's desires matched the blood and gore of campy horror films in another important way: they were, she said, "pure fiction, pretend, scary make-believe."[7]

While the "thought crimes" of Gilberto Valle raised important questions concerning privacy, distinctions between fantasy and reality, and the limits of the state's jurisdiction, my interest lies in the outrage, shock, and horror engendered by the hidden fantasy life of one of "New York's Finest." As one onlooker remarked, "the fact that this guy was a cop makes it especially disturbing. Here it is, a guy in uniform and someone who is to be the good guy. Behind those [sic] facade, he could be using his access to stalk any potential victims. The thoughts are just too scary."[8] In order to make his case, the state's prosecutor also zeroed in on the contradictions between Valle's "scary thoughts" and his chosen profession, condemning the man for betraying his solemn oath to the community:

There is a thin piece of metal that some members of our community are privileged to wear close to their heart. Some call it a shield. You may know it as a police badge, and it is the mark of an individual sworn to protect other members of the community . . . What you are going to learn during this trial is that

Officer Valle chose to *desecrate the trust that his community had placed in him.*[9]

Although the presiding judge, too, later took issue with the preju-dicial influence of Valle's employment, even he could not help but introduce the issue of "desecrated trust" in his early remarks, call-ing Valle's behavior "depraved, bizarre, aberrational and, as of now, entirely unexplained, particularly for someone who is a law-enforcement officer."[10] Yet given the rather long and growing list of killers who, by day, worked in some policing or law enforcement ca-pacity, to say nothing of the routine misdeeds of police, shouldn't we temper our collective shock at the notion of "desecrated trust"?[11] A history of bad men almost as long as the history of policing itself—the Florida cop Gerard John Schaefer, who may have murdered as many as thirty people; the Kansas serial killer Dennis Rader (BTK), who had a criminal justice degree and worked in civil code enforce-ment; the recently discovered "Golden State Killer," Joseph James DeAngelo, who also worked as a cop while committing multiple rapes and murders—confirms the idea that we should not, perhaps cannot trust the boys in blue.

Scary Thoughts

Like his murderous brethren, Valle did not simply desecrate the sanctity of the law and violate the community's trust. Gathering the sexual sadism of Ted Bundy and the cannibalism of Jeffrey Dahmer under the edifice of the policeman's badge, the "Cannibal Cop" stands as a uniquely potent monster figure, symbol of not only squandered trust but the collapse of liberalism's civilizing force par excellence—the police. While his repulsive fantasies do indeed place him in notorious company, my suspicion is that had Valle not been a cop, he would likely have not registered a blip on the cultural radar, instead being dismissed as yet another "internet pervert." In his summation, the prosecutor suggested just this, stating, "There is nothing about Mr. Valle that is special. At bottom he is a dirty cop. It is something we've seen a million times." Yet it is precisely because he "desecrated the public's trust" that this "dirty [cannibal] cop" re-mains fodder for tabloid media, true crime novels, television crime dramas, and documentary films, offering a grim warning of the horrors that inhabit our friends and neighbors, even those men licensed to "protect and serve."

For some insight into the outrage and disgust engendered by bad cops, even "cannibal cops" like Valle, we should revisit Julia Kristeva's influential *Powers of Horror*. As she famously proposes, horror emerges from encounters with the abject, those revolting things that expose and explode the presumed boundaries of identity and normality.[12] Cannibalism, even the fantasy cannibalism of Gilberto Valle, certainly fits Kristeva's understanding of the horror-inducing abject. Like a child who murders another child—a crime that crosses boundaries of capability and culpability—Valle's vicious fantasies, or even the mundane transgressions of a cop on the take, might be considered "doubly abject" as they shatter the limits of law and the strictures and expectations of the police, which for so many stand in for the social order itself. So while it is true that the Cannibal Cop, an abject chimera of cop/criminal, invokes a revolting sense of horror, as I will suggest in pages to follow, the bad cop, however abject, reveals an important contradiction and gap in the concept of police and its place within liberal social order. We are therefore obliged to ask: Just how abject are the crimes of police if they are actually "something we've seen a million times"? And then, if the figure of the bad cop is not horrific in and of itself, from where, if at all, does *the horror* emerge?

Toward untangling these and other questions, Eugene Thacker's *Horror of Philosophy* trilogy provides a useful framework of understanding. Employing horror fiction as an instrument to reveal contradictions, fault lines, and gaps in the ways we humans see the world, Thacker helps link the notion of violated trust to broader questions of ontology and symbolic order. He writes:

> The presumption of a consensual reality in which a set of natural laws govern the working of the world, the question of the reliability of the senses, the unstable relationships between the faculties of the imagination and reason, and the discrepancy between our everyday understanding of the world and the often obscure and counterintuitive descriptions provided by philosophy and the sciences. The fork in the road is not simply

between something existing or not existing, it is a wavering between two types of radical uncertainty: either demons do not
exist, but then my own senses are unreliable, or demons do
exist, but then the world is not as I thought it was. With the
fantastic—as with the horror genre itself—one is caught between two abysses, neither of which are comforting or particularly reassuring. *Either I do not know the world, or I do not know
myself.*[13]

For Thacker, the utility of horror, particularly the supernatural and
cosmic varieties of Edgar Allan Poe, Ambrose Bierce, and Howard
Phillips Lovecraft, lies in its ability to reveal antagonisms between
two ontological poles: *what I know of the world* and *what I know of
myself.* Put differently, at the genre's center are the questions *Do I
trust what I believe of the world? Or do I trust what I see of it?* This is
not simply the search for an empirical reality, something existing or
not existing, but an exercise that reveals the limits of human reason
and the boundaries of the *unthinkable*, the point at which our systems for making sense of the world fall apart. In the first lines of
volume 1 of this series, *In the Dust of This Planet*, he explains:

> The world is increasingly unthinkable—a world of planetary
> disasters, emerging pandemics, tectonic shifts, strange weather,
> oil-drenched seascapes, and the furtive always-looming threat
> of extinction. In spite of our daily concerns, wants, and desires,
> it is increasingly difficult to comprehend the world in which we
> live and of which we are a part. To confront this idea is to con-
> front an absolute limit to our ability to adequately understand
> the world at all—an idea that has been a central motif of the
> horror genre for some time.[14]

The enduring trope of horror fiction—the confrontation with the
unthinkable—Thacker transforms into a political exercise. Conspicuously absent from his inventory of the unthinkable, however, are the
killings, riots, and flames that interrupt our lives with increasing frequency. And so, to this unsettled world of looming disaster let us
add the police—the violence of the world made flesh[15]—and again
ask, *Do I trust what I believe of the world? Or do I trust what I see of it?*

Trust Us

Since the 2014 killing of Michael Brown by Ferguson, Missouri, cop Darren Wilson, similar killings have followed one after the other in a widely publicized and seemingly unending parade of state-sponsored violence and death. In the wake of Brown's killing, the most high-profile group to intervene, or at least the most highly placed, was the President's Task Force on Twenty-First Century Policing. Convened by President Obama in December 2014, the "blue-ribbon panel" of academics, police administrators, and activists submitted its final report to the president in May 2015, apparently resolving the eternal dysfunctions of police in just under six months. Of course, a chief area of concern—in fact, the first word of the panel's final report—was *trust.*

> Trust between law enforcement agencies and the people they protect and serve is essential in a democracy. It is key to the stability of our communities, the integrity of our criminal justice system, and the safe and effective delivery of policing services. Building trust and nurturing legitimacy on both sides of the police/citizen divide is the foundational principle underlying the nature of relations between law enforcement agencies and the communities they serve. Decades of research and practice support the premise that people are more likely to obey the law when they believe that those who are enforcing it have authority that is perceived as legitimate by those subject to the authority. The public confers legitimacy only on those whom they believe are acting in procedurally just ways. In addition, law enforcement cannot build community trust if it is seen as an occupying force coming in from outside to impose control on the community.[16]

Clearly, for the panel, compliance with and trust in the police was the important first step in reaffirming the consensual reality and symbolic order upon which community stability, institutional integrity, and democracy are thought to rest. Read cynically and alongside U.S. policing's history of crisis and reform, pleas of trust take on an entirely different tone. As if reciting the penance of the abuser, the report might just as well read: These killings were accidental, trust us. They will never happen again, trust us. You're not a cop, you can't understand, trust us.[17] Yet if we remain faithful to the abiding lessons of horror, we are obliged to ask: What if things are precisely as they appear? What if we saw what we saw?

Of course, policing's current crisis did not begin in 2014, 1914, or even 1814. Contrary to textbook accounts that mark the birth of the uniformed police in 1829 with Sir Robert Peel and the London Metropolitan Police Service and then in Boston nine years later, this history and, hence, the first demonic whispers of this book begin much earlier.[18] As feudalism collapsed across Europe, industrial capitalism rose in its stead, rising with it the police power as the primary means to transform once idle, free, and "masterless" men into proper working-class subjects bound to a new system of private property and wage labor.[19] Forced from subsistence on common lands by enclosure, the poor soon found themselves subject to the earliest incarnations of the police power, the "bloody legislations" of vagrancy laws that criminalized begging, charity, and the refusal of labor, among other things.[20] The masterless are harassed and corralled into the workhouses and "dark satanic mills" of capital, and it is here that a new political subjectivity is hammered into crude form.[21] As Mark Neocleous explains:

> The translation of "common rights" into "private property" required stamping out the customary practices around which such rights were organized such that what was once a custom became an illegality. This process, which was crucial in consolidating the wage form, took place through an operation of the police power on a massive scale. Indeed, the consolidation of the wage form and the development of the police power went hand in hand.[22]

A great leap in political consciousness begins when one abandons the notion that police exist to fight this abstraction we call crime. But by recognizing the police power as the primary instrument—through the monopoly on legitimate violence—by which states produce and uphold market relations and property rights, another even more harrowing leap in understanding is demanded. By tracing the power to shape, shackle, and in fact end the lives of others rather than the institutional form named "police," we draw a thick red line from the earliest vagrancy laws in England to the plantation and slave economy of the British colonies and later United States. It is here—more than a hundred years before police departments sprang up in Boston, New York, and Chicago—that we find the slave patrol, the police power made manifest not only to ensure the property rights of wealthy men but to produce and maintain new social distinctions drawn by race.[23]

Capitalism, it is said, is never not racial.[24] It is a system of wealth extraction and accumulation that functions by assigning differential value to human life and labor.[25] Any correct and properly critical theory of U.S. police, as Ben Brucato urges, must therefore take into account the ways that the police power is implicated in constituting racialized class formation and, indeed, race itself.[26] While there were initially no formal bases of racial distinction in the colonies, as landowners became increasingly outnumbered by African slaves, Maroon encampments, and hostile natives, fears of violent insurrection grew, and so, alongside the militia that pointed outward, they instituted a number of laws and practices meant to reproduce the internal order of the plantation economy.[27] As historian Robin D. G. Kelley describes:

> Unable to stop white servants and Africans from running away together, finding refuge in the swamps, hills, and among Native peoples, the landowning classes decided to free white servants and turn them into small property owners, proletarian citizens, and/or slave patrollers invested in the white Republic and the dream of attaining wealth and power for themselves.[28]

Seduced by the fantasy of transcending the station of their birth, poor Europeans, many of whom were bondsmen themselves, committed to this new order and set about policing what W. E. B. Du Bois later famously named the color line. In 1690, for instance, South Carolina passed the Act for Better Ordering Slaves, under which it became the duty of all European Christians to take part in the surveillance, harassment, and punishment of enslaved Black people, transforming the entire white population into "a community police force," in historian Sally Hadden's words.[29] Armed and on horseback, often riding in groups called "beat companies" (from which the police beat draws its name),[30] patrollers monitored public roads, stopped and questioned any Black person they encountered outside of their master's property, entered any property they thought might hold a fugitive slave, and claimed as contraband any property (food, weapons, books) that might indicate or encourage insubordination or escape.[31]

While it made itself known through this sort of incessant surveillance and inspection, the core of the patroller's authority was, of course, straightforward violence. And though poor whites who crossed the color line, fraternizing with or aiding upstart slaves, sometimes fell under their lash, it was always from Black skin that the patrollers drew the most blood. One seventeenth-century Virginia law held that Black and Native people adjudged guilty of petty crimes were to be stripped naked and whipped, while the very same law provided white servants the protection and dignity of clothing.[32] All of this was undertaken not simply as a crude plan to divide and conquer but as the continuation and rather logical development of an already existing system. "Police function to produce race, a category essential to the workings of the state-market under racial capitalism," writes historian Micol Seigel.[33] Across the southern colonies and states up to the end of the Civil War, the color line was policed by the slave patrol, making real the distinctions between white and Black, free and unfree, citizen and savage. It is through the everyday enforcement of these bloody divisions—administered in the interests of capital—that whiteness and the police power calcified together in violent opposition to Blackness.[34]

This brief and admittedly incomplete history does not end here. Ostensibly abolished during Reconstruction, the slave patrol was reborn as the Ku Klux Klan, carrying the mantle of organized terrorism and anti-Blackness into the new century. While the Klan operated under hoods and the cover of darkness, the color line was policed out in the open daylight by whites and the police forces that sprang up across the South to enforce the rising Jim Crow order and in the north to undermine organized labor.

From "bobbies" to "paddy rollers," Nathan Bedford Forrest to Bull Connor, beneath it all a fearsome, shape-shifting monster moving across centuries and continents: the police power. As the historian Walter Johnson adds, "from the slave trade and the Indian wars and down to the murder of Michael Brown and the Ferguson uprising . . . racial capitalism: the intertwined history of white supremacist ideology and the practices of empire, extraction and exploitation. Dynamic, unstable, ever-changing and world-making."[35] Since their twinned, cursed birth, the police power and racial capitalism have helped to bring this world with all its suffering and injustice into being. For many, this is an eye-rolling statement of the obvious. For many more, it might just as soon provoke an audible scoff. The latter, I contend, might help map the boundaries of a mode of understanding so horrifying that it imperils the very *worlds* we each inhabit.

Makers and Destroyers of Worlds

Setting out the first of three ontological positions, Thacker asks us to confront the human-centered world in which we live, what he calls the *world-for-us*. This *world*—always seen through human eyes—is an ontological prison of sorts, nearly impossible to escape, as it is we humans who think it. The world-for-us is one of subjective order, inseparable from, in fact made by, its economies, institutions, and police. While it is fundamentally subjective, it is necessary to add that in my application, Thacker's world-for-us is always a contingent, uneven world for *some of us*.

Where the police power is necessary to produce and sustain a supposedly civilized world of mass consumption and brutal privation, the limitations, failures, and absence of police reveal horizons of disorder, chaos, and anarchy—what Thacker calls the *world-in-itself*. This is an objective state of nature, one beyond the reach of human interference, or the world that returns following it. As we will see in chapters to follow, in order to glimpse the looming arrival or return of the world-in-itself, one need only consider a few of the many contemporary texts taking up disaster, the apocalyptic and dystopian. In Cormac McCarthy's novel *The Road*, for instance, the lawless violence of the postapocalyptic landscape can be read as precisely the inverse of the world-for-us. In the graphic novels and subsequent television series *The Walking Dead*, the struggle to reestablish social order amid hordes of rapacious "biters" is led by Rick Grimes, who before the fall worked as a small-town cop. Grimes, who commands and polices his fellow survivors and uses violence indiscriminately to ensure their survival, thereby reminds, not so subtly, that the violence and coercion of the police is essential to the reproduction or resuscitation of civilization. Yet even the apocalyptic imaginary, with its speculative attempts to imagine the (dis)orders that follow this one, still bears the weight of Cartesian subjectivity, as these stories rarely attend to the earth's objective qualities and instead attempt to imagine human experience after human civilization as we know it has ended. These desperate attempts to cling to this *world*, even while imagining its destruction, illustrate quite powerfully the difficulty of thinking outside the subject and subjective experience.

Irrevocably tied to the ontology of the world-for-us and at the center of the ceaseless struggle between order and chaos, the police power is indispensable. It is the force that brings this world into being, transforming once "masterless men" into proper political, hence civilized, human subjects. Still, if there is one fact that I suspect haunts the minds of even their most earnest supporters, it is this: the police offer no real protection and uphold the miseries of the present social order with coercion, violence, and murder. This is the unassailable limit of the police project—the horizon of its own possibility—the horror of police.

In his accounting of the vocabulary of horror, critic John Clute uses *vastation*—a traumatizing moment of revelation floating somewhere between terror and horror—to describe the moment of sober recognition when the cause of our fear is at last realized. Clute's understanding of this space is indebted to Ann Radcliffe, who, nearly two centuries before, wrote that whereas terror "expands the soul, and awakens the faculties to a higher degree of life," horror "contracts, freezes, and nearly annihilates them."[36] Fueled by the fear of the unknown, terror becomes horror when we glimpse "the atrocity of the thing itself." In this frozen moment, all previous systems of thought and extant forms of understanding are outmoded, *laid to waste* by the harrowing confrontation with a reality too abject, too revolting to have been previously contemplated.[37] This is perhaps what Jacques Derrida meant when he explained that the monster "simply, shows itself [elle se montre]—that is what the word monster means—it shows itself in something that is not yet shown and that therefore looks like a hallucination, it strikes the eye, it frightens precisely because no anticipation had prepared one to identify this figure."[38] It follows, then, that the whole point of horror as an artistic, aesthetic, and affective exercise is to find, face, and, often, make and name the monster.[39]

Fit to our pursuits, then, the horror that resides in the heart of the police is not merely born of the monstrous deeds of the bad cop, "something we've seen a million times." In an instant, as if donning glasses allowing us to see that which we could not or refused to see before, those we license to "protect and serve" become something more sinister, violent agents of a violent order. Here, between what appears and what is, the realization "you saw what you saw,"—the face of the monster is, in fact, the face of the police.

Monsters with Badges

In a July 1968 *Time* magazine cover feature titled "'The Police and the Ghetto," Tom Reddin, who followed the notorious William Parker as LAPD chief, is held up as an example of the promise of progressive police reform, described as the nation's only "top cop" with "mildly intellectual pursuits" and the foresight to enlist "psychiatrists" to bolster his police community relations program. The piece credits Reddin with modernizing Parker's "crusty authoritarianism" and being able to understand "the new problems caused by the postwar influx of Mexican-Americans and Negroes."[40] Of course, Reddin's subsequent performance and the ongoing legacy of the LAPD prove the feature's faith in a courageous reformer misguided, if not purposefully misleading.

Harmlessly tucked into the glowing puff piece is a brief description of the LAPD's nascent "Policeman Bill" program, a prototypical community policing (and therefore counterinsurgency) initiative intended to repair the torn relationship between the LAPD and the Black community, aiming specifically to pacify Black children. Under the heading "Monsters with Badges," the magazine tells how the department had designated fourteen "Policeman Bill" officers and assigned them to the first, second, and third grades of select "ghetto" schools: "It all sounds a little cloying," the article continues. "Even so, before one 'Policeman Bill's' visit, a survey showed, *ghetto children portrayed cops as monsters with whips and flashing silver badges.*

After he left, they scrawled kindly father figures. To woo teenagers, almost always the trouble makers in ghetto disturbances, the
L.A.P.D. has experimentally hired twelve youths for help on such
minor but ticklish assignments as mediating family disputes. The
program so far has shown encouraging signs of success." (Emphasis
mine.) Not only aligning with the theoretical and conceptual discus-
sions to follow, the tagline "Monsters with Badges" marks an important distinction in the ontological cleavage set out above. While
I will argue the horror of police resides in the fact that their monstrosity is rarely recognized as such, I do not in any way wish to suggest that the police are universally viewed in the same ways by all
people. Many among us—most of all the poor, people of color, and
so-called "ghetto children"—know all too well policing's true face.
As Matt Ruff, author of *Lovecraft Country*, put it, "when you're black
in America, there's always a monster. Sometimes it's Lovecraftian
Elder Gods; sometimes it's the police or the Klan, or the Register of
Voters."[41]

Appearing on a television program in 1963, the ever-prophetic
James Baldwin seemed to anticipate this horror. In Lorraine
Hansberry's famous meeting with Robert Kennedy in which she
begged for the administration's "moral commitment" to support
the burgeoning civil rights movement and to end the open violence
against Black people, Hansberry is said to have warned Kennedy
of the dire "state of the civilization which produced that photograph of the white cop standing on that Negro woman's neck in
Birmingham." Baldwin, too, remarked that he was terrified by the
moral apathy of white people who had "deluded themselves for so
long that they don't really think I am human." Repulsed by pictures
of police dogs sicced on protestors, Baldwin named the police, their
enablers, and, for their unwillingness to intervene, the Kennedys
themselves *"moral monsters."*[42]

Monsters by definition are abject; their unnatural bodies and
behaviors transgress and thus reveal and reaffirm the categorical
boundaries of natural order.[43] The power to identify and name the
monster, as well as to conceal one's own monstrosity, is a potent—
perhaps the ultimate—political act. There is, then, much to learn of
a political and social order by studying its monsters, as they map the
bleeding edge of human understanding and powerfully organize and

coalesce political power.[44] Consider, briefly, the Black Panthers' rationale for choosing to engineer *pig* as a subversive epithet for police. As Huey P. Newton explains in *Revolutionary Suicide*:

> "Pig" was perfect for several reasons. First of all, words like "swine," "hog," "sow," and "pig" have always had unpleasant connotations . . . The pig in reality is an ugly and offensive animal. It likes to root around in the mud, it makes hideous noises, it does not seem to relate to humans as other animals do. Further, anyone in the Black community can relate to the true characteristics of the pig because most of us come from rural backgrounds and have observed the nature of pigs. Many of the police, too, are hired right out of the South and are familiar with the behavior of pigs. They know exactly what the word implies. To call a policeman a pig conveys the idea of someone who is brutal, gross, and uncaring.[45]

Clearly, the Panthers' aim was to draw attention to the "brutal, gross, and uncaring" actions of the police and, by habituating the epithet, render them abject, inhuman, *monstrous*. Again, I point to the Panthers, Baldwin, and "ghetto children" who drew monsters with badges to be clear: the monstrosity of police is not some occulted knowledge, preached and possessed by a privileged few. Certainly, surviving members of the Bland, Crawford, Rice, Scott, Castile, Crutcher, McDonald, and countless other families are well versed in the teratology of police. Nevertheless, this is a critique I am compelled to make.

Despite periods of full-throated outrage, robust national surveys suggest that trust and confidence in police have nevertheless remained relatively stable for decades.[46] Even as it dipped significantly in esteem in 2015–16, the image of police had wholly rebounded by 2017 and markedly improved among whites, those fifty-five and older, and self-identified conservatives.[47] In other words, for overpoliced communities, the events of Ferguson and Baltimore were no revelation. For others, the ensuing backlash against police seems to have calcified more vociferous support around them.

What, then, keeps so many from apprehending policing's true face despite the parade of dysfunction, corruption, illegality, and violence? Toward an answer to these uneasy questions we must again ask, *What provisions have we made to shelter our minds from that which is too terrifying to confront?* In the opening sentences of *The Call of Cthulhu,* cosmic horror fiction forebear H. P. Lovecraft famously writes:

> The most merciful thing in the world, I think, is the inability of the human mind to correlate all its contents. We live on a placid island of ignorance in the midst of black seas of infinity, and it was not meant that we should voyage far. The sciences, each straining in its own direction, have hitherto harmed us little; but some day the piecing together of dissociated knowledge will open up such terrifying vistas of reality, and of our frightful position therein, that we shall either go mad from the revelation or flee from the light into the peace and safety of a new dark age.[48]

The most merciful thing in the world, as he puts it, is the shroud of mystification that keeps the human mind from connecting the dots, the ontological blinders that, for the sake of sanity, shield the eyes from seeing things as they truly are. Herein lie the seeds of Lovecraft's oeuvre and cosmic horror, the subgenre he is credited with founding. These "terrifying vistas of reality" for Lovecraft, like Thacker, lie not in the most violent and grotesque of human failings, or even in the anxious predilections of myth and superstition, but instead in the *unthinkable*: that which exists beyond everyday sight and human comprehension, the "boundless and hideous unknown, the shadow-haunted *Outside.*" Horror, then, for Lovecraft, is not the tearing of flesh, the flow of blood, or even abject boundaries of the human itself but the sober recognition that what we perceive to be real, what we rely upon to be true, is, at times, quite the opposite.

In his only nonfiction offering, *The Conspiracy against the Human Race*, contemporary horror fiction luminary Thomas Ligotti endorses Lovecraft's ruminations on the mercy of human ignorance, naming human consciousness the "parent of all horrors."[49] Drawing on the work of Norwegian philosopher Peter Wessel Zapffe, Ligotti details the ways that we humans shackle, or minimize, our consciousness in order to avoid the fear and horror of the unthinkable.[50]

Invoking the tone of Jackson and Lovecraft, he writes, "we cannot live except as self-deceivers who must lie to ourselves about ourselves, as well as about our unwinnable situation in this world."[51] For Ligotti, and likewise Thacker, horror—particularly supernatural and cosmic horror, with its other worldly monsters and "whole bestiary of impossible life forms"[52]—usefully undermines the anthropocentric foundations of much of contemporary thought, forcing the reader to consider, even if for a moment, this "unwinnable situation": a world, universe, cosmos that is indifferent, even hostile, to human understandings and desires. To begin to do away with our own practices of self-deception, we might then capture and slightly modify the long-standing anarchist refrain All Cops Are Bastards (ACAB) and instead, like the children, Baldwin, and the Panthers before us, insist that *All Cops Are Monsters*, a move that insists on their radical alterity and abiding indifference to the concerns of everyday people.

All Cops Are Monsters

In familiar Marxian prose, the polymath author and critic China Miéville writes, the "history of all hitherto-existing societies is the history of monsters. Homo sapiens is a bringer-forth of monsters as reason's dream. They are not pathologies but symptoms, diagnoses, glories, games, and terrors."[53] From the prototypical monsters of horror cinema's golden age to the slashers, ravenous corpses, and off-world chimeras of today, the genre generates its affective energies by introducing its readers and viewers to that which stands or crawls in opposition to natural and moral law, casting doubt on the existence of any inherent order at all.[54] Yet monstrosity's political utility is that it invariably doubles back to reaffirm the orders transgressed. This is why the monster emerges from within and is forever tied to the people who fear it, returning again and again to test and fortify the boundaries of the thinkable. The political theater of doing battle with and slaying the monster, likewise, works to position the injustices of a given social order outside itself and thereby reaffirm and redeem it.[55]

In a 1984 interview with the *Paris Review*, Baldwin again spoke of monsters, insisting that "insofar as the American public creates a monster, they are not about to recognize it. You create a monster and destroy it. It is part of the American way of life, if you like."⁵⁶ Like the dead who will not stay buried, monsters, as such, refuse to die, returning yet again to haunt and hunt the living.⁵⁷ As self-proclaimed "monster fighters," licensed to fight evil on our behalf, police are also always with us. Such is the eternal marriage of good and evil, friend and foe.

Given their insistence that they are "all that stands between the monsters and the weak," we might briefly consider just how efficient police are at fighting crime, let alone "fighting monsters." Aside from notorious killer/cops like Gerard John Schaefer and sadly common-place instances of lethal police violence, so-called "police deviance" is a well-established phenomenon. Even before delving into the academic literature on the subject, one might simply flip on the evening news or peruse social media to reckon the scope of police crimes. Whether planting drugs to make arrests, planting weapons to justify killings, extortion, theft, or outright robbery, for police no crime is off limits. To be fair, with more than seven hundred thousand sworn cops patrolling U.S. streets, it would be an impractical expectation for them to remain violation free. There are crimes, however, notably interpersonal and domestic violence, that occur at a greater rate among the police than in the general population.⁵⁸ Critics have also drawn attention to pervasive and often unreported sexual violence committed by cops. Long acknowledged with a wink and a nod, sexual favors are often demanded by cops in exchange for a pass on a traffic violation or minor arrest. In one particularly notorious "sex or jail" case, an Oklahoma cop named Daniel Holtzclaw was sentenced to 263 years in prison after being convicted of sexually assaulting nearly a dozen women.⁵⁹ As criminologist Philip Stinson and his colleagues who manage the Henry A. Wallace Police Crime Database find, U.S. police were formally charged with rape and sexual assault more than one thousand times between 2005 and 2013, a count that surely pales in comparison to the "dark figure" or true extent of sexual violence committed by cops.⁶⁰

While they are no doubt protected by their place within the broader system of U.S. justice, there is hardly a shortage of reporting on bad cops. Still, the failings of the institution are lesser known, albeit no less troubling. Readily available data collected by police agencies themselves shows them to be not particularly adept at solving

Blue Lives Matter ✓
@bluelivesmtr

"And maybe remind the few, if ill of us they speak, that we are all that stands between the monsters and the weak."
#BlueLivesMatter #BackTheBlue
#ThinBlueLine

The official Twitter account of Blue Lives Matter uses Michael Brown's killing to envision police as a thin blue line of heroic monster fighters.

crimes. Anyone who has had their home or car burglarized knows all too well that outside a stroke of luck, it is unlikely that they'll see their property again. Indeed, the 13 percent arrest rate for burglary bears this out. Even in cases of criminal homicide, where the circumstances of the crime make it more likely to identify the culprit, clearance rates hover around 60 percent, the vast majority of these cases solved not by stellar detective work as true crime television would have it, but in the moment at the scene or later by the loose lips of an accomplice.[61]

Just as the crime-solving acumen of police leaves us wanting, the institution's abilities to deter crime are also quite often overstated. Long ago, the Kansas City preventive patrol experiment strongly rebuked the widely held assumption that more cops equals less crime. The study, undertaken by the Kansas City Police Department (Missouri) in 1972–73 and later confirmed by independent evaluators, showed, among other things, that residents did not notice changes in police presence, that patrol patterns did not influence the rate at which crimes were reported, and that police presence did not significantly reduce burglary, car theft, robbery, or vandalism. Even more tellingly, increased police presence did not significantly reduce fear of crime, nor did it improve levels of "citizen satisfaction."[62] All of this is to say that the limits of police are no closely guarded secret.[63] Decades later, happenstance again underlined this open secret. When the NYPD fired Daniel Pantaleo in August 2019, more than five years after he choked Eric Garner to death, Patrick Lynch, president of the city's largest police union, urged its members to "slow down," make fewer arrests, and issue fewer summonses, with the idea that crime would immediately spike and New Yorkers would respond in outrage.[64] Much to Lynch's chagrin, the NYPD's slowdown resulted in not an increase but a decrease in serious violent crime.[65] While those employed as police commit plenty of crimes themselves, do a poor job of solving crimes, and are poorly equipped to intervene in crime more generally, this does not quite capture what I mean by the horror of police.

In his book by the same name, Calvin Warren uses the term *ontological terror* to describe "the terror the human feels with lack of security" and, more specifically, the terror engendered by a social order that denies the humanity of Black people. Using the demand "Black Lives Matter" to introduce his underlying claims, Warren argues:

A deep abyss, or a *terrifying question,* engenders the declaration "Black Lives Matter." The declaration, in fact, conceals this question even as it purports to have answered it resolutely.

"Black Lives Matter," then, carries a certain terror in its dissemination, a terror we dare to approach with uncertainty, urgency, and exhaustion. This question pertains to the "metaphysical infrastructure," as Nahum Chandler might call it, that conditions our world and our thinking about our world. "Black Lives Matter" is an important declaration, not just because it foregrounds the question of unbearable brutality, but also because it performs philosophical labor—it compels us to face the terrifying question, despite our desire to look away.[66]

Warren counters the prevailing humanist optimism with the pessimistic insistence that Black life simply cannot exist in an anti-Black world. After all, if this were not the case, would it be necessary to insist upon the dignity and value of Black lives? For Warren, that Black lives in fact do not matter engenders *terror*—"the terror that ontological security is gone, the terror that ethical claims no longer have an anchor, and the terror of inhabiting existence outside the precincts of humanity and its humanism."[67] The shuddering terror Warren describes bears some resemblance to the way I envision the horror of police. The sober recognition that the police offer no real protection and are in fact quite dangerous themselves is indeed terrifying. Yet where Warren's ontological terror is an ongoing state of fear and insecurity, the horror of police derives from the recognition of their true face—*the atrocity of the thing itself,* in Clute's words. "Terror is about the threat to life, of the knife behind you," writes Evan Calder Williams.

> Horror, conversely, is about the threat to understanding, of living to see the after-effects, of suddenly realizing that you were the one behind the knife all along. In this way horror is apocalyptic. It confronts us with the symptoms—and our complicity in reproducing them—and demands that we find a new set of instructions.[68]

Atrocity. Apocalypse. These attempts to narrate the dreadful truth we wish to avoid are of course drawn from or bear similarity to the Lacanian Real, the "unspeakable and horrifying disruption of our sense of reality."[69] Echoing the words of Jackson, Benjamin Noys reminds of the disavowed, disassociated knowledge that, if pieced together and reckoned as truth, "threatens us with madness." This pieced-together truth—this kernel of reality—is the horror of the Real. Like Jackson's larks and katydids, Noys suggests that we arrest our consciousness and flee this horror "into the 'dark age' of fantasy."[70] From Lacan and Noys to Jackson, Lovecraft, and Ligotti— who wrote, "Behind the scenes of life there is something pernicious that makes a nightmare of our world"[71]—there is a recognition that we collectively retreat into fantasy and restrain our own faculties so that we may avoid that which we know awaits us out in the darkness.

In addition to the limits and malevolence of police and the insecurity generated by the social order itself, there is the arresting horror that emerges from the elusive recognition that all this violence and brutality is born of failed and futile attempts to fashion a world around the unyielding desires of the human. Surrendering this anthropocentric ground, or stepping outside the subject, we become better equipped to confront an even more unthinkable and perhaps horrific universe utterly indifferent to the human and its world-making fictions: crime, criminal, law and order.[72] In the exercises to follow—which will require us to understand the police and social order as a pairing of the monster/ous and the horror/ific—we refigure the horror of police as not only an instantiation of our shared insecurities and our collective efforts to bend the material world into one built entirely for us, but as avenue to the unthinkable as well.

Police Horror Stories

By setting out the place of police, not just as a part of the overriding ideological and political order but as integral to the production of modern subjectivity and the ways we humans experience the world, we can begin to understand why large segments of the U.S. public turn away from policing's many misdeeds. Such a resignation may signal a collective indifference toward the predicament of the most vulnerable or an outright commitment to a racist, sexist, and generally unequal social order. Both of these possibilities are important to consider, of course, but the aim here is to reach a bit further than apathy and treachery. For subjects adrift in modernity's seemingly unpredictable and meaningless violence, to say nothing of its daily drudgeries and tremors of collapse, symbols of security, however inefficient, offer some a measure of comfort and relief. The police power, then, is for some the only means to achieve order in a disordered world, a necessary and righteous violence to balance the scales of not just legal but cosmic justice.

Despite their looming presence on the landscapes of U.S. social life, most of us, particularly our wealthy, white neighbors, will have scant meaningful contact with the agents of order. In their stead, a vibrant symbolic economy—a flow of texts and images, of social media news feeds, of true crime documentaries and reality television programs—draws us into the drama of crime and violence and the political theater of police. All this imaginative work forms the basis of what Christopher P. Wilson calls *cop knowledge*: "the literary, journalistic, and mass-cultural encounters with everyday police authority."[73] I deploy the complementary term *police stories* to describe a broad array of texts communicating and carrying Wilson's cop knowledge. While this includes what is said of and by police in the everyday, when it comes to our culture industries, so long as police are central, something may be considered a police story. Admittedly, this strategy makes the category an expansive one, overlapping related literary and filmic genres, from 1950s detective fiction and southern gothic noir to crime-scene investigation dramas, police memoirs, podcasts, and reality television. This strategy may ruffle some feathers. But my aim is not to explode categories for explosion's sake but rather to take seriously the incredible amount of material poured into and spilling from our vernacular police stories.

But what of the players in these stories? *Police* in my usage tends to denote the local, state, and federal agencies, some eighteen thousand of them in the United States, that fashion the institution itself, while *cop* refers to those who do the work of *policing*. I prefer "cop" and sometimes "agent" over "law enforcement" or "officer" for a number of reasons. Outside of the deficiencies noted above, as has long been acknowledged by even their most ardent defenders, much of what the police do actually has very little to do with responding to crime or enforcing law.[74] Police, in fact, routinely underenforce the law, acting instead as "street-level bureaucrats" armed with discretion to rule on crime in the moment as they see fit.[75] Even more provocatively, David Correia and Tyler Wall suggest the moniker "cop" likely derives from the Middle French *caper* or Latin *capere*, meaning to capture and to seize or grasp. Referring to the ability to seize control of property and the body, the midcentury slang "to cop" or "cop a feel" describes unwanted taking and contact, thereby reminding that *the cop* is not always on the right side of the law.[76] Given the countless sexual assaults cops commit each year—perversely exemplified by David Rojas of the LAPD, who was caught on his own body-worn camera fondling the body of a dead woman—to say nothing of the "civil asset forfeiture" and outright robbery that rakes in untold millions each year,[77] cop is arguably a remarkably accurate and apt descriptor.[78]

In his survey of U.S. cop action films, sociologist Neal King insists that "cop" is a useful descriptor of the "white middle class protector" institutionalized in and by the genre with the arrival of Clint Eastwood's "Dirty Harry" Callahan in 1971.[79] Around this time, aided by the anticommunist work of the John Birch Society, cops on the street coalesced as a powerful symbol of the conservative end of the white working class.[80] In this use, cops are thought to stand against the tide of amoral anti-Americanism that supposedly washed over the country and culture in the late 1960s and cut through the bureaucratic quagmire of a liberal legal system intent on protecting the rights of criminals over the lives of innocent middle-class white people.[81] Even when a police story features a Black cop, adds Jared Sexton, it nevertheless advances the unrelenting whiteness of police—a violent power meant to reproduce an unequal, racist social order.[82] Much the same can be said of women like *Law and Order's* Olivia Benson, who, while tasked with gendered duties of working "sex crimes" and caring for victimized women and children, are nevertheless imagined and represented in decidedly masculine and violent ways.[83] While the cops of our imagination have always been overwhelmingly white and male, the cops on our streets are equally so, comprising roughly 75 percent white and 85 percent men.[84] Reflecting both representation and demographics, I therefore conceive of the police power as white and male power, acknowledging, as legal theorist Markus Dirk Dubber points out, the fundamentally patriarchal nature of the police power itself.[85]

Now, some might again scoff at the bold line I draw between the police of our imaginations and the workings of actual police, insisting that fantasy, as such, should never be confused with nor take precedent over reality's hard edges. To such a skeptic I could, of course, point to the mountainous body of scholarly writing taking up questions of how we humans use culture to make sense of our lives and of the world. I might also remind the dubious that police themselves admit to being drawn to the job and to modeling themselves after fantasy cops like Dirty Harry.[86] But to save time, we can simply read the words of Bill Barr, U.S. attorney general and thus the nation's top cop under George H. W. Bush and Donald Trump. While a guest on a true crime podcast, Barr discussed his stint as a consultant for a network crime drama and spoke directly to the ways the police story is implicated in an imaginative sort of vengeful catharsis "hardwired" into humans:

> I believe a sense of justice is hardwired into human beings. Don't ask me why, but it is there and it's satisfying to see justice done. And we feel angry when we see injustice that isn't rectified . . . in the Dirty Harry movies and so forth. What was that movie with Bronson? *Death* . . . *Death Wish*, yeah. That kind of thing that gives people a sense of satisfaction when they see it . . . There's that scene in *Dirty Harry* where I think the guy has kidnapped somebody who is running out of oxygen, has a few minutes to live. Dirty Harry asks, "Where is she?" And the other guy smirks at him and he shoots him in the leg or something and the guy tells him where it is. I say, now, was that an unjust or morally repellent act? Is the reason that the audience applauds when that happens because the audience is morally bankrupt? Or is there something else going on there? So I think these are interesting issues.[87]

Despite Barr's fuzzy recall and equally dull analysis, he nevertheless demonstrates a certitude in vindictive human drives satiated by the police story. Such a view aligns with a mode of sociality organized around violence, tragedy, and death.[88] From Twitter feeds exploding with carnage to the ever-blossoming genre of true crime, we come to know ourselves, each other, and our unique place in the world through mediated experiences of violence, crime, and disorder. All the while, police, the workaday arbiters of these bloody social wounds, skulk in the background.

Some critics of our collective crime obsession are quick to frame it as an artifact wholly of the present, a rhetoric of decadence signaling, somehow, the degradation of a culture teetering into madness.[89] However, citing examples from the captivity narrative of Mary Rowlandson to the writing of Charles Brockden Brown, Washington Irving, Herman Melville, and, of course, Edgar Allan Poe, professor of American literature Harold Schechter—himself a prodigious true crime writer—demonstrates in his book *Savage Pastimes* how violence and gore have long been a part of American culture and, while they may be technologically sophisticated, today's offerings are not by any stretch more brutal.[90] Schechter's observations are confined neither to the contemporary moment nor to American culture. In 1764, for instance, appeared an anonymously authored four-volume collection, *The Bloody Register . . . A Select and Judicious Collection of the Most Remarkable Trials for Murder, Treason, Rape, Sodomy, Highway Robbery, Piracy . . . From the Year 1700 to the Year 1764, Inclusive*, published in London by E. and M. Viney. As one might surmise from the lengthy and garish title, the work gathered the most alarming offenses from England of the day. From petty robbery and "house breaking" to high treason, murder, and the trial of the legendary pirate Captain Kidd, the entries of the *Bloody Register* bear as much resemblance to the catchpenny accounts of their day as they do the lurid supermarket tabloids of today. Interesting, however, is that the collection's authors billed their work as public service, explaining in the preface, "great good we hope to accrue to mankind from perusing the following work; by which the rising generation will be deterred from launching out into the world of vice, if with attention they consider the miserable fate of the many unhappy wretches who have suffered for committing the crimes herein related." For its anonymous authors, the collection was ostensibly meant to provide instruction, above and beyond the good book, in morality and deter its readers from a life of crime and disrepute. Yet, as many an honest reader knows, these stories are never as much a deterrent as they are avenues to desire. As the writer and critic Leslie Fiedler puts it, stories such as these persist "not merely because they instruct us morally or delight us with their formal felicities, but because they allow us, in waking reverie, to murder our fathers and marry our mothers with Oedipus; to kill a king with the Macbeths, or our own children with Medea."[91]

Today, the ever-proliferating police story acts, in Wilson's words, as the "crucible vehicle for authoritarian populism," providing the cathartic narrative of violent disorder met by equally violent retribution.[92] From a veritable assembly line, new vehicles emerge, advancing this cause into new spaces: wildly popular series such as Netflix's *Making a Murderer* and *Tiger King: Murder, Mayhem, and Madness* and HBO's *The Jinx* and *I'll Be Gone in the Dark*; podcasts such as *Serial*, *Criminal*, and *S-Town*, which reach tens of millions; and the innovative true crime convention CrimeCon, which caters to the "crime-obsessed" and purports to bring the genre alive "through immersive experiences, incredible guests," and "nerdy deep-dives into tactics and cases." Mirroring Comic-Con and other consumer-driven conventions where attendees purchase memorabilia, rub elbows, seek autographs, and take selfies with their heroes, the inaugural CrimeCon in Indianapolis, Indiana, featured crime-culture personalities like attorney F. Lee Bailey, author and television personality Aphrodite Jones, *Dateline NBC*'s Josh Mankiewicz, and the true crime carnival barker Nancy Grace. With attendees reported as being more than 80 percent women, it captures an interesting and understudied phenomenon: by a large margin, women are the top consumers of true crime.[93] Of the few studies to take up the question systematically, one finds that when it comes to violent entertainment, women prefer stories of interpersonal violence, enjoy speculating about the psychological motivations of violent people, and look to true crime content for instruction on how to prevent becoming victims themselves.[94] Laura Browder, who questioned women on their interests in true crime, draws interesting parallels to the romance novel. Where romance novels engage the drive for consummation, she sees true crime satisfying drives for revenge and punishment.[95] Conventioners I interviewed in Indianapolis supported these assertions and reaffirmed the notion that police stories, and true crime more generally, provide a narrative that, in the words of one woman, "set the world right again." While true crime products are first and foremost moneymaking ventures, the immense viewership and public attention they generate have had some tangible effects. Attention drawn by *Making a Murderer* and *Serial* instigated new legal proceedings. In the case of *The Keepers,* which focuses on the efforts of two women to solve the 1969 murder of their teacher, Sister Catherine Cesnik, the pair's Facebook group has brought together tens of thousands of amateur "websleuths" and self-described "murderinos" hoping to do the same. Speaking to her personal engagement with the genre, Georgia Hardstark, one half of the popular "true crime comedy podcast" *My Favorite Murder* and coauthor of the memoir *Stay Sexy and Don't Get Murdered,* told the *Los Angeles Times* that for her, it's neither fantasy nor fiction but somehow "comforting to learn as much as I can about [crime, violence, murder] because it makes me feel a little more in control of my life, in control of what happens to me."[96] These new interactive formats, which allow participants to step into the fantasy role of police and to write and perhaps solve the story themselves, detail further the ways the genre helps subjects make sense of the world.[97]

All of this is not to suggest that women might be more susceptible to the gratuitous titillation and ideological fodder of the police story but to demonstrate how it might be an instrument useful to our own psychic survival. As criminologist Elizabeth Yardley and her colleagues have suggested, the violent fantasy world of police stories—so, too, police themselves—provides a powerful mechanism to reproduce a coherent symbolic order, in which police avenge the innocent and punish the violator. Yet it is precisely to this vibrant interior fantasy world that some flee in order to avoid an encounter with more uncomfortable realities.[98] In Stephen King's words, "we take refuge in make-believe terrors so the real ones don't overwhelm us."[99] Here we can say the overriding narrative that places the valiant cop at the center of a consistent and predictable social order is but one tool that helps us disown what we know to be true.

To restrain our own consciousness—the parent of all horrors—we humans isolate our troubling thoughts or deny their existence, distract ourselves with our pet obsessions, anchor ourselves in the greater good of "God" or "Nation," or sublimate the horror that surrounds us by embracing the cold impartiality of the universe or the disinterest of a God that "works in mysterious ways."[100] And so the police story, with its allusions to primordial evil, disorder, and madness, is overlaid onto countless lives as an avenue to desire and as an ontological crutch—a calming guidebook for troubled times. Moving back and forth from the cops of our imagination to the cops on our streets, the chapters that follow each seek to explore and elaborate upon the many ways in which we collectively, as subjects, actively endorse and reproduce the police as a social institution and a key instrument of ontological ordering.

Chapter 1, "Bad Cops and True Detectives," brings together and elaborates some of the concepts set out above and reads them through the first season of HBO's much-liked *True Detective* series. Like that of all police stories, the world of *True Detective* is beset by killers and monsters of all kinds. Much like the world we presently inhabit, it is perpetually wrestled from the brink of chaos and disorder by a greater monster—the police.

Building from there, the next two chapters are organized around the mutually constitutive dialectic of the barbarism of disorder and the barbarism of order.[101] Chapter 2, "The Police at the End of the World, or The Political Theology of the Thin Blue Line," engages the apocalyptic imaginary to demonstrate the ways in which police are imagined as indispensable to the continuation of a secure world-for-us. Drawing on contemporary police culture and readings of Thomas Hobbes and Carl Schmitt, the chapter outlines an epistemology of enmity and ontology of war, affirming the position of police as the hero/god figures of Western modernity. As its counterpoint, chapter 3, "RoboCop, or Modern Prometheus," considers the barbarism of order through ongoing debates about police repression, particularly those concerning nascent police technology and its attendant militarization. Reading the police story and science fiction with and against contemporary social theory—phenomenology and transcendental and new materialisms—the chapter offers three ways to trouble the technological determinism inherent to the critique of police militarization and demonstrates how this seemingly progressive critique actually reaffirms the police power.

Chapter 4, "Monsters Are Real," combines the positions sketched out in the previous two chapters and reads them from the vantage of the police. As we know from countless examples, police must simply suggest they "feared for their lives" in order to excuse their knee-jerk reactions and devastating lethality. Taking their claims seriously, the chapter considers not only the horror engendered by police but the police as *horrified* subjects themselves. Finally, chapter 5, "The Unthinkable World," uses the ongoing debates over defunding and abolishing the police as an avenue to the *unthinkable*: a world without police.

CHAPTER 1

Bad Cops and True Detectives

The monster always calls forth the police.

—Mark Neocleous, *Universal Adversary: Security,
Capital, and "the Enemies of All Mankind"*

In the title role of the 1992 film *Bad Lieutenant*, Harvey Keitel plays a vicious and deeply compromised NYPD detective. Known only as "the lieutenant" (a move that announces and affirms his alterity), he engages in all the behaviors police insist they guard against. Alcohol abuse, drugs, gambling, theft, rape, racism—there is no bridge too far. This is not a man with a name, this is a cop. A *bad cop*. Assigned to investigate the brutal rape of a Catholic nun, the lieutenant metes out his own brand of street justice while juggling his estranged family, sex and drug habits, and gambling debts. One critic remarked that in a world where "everyone seems to do drugs" and the "system lets young hoodlums walk and no one cares, he may be a bad cop, but he's just one of many."[1] The brutality and desperation embodied by the lieutenant distinguished the film as an edgy departure from its genre contemporaries, winning it critical praise and a sustained cult following.

While it was perhaps meant to be a journey into one man's self-degradation and death, there is another reading of *Bad Lieutenant*, which haunts all police stories. Though clearly not a "good cop" by any measure, waging revanchist war in dogged pursuit of two street kids, the lieutenant remains indisputably *a cop*. With few exceptions, this rule guides the police story: no matter how bad the cop, the violence of liberal law and order remains its symbolic core. This is why police, as theatrical prop and material practice, are indispensable for political power. Police stories, then, even those featuring cops as depraved as the lieutenant, tend to somehow reaffirm the symbolic order of a world divided neatly between good and evil, cop and criminal.[2] Yet we should resist reducing the police story to a simple vehicle for the expression and reproduction of political power, as yet another reading hints at more troubling ontological tangles.

Bad Cops

The failures, limitations, and outright illegality of police, the "something rotten in law" famously diagnosed by Walter Benjamin, are well-worn territory in scholarly critiques of police and state power.[3] While often the core of the "bad apple" narrative, and at other times simply ignored, policing's festering rot nevertheless abounds within its cinematic and televisual representations. Openly fraught and contradictory, the police story operates as part of the imaginary[4]—the realm of misidentification and self-deception—affirming, however subtly, what Benjamin saw as the law-making and law-preserving function of police violence, marking the very moment at which the state's authority and social order begin to break down.[5] Like Keitel's lieutenant, a cop who remains ostensibly in service of the law while operating outside of it, Detective Jimmy McNulty (Dominic West) of HBO's much-lauded crime drama *The Wire* provides another example of the contradictory figure that breaks the law to uphold the law. Called a "sociopathic enforcer" by theorist Adam Kotsko, McNulty is the familiar rogue figure whose violence and transgressions are essential skills employed for a higher calling—*social order*.[6] In one exchange with Lester, a seasoned and particularly wise colleague, the brash McNulty sets the two out as different, part of a rare few *natural police*:

> MCNULTY: You know something, Lester, I do believe there
> aren't five swingin' dicks in this entire department who can
> do what we do. I'm not sayin' like all chest out and shit. It's
> just, you think about it. There's maybe, what, three thousand
> sworn, right? Hundred or so are bosses, so not a fucking clue
> there. A few more hundred is sergeants and lieutenants, most

of them wanna be bosses one day, so they're just as fucked. Then there's six or seven hundred fuckin' housecats, you know, deskmen. And in the patrol division, there's probably a little bit of talent there, but the way the city is right now, that's fifteen hundred guys chasin' calls and clearin' corners. I mean, nobody's knowing his post, nobody's building nothing, right? And CID is the same. Catching calls, chasing quick clearances keeping everything in the shallow end, I mean who is it out there can do what we do with a case? How many are there, really? Don Worden, Ed Burns, Gary Childs out in the county. John O'Neil and Steve Cleary over at Woodlawn. Oh, they bring it in, but there's not many. There's not many. We're good at this, Lester. In this town, we're as good as it gets.

LESTER: Natural police.

MCNULTY: Fuck yes! *Natural police.*[7]

Whereas Benjamin would see all police as agents who, through the force of legitimate violence, reproduce the law, McNulty's rant advances the notion that only he, Lester, and a few other "natural police" possess the attributes (or perhaps will) to act, however violently, on behalf of the community and social order. Again, this understanding of the police power can be traced in its filmic form to the archetype natural police or rogue cop, Harry Callahan (Clint Eastwood) of the 1970s *Dirty Harry* franchise.[8] In her well-regarded book *Shots in the Mirror,* criminologist Nicole Rafter argues that *Dirty Harry* marks a departure from staid television serials like *Dragnet* and *Mayberry RFD* and films that tended to position police as unsophisticated beat cops, crusading G-men, or dashing private eyes.[9] Emerging at a time of marked social discord alongside a conservative tough-on-crime politics and the war on drugs, *Dirty Harry* represented a new kind of cop, tailored perfectly for the rising tide of authoritarian populism and powerfully foreshadowing the growing centrality of police in U.S. social life. As Neal King insists, from *Dirty Harry* henceforth, the cop film genre reflects a stridently conservative, revanchist vision where "working-class community protectors—cops, for short—blow through racial guilt, sexual hostility, and class resentment with wise-cracking defiance and a lot of firepower."[10]

However, in *Bad Lieutenant* and other films like *To Live and Die in L.A.* (1985) and *State of Grace* (1990), Rafter marks a departure from the working-class-protecting *Dirty Harry* rogue and, accordingly, a critique of the police power. For her, *Bad Lieutenant* is not simply a graphic film about a bad cop but instead an altogether unique development in the genre, a category she calls alternative-tradition or critical cop films. Set apart from the seduction and shadow of noir and postmodern films somehow altogether absent of heroes, these alternative-tradition/critical cop films "aim at negating the very idea of a hero." For Rafter, then, films such as these make the singular point that "there is no such thing as a good cop" and, by implication, "no such thing as a good man."[11] While some films do, perhaps, offer a more nuanced critique of police, as we have seen with *Bad Lieutenant*, violence and illegality in service to broader understandings of security, law, and order nevertheless remain the narrative core of even the darkest police story. Not just pop culture kitsch, police stories are, as Giorgio Agamben puts it, "the place where the proximity and the almost constitutive exchange between violence and right that characterizes the figure of the sovereign is shown more nakedly and clearly than anywhere else."[12] Even Georges Bataille saw the police story as a site of order reaffirming spectatorship, offering the relatively safe, vicarious experience of criminal transgression and the righteousness of punishment.[13] As such, the misdeeds of even the most irredeemable cop remain part of a symbolic order that reaffirms the unavoidable necessity of police violence as an indispensable instrument of sovereign power.

Implicit in the very notion of the "bad apple" is the understanding that the "good apples" protect and serve benevolently. As *Dirty Harry* was meant to suggest, bad cops offer an antidote to the failures of a liberal criminal justice system so tangled in due process and bureaucracy that it repeatedly fails to protect the innocent, act on behalf of the aggrieved, and punish the wicked. But even then, in the cinematic imagination as well as the actual workings of this world-for-us, the political theater of singling out, punishing, and expelling the rogue, bad cop shields the policing institution from scrutiny, allowing it to, in Kotsko's words, "recover and return to its old path . . . stronger than ever."[14]

Whether it emerges from the imagination or the shadowy terrains of city streets, scaffolding the view of the bad cop as a necessary evil is the objectless anxiety born of the always-present and yet-to-arrive threat of crime and violence. Like Agamben and Bataille, Jean and John Comaroff see the tidy narratives of police procedurals, hypermasculine "supercops," and crime scenes deconstructed with "magico-scientistic" precision, conjuring a world where no mystery goes unsolved and the wicked never elude justice, thereby performing, "over and over, the phantasm of sovereign authority."[15] The symbiosis between police, however violent and corrupt, and their fearsome adversaries bears some resemblance to what literary critic Franco Moretti famously called the dialectic of fear. For Moretti, the monsters of the gothic imagination usefully diagnose the nascent anxieties of bourgeois modernity. Reading Shelley's *Frankenstein* as the portents of scientific rationality and Stoker's *Dracula* as the horrors of vampiric landlordism, the gothic "literature of terror" documents the tremors of an emerging capitalist dystopia.[16] As Mark Steven puts it, the dialectic of "vampire and monster, propertied and propertyless, bourgeoisie and dispossessed" powerfully depict the two poles of capitalist society.[17] He writes:

> Frankenstein's nameless monster is literally stitched together from deceased members of a blighted underclass. He is an embodiment of the proletariat, the ungodly collectivization of otherwise disaggregated subjects into a single, productive and altogether menacing entity. Dracula, inversely, is less the feudal aristocrat that his title might imply than he is a monopoly capitalist, whose migration from Transylvania to London is one of imperial expansion.[18]

If the hulking wretch and bloodsucking landlord diagnose the anxieties of their day, what, then, can be said of their antagonists? In Moretti's words, "whoever dares to fight the monster automatically becomes the representative of the species, of the whole of society."[19] In other words, the enemy of the monster is always a stand-in for the social order. In the case of Shelley and Stoker, their monsters' rivals approximate the whole of nineteenth-century mediocrity with its backwards nationalism, racism, superstition, and ill-informed hubris. From the villains of Poe and Doyle to the psychopaths and gangsters of Hammett and Chandler on through to the serial killers and terrorists of the present, in the police story, the police have stood in heroic opposition to their monstrous adversaries. This is precisely the point made by Neocleous when he insists that "the monster always calls forth the police."[20] Even the early U.S. police sociologist Egon Bittner invoked the dialectic between monster and monster fighter—in his case the dragon and the dragon slayer—to describe the relationship between cop and criminal. Literary critic Leo Braudy, too, sees the monster and the police dialectically, writing:

> The monster and the detective are opposite sides of the same coin: the monster is the embodiment of disorder, an eruption into the world of normality, coming from some alien place, from hell, from outer space, from wherever and whatever is not normal. The detective by contrast is the seeker for order. Instead of the unprecedented monster, the detective's quarry is the criminal, the monster reduced to a human scale.[21]

Taking up the television series *Dexter*, which revolves around a serial killer–cum–crime scene technician, Neocleous likewise shows how the monstrous is bound up with the fundamental police problem, the question of order.[22] From this view, the beat cop who chases petty criminals and the serial killer who preys upon the lost and dispossessed pursue the same ends: disposal of social refuse—cleaning up the streets. Where Neocleous and Braudy diverge, however, is on the composition of police and their proximity to the monster. Through a reading of Thomas Hobbes's *Leviathan* and *Behemoth*, Neocleous focuses our attention on the violent monstrosity of sovereign power. As Moretti similarly suggests, rapt by the horrors of the monster, liberal subjects must accept the vices of its destroyer, thereby displacing the violent monstrosity of the social order and outside society itself. While Neocleous offers several examples where police, as self-proclaimed "dragon slayers" or "monster fighters," seem to have slipped over the Nietzschean precipice and become monsters themselves, we should be clear in the view, as is he, that whoever occupies the figure of police *is always already a monster*. In other words, the fear and insecurity that characterize bourgeois modernity stitch together and rely upon the terrible unity of monster *and* police.

Consider *Training Day* (2001), which won Denzel Washington an Academy Award for his portrayal of a villainous LAPD detective, Alonzo Harris. Reaffirming the fluidity between the police of our imagination and the police on our streets, Harris was based on Rafael Pérez and David Mack, two LAPD cops at the center of the notorious Rampart scandal. As one analysis of the film and its real-life analogues described, Harris is an amalgam of "Rampart villains Perez and Mack: both Latino and African American, part cop and part gang-banger."[23] In the film's decisive scene, when the street gang he has long bullied into doing his bidding refuses to murder his trainee Jake Hoyt (Ethan Hawke) and Harris launches into a now-famous tirade, the monster *in* police comes into full view:

> Aww, you motherfuckers. Okay. Alright. I'm putting cases on all you bitches. Huh. You think you can do this shit . . . Jake? You think you can do this to me? You motherfuckers will be playing basketball in Pelican Bay when I get finished with you. SHU program, nigga. Twenty-three-hour lockdown. I'm the man up in this piece. You'll never see the light of . . . who the fuck do you think you're fucking with? I'm the police. I run shit around here. You just live here. Yeah, that's right, you better walk away. Go on and walk away, 'cause I'm gonna burn this motherfucker down. *King Kong ain't got shit on me!* That's right, that's right. Shit, I don't—fuck. I'm winning anyway, I'm winning . . . I'm winning any motherfucking way. I can't lose. Yeah, you can shoot me, but you can't kill me.[24]

Like Hobbes's Leviathan, Harris's King Kong looms above the landscape, promising punishment and death to his unruly subjects.

The monster in police is named even more explicitly in the 2016 crime thriller *Triple 9*. In an all-too-familiar scene, a grizzled veteran, Jeffrey Allen (Woody Harrelson), counsels a hopeful upstart, Chris Allen (Casey Affleck), on the ins and outs of police work and calls forth the monster.

> JEFFREY ALLEN: How's your job going?
>
> CHRIS ALLEN: You know, spend my time trying to make a difference. I know how that sounds.

JEFFREY ALLEN: You're gonna make a difference? You ain't
gonna make a fucking difference. Forget about that. Your job:
out-monster the monster, then get home at the end of the night.
Out here there is no good, there is no bad. To survive out
here you gotta *out-monster the monster*. Can you do that?[25]

It bears repeating: *All Cops Are Monsters*. Instead of liberalism's
dream of law and order, in this rendering, policing is simply a project
of superior violence and firepower. Here, beyond good and evil, the
biggest monster wins.

Reading Slavoj Žižek's oeuvre for its modern gothic elements,
Benjamin Noys suggests that on the one hand is the Real, the monstrous outside, the unknowable "Thing," against which we guard ourselves through the flight or retreat into fantasy. On the other hand,
following Žižek, he suggests the monster is always "a projection of
our own excesses, as our own refusal to admit the negativity at the
heart of our existence."[26] In other words, the horror of the Real is
the recognition of our own monstrosity, the terrifying realization of
our own abiding connections to the monster and monstrous. This,
of course, includes the violent monstrosity of the system we have devised to ensure security and civil peace—*the police*.

Encounters with the unthinkable, supernatural, and monstrous,
as Thacker reminds, invite a competition between two poles of ontological uncertainty: "either I do not know the world, or I do not
know myself."[27] His point, again, is that horror lies not in the suspicion that one is insane, but rather in the realization that one is
not insane. Fit to the question of the police, it is not necessarily the
abhorrent acts of the bad cop that are horrific, but rather the sober
recognition that the police are not what they insist they are and
that their violence, coercion, and murder are routine practices. On
the street and in the imagination, liberal subjects encounter police
empowered to act on their own volition and discretion, employing
violence and coercion with impunity. Whether or not it is justified
or admitted, the violence of police appears as an unavoidable consequence of the present social order, this world-for-us, which has
only ever been for some of us. As Sarah Schulman puts it in her
book *Conflict Is Not Abuse*, the police have gained control over the
discourse of violence, the means to end it, and, through direct part-

nerships with media members and institutions, its expression in the popular imagination. She writes:

> Television shows like *Law and Order: Special Victims Unit* surfaced with a focus on sex crimes and family violence. In a typical episode, a purely innocent victim, who does not participate in creating conflict and is inherently good, is stalked/abused/attacked by a purely and inherently evil predator. The answer to the conundrum is the police. Popular mass entertainment, a corporate entity that is not self-critical, makes the message clear: people are either victims or predators, and therefore the answer is always the police, who are also not self-critical.[28]

When viewed critically, however, the victims left in crime's wake impart the worrisome reminder that police rarely prevent crime, appear only after the damage is done, and often inflict damage of their own. Again, the admission is that police cannot keep you safe, are in fact under no obligation to do so, and quite often view you and your kind as threats or, worse, enemies.[29]

The horrifying recognition that this world is unthinkable apart from the violence and coercion of police shares obvious conceptual terrain with Mark Fisher's *Capitalist Realism*.[30] Drawing inspiration from Fredric Jameson's well-known suggestion that it is, for some, easier to imagine the end of the world than the end of capitalism, Fisher diagnoses the pervasive sense "that not only is capitalism the only viable political and economic system, but also that it is now impossible to even imagine a coherent alternative to it."[31] To elaborate his position, Fisher looks to dystopian fictions, which were once sites to imagine avoidable futures, and instead finds in films like *Children of Men* an extrapolation or exacerbation of our present. "In this world, as in ours," he writes, ultra-authoritarianism and capital have fashioned circumstances where internment camps and franchise coffee bars exist alongside one another, public space has been abandoned to "garbage and stalking animals," and—much to the glee of "neoliberals, the capitalist realists par excellence"—the state soldiers on, stripped bare to reveal its core military and police functions.[32] While capitalist realism usefully marks the boundaries of the thinkable, these boundaries can also operate theoretically and politically, demonstrating the ways that representation can open space for the imagination of new worlds.[33] As Noys suggests, "we can read theory as fiction and fiction as theory by holding them together through a 'parallax view' whose vanishing point is the moment of the 'Real.'"[34] In this spirit, we carry on with our purposeful misreading of the police story, not as mystery or drama but as *horror*. After all, the basic definition of any horror text, as film scholar David Russell insists, is the monster and the conflict arising from the unreal monster's relationship with normality.[35]

True Detective: Bad Men at the Door

For purposes of brevity and clarity, the rest of this chapter focuses on the eight episodes of the first season of *True Detective*. Written by Nic Pizzolatto, the season, which aired on HBO in early 2014, stars Matthew McConaughey as Rustin Cohle and Woody Harrelson as Martin Hart, two Louisiana State Police detectives set to solve a string of bizarre, ritualistic murders. While at its core *True Detective* is a boilerplate buddy-cop police procedural,[36] a number of distinct aesthetic and narrative elements make it a particularly useful text for our purposes.[37] Most notably, Pizzolatto's foray into weird and speculative fiction—his nod to the horror fiction of H. P. Lovecraft and Robert W. Chambers and the obvious influence of Thomas Ligotti's philosophical pessimism—sets the series apart from the typical procedural.

The weird, as Lovecraft famously defined, "has something more than secret murder, bloody bones, or a sheeted form clanking chains." As a rule, a "certain atmosphere of breathless and unexplainable dread of outer, unknown forces must be present; and there must be a hint, expressed with a seriousness and portentousness becoming its subject, of that most terrible conception of the human brain—a malign and particular suspension or defeat of those fixed laws of Nature which are our only safeguard against the assaults of chaos and the daemons of unplumbed space."[38]

Animating the dread of the unknown and the outside are Louisiana's bleak bayous and swamps, alien landscapes upon which, as Cohle observes, "nothing grows in the right direction." Not simply a scenographic backdrop, from Pizzolatto's imagination springs a menacing *earth*, seemingly possessing a will of its own. As he himself describes, this is a world where "the weak (physically or economically) are lost, ground under by perfidious wheels that lie somewhere behind the visible, wheels powered by greed, perversity, and irrational belief systems, and these lost souls dwell on an exhausted frontier, a fractured coastline beleaguered by industrial pollution and detritus, slowly sinking into the Gulf of Mexico. *There's a sense here that the apocalypse already happened.*"[39]

Disembodied aerial shots of Cohle and Hart's car knifing through endless stretches of swamps and bayous abandoned to the petroleum industry and encroaching sea call forth the sense that the inhabitants of this world, again in Cohle's words, "don't even know the outside world exists" and "might as well be living on the fucking moon." Cohle and Hart's preserve, then, is not the familiar city of crime fiction or even the balmy South of *In the Heat of the Night* (1967) but an uncanny and emergent world-in-itself, a world that, as Thacker warns, *bites back*. Distinguishing the series further still, Cohle's pessimistic view of humanity as a "tragic misstep in evolution" runs dead-on into the aims of liberal order, rendering the act of detection a seemingly futile endeavor.

While the weird might set it apart from the typical cop drama, *True Detective*, like all police stories, turns on the figure of an enemy. In the opening minutes of its first episode, Cohle and Hart catch a glimpse of their illusory, faceless adversary. Called by local police to an impenetrable cane field punctured by a single tree, the pair finds a murdered woman posed as if kneeling at a prie-dieu, a crude crown of deer antlers and vines fixed atop her head. Observing the scene littered with strange symbols and twists of twigs and vines called devil nets, a local cop blurts out, "Them symbols, they're satanic—they had a 20/20 on it a few years back." Reciting the profiler's monologue, Cohle's on-scene analysis begins to sketch the killer's outline across the body of yet another dead woman:

Ligature marks on her wrists, ankles, and knees. Multiple shallow stab wounds to the abdomen. Hemorrhaging around throat, lividity at the shoulders, thighs, and torso. She'd been on her back awhile before he moved her. This is gonna happen again, or it's happened before. Both. It's fantasy enactment. Ritual.

Fetishization. Iconography. This is his vision. Her body is a paraphilic love map. An attachment of physical lust to fantasy and practices forbidden by society. Her knees are abraded. Rug burns on her back. Cold sores, gumline recession, bad teeth—there's decent odds she was a prost'. He might not have known her, but this idea goes way back with him. This kind of thing does not happen in a vacuum. I guarantee this wasn't his first. It's too specific.[40]

Authoring this particular killer, *True Detective* advances a well-worn narrative pitting cops, whether patrolman or profiler, against a spectral, sometimes supernatural adversary.[41] With the initiation of the investigation in 1995, the series sits on the tail end of the so-called Satanic Panic that seized the U.S. imagination in the mid-1980s and saw a cottage industry of social workers, therapists, and specialist "cult cops" spring up in opposition to an imagined network of child-murdering occultists.[42] Despite failing to substantiate any such conspiracy, fears of "ritual satanic abuse" nevertheless resulted in numerous criminal trials—the most notable being those of the McMartin preschool case—and, in some instances, lengthy prison sentences for the wrongly accused.[43] While the "panic" was by definition overstated, we should not dismiss *True Detective*'s satanic adversary as simply clichéd fantasy. In his work on the series, Joseph Laycock, a scholar of religion, suggests that police stories that pit cops against an imagined evil, however fantastic, provide plausibility structures that reaffirm a decidedly binary and Manichean ontology.[44] As the history of the Satanic Panic shows, a pastiche of innocuous youth fads—role-playing games, tarot cards, Ouija boards, heavy metal music[45]—were even seen as symptoms and evidence of this particular iteration of policing's battle with evil.[46]

Reaching deeper into the cultural register, historian Philip Jenkins traces the panic and "virtually every allegation about real-life American Satanism" to the dubious anthropology of Margaret Murray, the weird fiction of Lovecraft, and Herbert S. Gorman's *The Place Called Dagon*.[47] Much like the *Necronomicon*, a fictional grimoire that escaped Lovecraft's imagination to become, according to some police and "occult specialists," a real book used in satanic rituals, Murray's discredited *The Witch-Cult in Western Europe*[48] and the weird tales and horror fiction it inspired initiated, according to Jenkins, a cultural vocabulary and "body of memories" that have been put to work by police and prosecutors at various times over the last century. A tremendous, or rather tragic, example of the consequences of policing's dubious occult expertise is detailed in the West Memphis Three case, widely publicized by the HBO documentary series *Paradise Lost*. In this case, three teen boys from the wrong side of West Memphis, Arkansas, were convicted of the murders of three grade-school boys also from impoverished families. Based on a confession that police coerced from one of the accused, circumstantial evidence, and outrageous links to satanism made by police and, notably, an "occult specialist" hired by the state who had attained his certification via mail order, two of the boys received life sentences without the possibility of parole, while the third was sentenced to die. With the help of celebrity activists and a dogged defense team that secured exculpatory evidence, the three were finally released after more than eighteen years in prison, but the "Child Murders at Robin Hood Hills" remain unsolved.

Light versus Dark

While *True Detective* is certainly part of a longer cultural and literary lineage, the roots of its satanic adversary run far deeper than the swirling cauldron of panic, dubious scholarship, and pulp fiction kitsch that boiled over in the late 1980s. In his writing on the fifteenth-century French child killer Gilles de Rais, Bataille insists that the murderer's crimes call forth the grace of compassion and make possible the Christian duties of confession and forgiveness.[49] Even the obscene crimes of this bloodthirsty "sacred monster," Bataille writes,

> are not contrary to the "truest Christianity," which is always—be it frightening! be it Gilles de Rais'!—ready to forgive crime. Perhaps Christianity is even fundamentally the pressing demand for crime, the demand for the horror that in a sense it needs in order to forgive. It is in this vein that I believe we must take Saint Augustine's exclamation, "Felix culpa!," Oh happy fault!, which blossoms into meaning in the face of inexpiable crime. Christianity implies a human nature which harbors this

hallucinatory extremity, which it alone has allowed to flourish. Likewise, with the extreme violence we are provided with in the crimes of one Gilles de Rais, could we understand Christianity? Perhaps Christianity is above all bound to an archaic human nature, one unrestrainedly open to violence?[50]

Adopting elements of Max Horkheimer and Theodor Adorno's *Dialectic of Enlightenment*, Paul O'Brien similarly suggests that numerous cultural forms, including the satanic killer, emerge from a mutually reinforcing doctrine that positions Christian ethics alongside a belief in God's satanic adversary and the righteousness of eternal damnation for those who run afoul of Christian law. He writes:

> On the positive, as noted already, Christianity foregrounded the values of altruism, reciprocity and mutual concern that inform the liberal values of the West (including, largely and often unconsciously, the values of those atheists and humanists who ostensibly reject it). On the negative side, it unleashes the fury of pathic projection with its teaching of, on the one hand, Evil/Satan as an opposing power to God, and on the other hand, eternal punishment for offenders and unbelievers.[51]

Much like Moretti's *dialectic of fear*, Hart and Cohle's battle with a satanic adversary invokes a *dialectic of Christianity* that draws upon and reinforces decidedly Western Christian understandings of social order and, of course, the police power. But this is not simply a narrative device or cinematic motif. As Neocleous argues in his book *The Universal Adversary*, the theology of evil, particularly Christian understandings of the devil, have always been central to Western political power. Leaders of nascent state formations in Europe quickly learned that their legitimacy was bolstered by tying their authority to divine right, with claims that they were "co-ordinating the war on the Devil as the Enemy of All Mankind as well as the Enemy of God."[52] *True Detective* presents this imagined battle with evil and "war on the Devil" similarly when, in the first episode, Reverend Billy Lee Tuttle, a powerful, politically connected church leader who has pressured the police into launching a task force investigating crimes with an "anti-Christian connotation," warns Hart and Cohle that "there is a war happening behind things." Of course, Cohle, ever the atheist pessimist, decries the superstition of satanism (at least initially) and quips, "You know me. I don't see the connection between two dead cats and a murdered woman, but I'm from Texas."[53] The dialectic of Christianity invoked by an imagined "war" between the righteous (police) and the wicked (killer) reveals the outlines of what I call the *political theology of the thin blue line*. Political theology as proposed by the reactionary legal theorist Carl Schmitt holds that the theories of modern state formations are in essence secularized theology, in both their historical development and contemporary practice.[54] So, as Schmitt famously put it, political power transferred from theology to the theory of the state, "whereby, for example, the omnipotent God became the omnipotent lawgiver," the most immediately recognizable of which is, of course, the police.[55] As we have seen, the political theology of the thin blue line extends beyond cinematic representations to the theatrics of actual police who see themselves as holy warriors locked in a spiritual battle for civilization's salvation. As if parroting Schmitt, in his reimagining of the police power as cynegetic, or hunting, power, philosopher Grégoire Chamayou suggests that the power assumed by the modern police force developed independently of the laws that now justify and loose it upon the world, *a righteous hunter of man*.

> Whence the antinomy, constantly staged in contemporary cinematic fiction, between the requirements of police pursuit and the principles of the law. To be an efficient hunter, one must pursue the prey despite the law, and even against it. But this antinomy was not born in the imaginations of scriptwriters. In passing from the law to the police, we pass from one sphere of sovereignty to another, from the theology of the state—the legal system—to its material form—the police. From its spiritual existence to secular arm.[56]

Through its imagined battles with a satanic adversary, the police story positions police as both the omnipotent lawgiver and adjunct of a decidedly Western Christian understanding of God and of cosmic order.[57]

When, in "The Locked Room" (episode three), a lead takes the pair to an Evangelical tent revival and Hart offers Cohle his take on the functionalism of religion, the political theology of the thin blue line is plainly spelled out.

> HART: I mean, can you imagine if people didn't believe, what things they'd get up to?
>
> COHLE: Exact same thing they do now. Just out in the open.
>
> HART: Bullshit. It'd be a fucking freak show of murder and debauchery and you know it.
>
> COHLE: If the only thing keeping a person decent is the expectation of divine reward, then, brother, that person is a piece of shit and I'd like to get as many of them out in the open as possible.
>
> HART: Well, I guess your judgment is infallible, piece-of-shit-wise. You think that notebook is a stone tablet?
>
> COHLE: What's it say about life, huh? You gotta get together, tell yourself stories that violate every law of the universe just to get through the goddamn day. Nah. What's that say about your reality, Marty?[58]

We can assume that Hart sees himself and others of his kind fashioning a thin blue line, which, like belief in God, holds back a swelling tide of evil, "murder and debauchery." Despite their tensions, Cohle and Hart are not far from agreement. The difference, it seems to me, is that where Hart believes that divine law and man's law keep the rabble in line, Cohle sees law as superfluous, as those who follow moral law will do so of their own accord. It follows, then, that where Hart might view himself as a dispassionate administrator and enforcer of law, Cohle more honestly identifies with Chamayou's hunter, "getting out in the open" those "pieces of shit" like their faceless adversary, not restrained by self or social convention. As we will soon see, this fearful hunter of men and monsters is well represented by those cops who do the actual work of policing.

In *True Detective* as it is at this very moment, the freak show of debauchery and murder is distilled down to its terrifying core: the serial killer, a figure that projects a society's blackest desires and elicits its most righteous vengeance simultaneously.[59] One need only peruse Netflix's mass catalogue of serial-killer documentaries and dramas to reckon the immense popularity and profitability of this particular corner of the true crime genre, what cultural theorist Brian Jarvis has called "Monsters Inc."[60] Present in the first scenes but not revealed until the final episode, Cohle and Hart's adversary stalks the otherworldly Louisiana bayous hiding in the dark like, in Pizzolatto's words, "a creature out in the tall grass that you can't see."[61] But because the monster/enemy/adversary is unnamed through most of the series, the project of true detection is more accurately one of true conjecture, projecting the killer's shifting, sinister shadow across each of its eight episodes. What this demonstrates is that in order for the police story to deliver on its powerful ideological message, it is not necessary to solve the crime or bring the killer to justice, as those who study the producers and consumers of true crime suggest; instead, the police story must simply invoke the *imagination* of an enemy.[62] This is perhaps why Pizzolatto says that he meant more for the series to "take the form of a manhunt . . . than any kind of a whodunit."[63] Which is to say that the form the enemy assumes actually matters little to the mobilization of the police story, and likewise police power—the point is that there is a monster somewhere, whether hiding in the tall grass or standing in plain view. As Chamayou similarly reminds, the police power is a power of pursuit: it does not deal with "legal subjects but rather bodies in movement, bodies that escape and that it must catch, bodies that pass by and that it must intercept."[64] The ongoing and perpetual *hunt for the monster*—in the mind and on the streets—calls forth and reproduces the police power.

As Cohle plainly admits, the world of police is a world *where nothing is ever solved*. Whether the killer escapes or is brought to justice, the theatrics of police detection always leave some questions unanswered, just as it creates or uncovers altogether new questions. What were the killer's motivations? Did he have help? Are there more like him? That policing—real and imagined—always manages to create more questions than it answers and identifies more suspects than it apprehends is at once one of its most deeply held secrets and repugnant horrors. For it to endure, the police power must have an enemy; it must create a monster to find and fight, kill, or cage.

The Monster at the End

Despite persistent allusions to some otherworldly horror, *True Detective* fails to deliver the supernatural. Questions of Carcosa and the King in Yellow instead dissolve into Errol Childress, an unhinged but apparently ordinary man living with his wife/sister on a rotting plantation deep in the bayou. Authoring this particular enemy, *True Detective* lazily draws upon and reaffirms a clichéd and conservative narrative built upon the supposed biological inferiority of the rural poor and the overstated but tidy causality of interfamily sexual abuse and violence found elsewhere in films like *Deliverance* and enshrined in the sociobiology "family studies" of early American eugenics. Such is the function of the hunt for the enemy, distilling and reproducing the symbols, language, and names of abjection, radical alterity, and monstrosity.

But again, the enemy is always an incidental prop establishing the necessity of an even more fearsome figure, the police. All of this is, of course, readily apparent in *True Detective*. In one scene, for instance, Marty, having committed yet another offense against his wife and family, self-loathingly asks Cohle, "Do you wonder ever if you're a bad man?" to which Cohle replies, "No. I don't wonder, Marty. The world needs bad men. *We keep the other bad men from the door.*"[65] Again, we are not simply informed of the existence of the monstrosity in police but warned of its absolute necessity. Contradicting his pessimistic, nihilistic façade, Cohle endorses the rogue's notion of breaking the law to uphold the law, advancing a fundamentally Hobbesian view of social order—a world occupied, ordered, and ruled by *bad men*.

Like the "ghetto children" who drew monsters with badges, the monster in police, or in this instance the monstrous face of police hidden behind a human mask, is a metaphor dropped at several points throughout the series. Returning to the Evangelical tent revival in episode three, the imagery in the fiery sermon of preacher Joel Theriot (Shea Whigham) foreshadows this important theme:

> Now, I'm here today to talk to you about reality. I'm here to tell you about what you already know. That this, all this, is not real. It is merely the limitation of our senses, which are meager

devices. Your angers and your griefs and your separations are a fevered hallucination once suffered by us all, we prisoners of light and matter. And there we all are, our faces pressed to the bars, looking out, looking up, asking the question, begging the question: Are you there? . . . If ever your sorrow becomes such a burden that you forget yourself, forget this world, I want you to remember this truth. It's as indelible as the sun in the sky and the ground beneath your feet: *this world is a veil, and the face you wear is not your own.*[66]

Begging his parishioners to consider the unseen and outside, Theriot channels a Lovecraftian ontology in which unknowing subjects, "faces pressed to the bars, looking out," are imprisoned on a "placid island of ignorance in the midst of black seas of infinity." And just as these subjects can never know the true nature of their own reality, as inhabitants of the subjective world-for-us, they cannot know themselves, either. Later in the same episode, in an extended monologue in an interrogation room, Cohle sketches out his theory of subjectivity more fully.

You see, we all got what I call a life trap—a gene-deep certainty that things will be different, that you'll move to another city and meet the people that'll be the friends for the rest of your life, that you'll fall in love and be fulfilled. Fucking fulfillment, and closure, whatever the fuck, those two fuckin' empty jars to hold this shit storm. Nothing's ever fulfilled, not until the very end. And closure—nothing is ever over . . .

People . . . I have seen the finale of thousands of lives, man. Young, old, each one was so sure of their realness. That their sensory experience constituted a unique individual. Purpose, meaning. So certain that they were more than a biological puppet. Truth wills out, everybody sees once the strings are cut, all fall down.

This . . . This is what I'm talking about. This is what I mean when I'm talkin' about time, and death, and futility. Alright, there are broader ideas at work, mainly what is owed between us as a society for our mutual illusions. Fourteen straight hours of

staring at DBs—these are the things ya think of. You ever done
that? You look in their eyes, even in a picture, doesn't matter if
they're dead or alive, you can still read 'em. You know what you
see? They welcomed it . . . Not at first, but . . . right there in
the last instant. It's an unmistakable relief. See, 'cause they were
afraid, and now they saw for the very first time how easy it was
to just . . . let go. Yeah, they saw, in that last nanosecond, they
saw . . . what they were. You, yourself, this whole big drama, it
was never more than a jerry-rig of presumption and dumb will,
and you could just let go. To finally know that you didn't have
to hold on so tight. To realize that all your life, you know, all
your love, all your hate, all your memories, all your pain, it was
all the same thing. It was all the same dream, a dream that you
had inside a locked room, a dream about being a person. And
like a lot of dreams, there's a monster at the end of it.

Attacking the Cartesian subject, Cohle imagines an experiential and
sensory dreamworld where the subject is trapped in a room or prison
of their own making, a world of joy and pain, of fear and desire.[67] The
monster at the end to which Cohle refers, at least in the narrative of
the series, refers to his enemy, the criminal. But more subtly, he is in
fact referring to his own subjectivity, the real face that hides behind
the mask that he, other police, and all who inhabit this world wear.
When Cohle finally confronts Childress, this is perhaps confirmed.
With the two locked in battle, Childress leans in and whispers *"Take
off your mask, little priest,"* begging Cohle to reveal or perhaps confront
the monstrous face hidden behind the mask of human *and* police.

  With Cohle beating information out of suspects and Hart exact-
ing bloody revenge on two boys caught in congress with his underage
daughter—to say nothing of their cold-blooded executions of two
meth-cooking child molesters—the monstrous violence of police is
laid bare throughout the series. In fact, one analysis went so far as
to record fifty-seven individual crimes committed by Cohle alone
and to estimate a cumulative prison sentence of 781 years under the
Louisiana criminal code.[68] In another scene, where Cohle rousts
Lucy, a truck-stop sex worker, he even more plainly admits the monstrosity of the police power and the *bad*, or what Hobbes might call
the *darkness*[69] of his own character.

LUCY: I thought you were gonna bust me.

COHLE: I told you, I'm not interested.

LUCY: Yeah, I know. You're kinda strange, like you might be
dangerous.

COHLE: *Of course I'm dangerous. I'm police. I can do terrible
things to people with impunity.*[70]

That police are empowered to *do terrible things to people with impunity* is precisely the sublimated *horror of police*. And because it is so tightly bound up with the Cartesian subject/object correlation and the ontology of the world-for-us, it is a horror that few are willing to entertain, let alone openly admit. Yet the horror of police is not simply a matter of denial, as plainly depicted in myriad cultural texts: police are the monsters *preferred* over others—Leviathan over Behemoth—the *bad men* who guard the door.

Cohle's "life trap" shows how his subjectivity is produced. Rather than simply being victims of an inescapable ideology that dictates the benevolence of police, political subjects are active participants in the production of their own subjectivity and relationship to power. In order to avoid an encounter with the Real, political subjects solicit the trap of a coherent symbolic order, reaffirming its coherence by resigning themselves to the order of things—a violent world of competition and exploitation, tamed, or at least administered, by the superior violence of police.[71] In other words, the ideology that glosses over policing's many contradictions and failures is not simply imposed by political power from above but is also actively produced by those who make the Faustian bargain, choosing the violence of police in order to avoid the more horrifying realities of an inherently inhospitable and insecure world.

In another of his many rants against religion, Cohle diagnoses this dynamic subjectifying process in what he calls our shared capacity for illusion.

The ontological fallacy of expecting a light at the end of the tunnel, well, that's what the preacher sells, same as a shrink. See, the preacher, he encourages your capacity for illusion. Then he tells you it's a fucking virtue. Always a buck to be had doing that, and it's such a desperate sense of entitlement, isn't it?[72]

Not unlike the self-deception identified by Ligotti, Žižek, and Peter Wessel Zapffe that we humans enlist to restrain the horrors of our own consciousness, Cohle finds in religion an instrument that allows people to continue to persist despite human failings and the horror of their own mortality. As a cop, Cohle should have counted himself among the preacher and shrink as another who sells the illusion of a coherent symbolic order, when he in fact knows all too well that this is a *world where nothing is ever solved*.

In the end, then, the first season of *True Detective* is not a Nietzschean fantasy of men "who hunt monsters and become monsters themselves" after all; as police, Hart and Cohle were always already monsters. What it offers is instead another iteration of the intoxicating yet dangerous mythology of the police story. The "macho nonsense" of Cohle and Hart, their violence and crimes, all justified by a Manichean ontology that positions the police as the thin blue line between goodness and evil.[73] If we stopped here, *True Detective* would still be a useful but not necessarily unique journey into the noxious ideology of the police story. Yet it is Cohle's philosophical pessimism and the paradox of a nihilist policeman that provide one final and particularly useful avenue for critique.

The Unthinkable World

The obvious task here is to square the disjuncture between Cohle's philosophical positions and his chosen profession. Why would an antinatalist pessimist endeavor to solve crimes, avenge the wronged, punish the violator? Early on, when Hart and Cohle are getting to know each other, we are given a direct answer to these questions.

HART: Can I ask you something? You're Christian, yeah?

COHLE: No.

HART: Well, what do you got the cross for in your apartment?

COHLE: That's a form of meditation.

HART: How's that?

COHLE: I contemplate the moment in the garden. The idea of allowing your own crucifixion.

HART: But you're not a Christian, so what do you believe?

COHLE: I believe that people shouldn't talk about this type of shit at work.

HART: Hold on, hold on. Three months we been together, I get nothing from you. Today, what we're into now, do me a courtesy, okay? I'm not trying to convert you.

COHLE: I'd consider myself a realist, but in philosophical terms I'm what's called a pessimist.

HART: Okay, what's that mean?

COHLE: It means I'm bad at parties.

HART: Let me tell you, you ain't great outside of parties, either.

COHLE: I think human consciousness is a tragic misstep in evolution. We became too self-aware. Nature created an aspect separated from itself. We are creatures that should not exist by natural law.

HART: Well that sounds god-fucking-awful, Rust.

COHLE: We are things that labor under the illusion of having a self. This accretion of sensory experience and feeling, programmed, with total assurance, that we're each somebody. When, in fact, everybody's nobody.

HART: I wouldn't go around spouting that shit if I was you. People around here don't think that way. I don't think that way.

COHLE: I think the honorable thing for our species to do is deny our programming. Stop reproducing. Walk hand in hand into extinction.

HART: So what's the point of getting out of bed in the morning?

COHLE: I tell myself I bear witness, but the real answer is that it's obviously my *programming*, and I lack the constitution for suicide.[74]

Even Cohle, a man who believes humankind to be a "tragic misstep in evolution," who openly decries the futility of existence, and who advocates planned extinction, cannot deny his *programming* and the compulsive solicitation of the trap of a coherent symbolic order. Despite all his blustering nihilism, Cohle himself "labors under the illusion of having a self," is "programmed with total assurance" that he is in fact *somebody*—a subject of liberal capitalist social order. As a representative of that order, Cohle cannot escape the Cartesian world-for-us and its Manichean ontology, pitting police against an ambiguous and spectral but ever-present evil.

In the waning minutes of the season, as the pair revisit their near-deaths resulting from their confrontation with Childress, Cohle's subjectivity is further revealed as his nihilism finally gives way.

> COHLE: I tell you, Marty, I been up in that room looking out those windows every night here just thinking, it's just one story. The oldest.
>
> HART: What's that?
>
> COHLE: Light versus dark.
>
> HART: Well, I know we ain't in Alaska, but it appears to me that the dark has a lot more territory.
>
> COHLE: Yeah, you're right about that. You're looking at it wrong, the sky thing.
>
> HART: How's that?
>
> COHLE: Well, once there was only dark. You ask me, the light's winning.[75]

In her critique of the series, Erin K. Stapleton suggests that Cohle has "softened his horror for the uselessness of life" and the spirituality of his near-death experience has reawakened a "latent nostalgia for the monotheistic dialectic between 'good' and 'evil.'"[76] But this is hardly nostalgia, and Cohle's is no conversion. Rather, he simply reaffirms the position of the police within the "oldest story," the story of light versus dark, good versus evil—a story that he and Marty, as always already subjects and servants of the world-for-us, were doomed to play out.

Just as Hart and Cohle are programmed in service of a particular type of order, so, too, are liberal subjects who disavow the inherent violence of police and actively solicit the trap of a coherent symbolic order and the place of police within the ontologies of *world* and *earth*. In regard to the former, as those who enforce the wage, protect private property, and produce an unequal racial order, the police are vital to the creation and continuation of the late-capitalist *world*, one that is always imagined as being for some of us. That the police are inseparable from this world is all the more apparent in attempts to imagine an objective *earth*. As Thacker is clear to point out, while we might be able to imagine the objective thing in itself, the paradox is that "the moment we think it and attempt to act on it, it ceases to be the world-in-itself and becomes the world-for-us."[77]

As will be explored in the following chapters, this paradox is neatly illustrated by the place of the police within the apocalyptic and dystopian imaginaries. Where the apocalyptic imaginary portends the lawless barbarism of disorder, dystopian texts like *1984* and *Fahrenheit 451* depict the barbarism of order, warning of a world beset by far too many, or perhaps the wrong kind of, police (i.e., "militarized"). Even more subtly, films that employ an asteroid strike or earthquake to invoke the apocalyptic powerfully illustrate the horror of policing's impotence through the singular warning that there are some, in fact many, things for which they are simply of no use. In the zombie film *World War Z* (2013), for instance, when, in the midst of panic and looting, the film's protagonist (Brad Pitt) kills two men who were attacking his wife and immediately submits to a responding police agent, he quickly learns that the agent is also looting and offers no protection. The representation of policing's human fallibility and impotence again illustrates the many ways that policing is tied to the collapse or continuation of the symbolic order. Together, the abject concrete universal, the undeniable truth, is this: police are often not there when you need them, around when you don't, and ultimately of no use either way.

Capitalist realism, as Fisher reminds, occupies the horizons of the thinkable, even the boundaries of the apocalyptic and dystopian.[78] To imagine the end of this world, or the end of capitalism, we must also imagine the end of police. The challenge, then, for those who hope for a world free of the violence of capital and police is how to escape this ontological trap. The Lovecraftian weird, which has been touted by Thacker and others for its ability to help contemplate the unthinkable, offers a clue. Despite his odious racism, Lovecraft's oeuvre is a heuristic for those working within the varied fields of critical animal studies, posthumanism, new materialism, speculative realism, and object-oriented ontology. With the help of the weird, philosopher Graham Harman proposes an object-oriented ontology intent on challenging the correlation between thinking and being and the anthropocentric assumption that the things that exist do so only *for us*.[79] As deployed by Pizzolatto in *True Detective*, Harman sees the Lovecraftian weird, inhabited by indescribable monsters and otherworldly forces defying human comprehension, as productive of the gaps between objects and their unknowable qualities. This sort of speculative realism "does not mean that we are able to state correct propositions about the real world" but instead concedes that (noumenal) "reality is too real to be translated without remainder into any sentence, perception, practical action, or anything else."[80] For Harman and other thinkers of his variety, the promise of this sort of speculative thought lies in its ability to undermine anthropocentric human exceptionalism and offer a starting point for a more munificent engagement with the world that each of us create and inhabit.

Criminologists Steve Hall and Simon Winlow insist that those who theorize about the causes and consequences of crime may benefit from such a speculative position, one that could "dispassionately and without optimism" apprehend the present and its consequences "as contingent realities in the 'cold world,' and reflect on our role in their causation, and speculate freely on how things might have turned out differently and might turn out differently, should we choose to change our way of doing things."[81] Elsewhere, Winlow[82] calls for an enlightened catastrophism that abandons the myth of reform, incremental progress, and easy solutions for the clarity of a grim realism better equipped to imagine the dystopian future, or perhaps reckon the dystopian *present*.[83] "Once we have imagined this future," he writes, a "shock of recognition and conscious acceptance" must and will compel us to "be brave enough to face the future and look it square in the face, and then join with others to fashion the forms of intervention that can arrest our slow descent into the chaos of the future." Turning the capitalist realist imaginary back on itself, a purposeful misreading of its own texts—those of the supposed Hobbesian necessity of the brutal criminality of the monster-fighter "bad cop"—opens a parallax view of the horrific present fabricated and occupied by always already militarized forces of armed men, organized to uphold the racial capitalist order. If the contemporary police story helps reaffirm the Hobbesian view that the police are always necessary and redeemable, perhaps what is offered by the horror of police is the pessimistic view that the police are, in fact, irredeemable. Here in the cold light of day, we better apprehend how and why liberal subjects—beset by an objectless anxiety and fear of the monster—cling to and actively solicit the solipsistic Cartesian ontology of the world-for-us and its intractable violence and inequality.

Because the gap between appearance and essence is irreducible, the best way forward is to formulate the antagonisms necessary to better understand a certain social order. The police story and the antagonisms found therein clearly illustrate the fantasies that reproduce the dystopian present. The challenge, which we will return to by the book's end, is to think outside the subject in order to imagine the unthinkable, a *world-without-police*.[84] Characterized by the radical negation of the self, the subject, and its institutions, such a world perhaps then portends what Henri Lefebvre saw as the "arrival of a new kind of thinking": that which "does not shy away from the horror of the world, the darkness, but looks it straight in the face, and thus passes over into a different kingdom, which is not the kingdom of darkness."[85] But for now, let us turn to the barbarism of disorder and ponder the ways that the police power is reaffirmed by the apocalyptic imaginary and the seemingly irrepressible fantasies of the end of the world.

CHAPTER 2

The Police at the End of the World, or The Political Theology of the Thin Blue Line

> It is estimated that by 1970, 45 percent of the metropolitan area of Los Angeles will be Negro . . . If you want any protection for your home and family . . . you're going to have to get in and support a strong Police Department. If you don't, come 1970, God help you.
>
> —LAPD Chief William H. Parker, televised address during the Watts Rebellion, August 1965

Hollywood tastemakers, it seems, are quick to bet on the end of the world. From plagues and pandemics to comets, meteors, zombies, and alien invasions, whatever the calamity is will be knocked down by human ingenuity, solidarity, and will—and usually inside the space of two hours. Of the many to perform this filmic ritual of death and rebirth, the big-budget CGI spectacle *2012*, which features a coronal mass ejection and full polar reversal as its engine of demise, is exemplary in terms of the scale and manner in which the end is realized. As if cribbed from Mike Davis's masterful *Ecology of Fear*, *2012*'s apocalyptic fantasy is captured in the utter decimation of Los Angeles.[1] Landmark buildings topple, mountains rise from the pavement, and the city slides into the Pacific, sliding along with it the detritus of Western modernity. Not so fast, says a multinational team of scientists who have engineered a fleet of giant arks on which heads of state and global elites will ride out the storm.

Given that the film was released in 2009, well ahead of the 2012 apocalypse anticipated by interpreters and adherents of the Mesoamerican Long Count (Mayan) calendar but dead center in a financial apocalypse triggered by unrestrained speculation and manipulation of the U.S. housing market, it is little wonder that this particular rendering of the end of the world finished fifth among the highest-grossing films that year. Like others of its kind, *2012* is less a fantasy projection of latent anxieties and more a distillation or exacerbation of the present, ending as it does with the surviving band of politicians, super-rich passengers, and a few soldiers, servants, and stowaway commoners set to colonize a newly formed African supercontinent; the rest of Earth's wretched souls have been, as the late, great comedian George Carlin once predicted, "sloughed off like a bad case of fleas." Whether brought on by solar flares or credit default swaps—as the unhinged conspiracy theorist who correctly predicted the film's apocalypse put it—at the end of the world, only "Bill Gates, Rupert Murdoch, or some Russian billionaire" stands a chance.

Returning to the smoldering present, the California wildfires suggest just this, as the estates of Kanye and Kim Kardashian West and other wealthy residents of Malibu are perennially spared by their own private firefighting and security forces. The uneven apocalypse, to use Evan Calder Williams's useful phrase, engineered by California's elite follows a trend that Evan Osnos reported on for the *New Yorker* in 2017. In his article "Doomsday Prep for the Super Rich," Osnos describes how many of the world's elite are prepping, planning, and, indeed, investing in civilization's coming "crackup."[2] With private security forces and private jets on standby to deliver them to the Midwest and defunct ICBM silos retrofitted as luxury blastproof condos, or to stocked and fortified estates in New Zealand, these super-rich superpreppers seem to be in on a secret that eludes the peasantry. Warning of the "thin cultural ice" on which society presently skates, one former Facebook executive whom Osnos interviewed explained, "when society loses a healthy founding myth, it descends into chaos." With the shorthand WROL (without the rule of law), the founding myth to which he refers is, of course, the myth of liberal order. Under such conditions, the executive continued, no matter how wealthy, "one guy alone" will not outlast the mob unaided by armed militia or private police. This is hardly the admission of some closely guarded secret, as the stockpiling of weapons and ammo and the preparation of tactics and fortifications are among the chief tasks of all preppers, elite or common. There is, however, an important distinction to be made here. These wealthy preppers are concerned with not simply the dissolution of law but more precisely the dissolution of the *rule* of law backed by police who secure their lives and property at the point of a gun. We should therefore not overlook the underlying and deeply held belief of some that the ability to administer violence and impose order is as necessary to the resuscitation of civilization, or at least an individual's survival, as are food, shelter, and clothing.

For some dissent, Osnos sought out Max Levchin, who, unlike his fellow PayPal cofounder Peter Thiel, is among the few from within the Silicon Valley tech crowd openly critical of the growing trend toward luxury survivalism. Of his wealthy brethren "worried about the pitchforks," Levchin asks, how many support charities for homeless people or pay income inequality, even within their own companies, more than lip service? Robert Johnson, head of the nonprofit think tank Institute for New Economic Thinking, assembled after the 2008 crash, seems to agree, insisting that funded and functional public education, universal health care, or even arts and recreation could perhaps begin to pacify the incendiary potentials of the dispossessed. However, just as with those set to ride out the crisis in a boutique bunker, Levchin and Johnson, whether motivated by kindness or simply hoping to mitigate the inevitable, clearly feel the tremors of the gathering angry mob. From either perspective, then, the question is not when it will finally kick off but what to do when it does.

Continuing on with themes raised in the previous chapter, my contention here is that while often absent in the fantasy projection of civilization's crackup, in the subsequent attempts to reassemble its scattered shards, it is the police who emerge as central, if not unavoidable, figures. In his book *Crime and the Imaginary of Disaster*, Majid Yar sees postapocalyptic fictions depicting the fragility of liberal order as diagnostic of widespread anxieties concerning a world of seemingly increasing violence, war, and unrest.[3] For Yar, the films and texts of the apocalyptic imaginary open up productive space in the ceaseless debates surrounding the crisis of law and order, characterized, as they often are, by urban hellscapes beset by lawlessness and violent predation. Departing ever so slightly, my suggestion is that our shared understandings of civilization, particularly those of Western liberal democracies, are inseparable from the police, as it is they who are thought not only to deliver us from atavistic, precivilized savagery but, in fabricating social order, to actively transform once "masterless men" into proper political, hence *civilized*, human subjects.[4]

As evinced by 2012 and examples to follow, while police are sometimes conspicuously absent or impotent as civilization dissolves into chaos, they nevertheless play a central role in restoring the old order—a world for *some* of us. Take, for instance, the speculative position of police within the unfolding horrors of global climate change. With a veritable apocalypse lining up for decades, rather than raising a global movement of mutual aid to meet the looming crisis, the best the U.S. government has been able to muster is a disparate collection of toothless coalitions and some minor legal restrictions enforced by economic penalties (most of which were evacuated under the Trump administration)—essentially relying on the police power to force begrudging compliance. Recognizing the enormity of the problems that lie ahead, but with little faith in the ability of mass movements to thwart the interests of capital, Geoff Mann and Joel Wainwright in their book *Climate Leviathan* go so far as to predict, perhaps hope for, the rise of a collective global order, a sort of Hobbesian "planetary sovereignty, defined by an exception proclaimed in the name of preserving life on Earth." They argue science, evidence, and reason have, thus far, failed to marshal a sustained opposition to the challenges we collectively face; as a last-ditch effort, the pair foresee the rise of a multinational sovereign power, invested with the authority to decide "what measures are necessary and what and who must be sacrificed in the interests of life on Earth."[5] In other words, on the road to environmental ruin—at the literal end of the line—again looms the monstrous violence of the sovereign and its twin powers, war and police.

Despite Mann and Wainwright's convincing argument, one might ask just how likely such a power is to emerge and just how effective it might be in the face of powerful interests, let alone in the face of a natural world increasingly, in Thacker's language, *not-for-us*. In late September 2018, Eric Levitz wrote in *New York Magazine* how a study recently released by the Trump administration had predicted a catastrophic rise in global temperature of between 4 and 7 degrees Celsius by century's end. Such jump in global temperature—well beyond the point of no return, commonly set at a rise of 2 degrees Celsius—would leave low-lying coastal areas along the U.S. Eastern Seaboard, notably Manhattan, submerged. Stunning as the forecasts were, even more so was the Trump administration's decision to use the report to justify the repeal of federal fuel efficiency guidelines established by the Obama administration. The precautionary logic, apparently, was that since the proposed guidelines could not halt the predicted rise in temperature on their own, why bother? It was as though, as Levitz speculated, the administration had declared the future lost and had decided to accelerate through to the end. Not unlike the super rich withdrawing, ahead of revolution, to bespoke bunkers and private islands, Mike Davis sees a privileged elite planning similarly for life on an increasingly inhospitable planet. Contrary to Mann and Wainwright's global Leviathan, Davis suggests that as the symptoms of climate change become more apparent, those with means will attempt to insulate themselves from the panicked scramble for resources and solid ground. Efforts toward mitigation, he suggests, will likely be abandoned for a sort of triage, predictably placing "Earth's first-class passengers" at the front of the line for "green and gated oases of permanent affluence on an otherwise stricken planet."[6] The future foretold by Davis and demonstrated by the Trump administration is less a form of Mark Fisher's capitalist realism and perhaps more akin to *capitalist nihilism*.[7] Unlike the well-worn observation that it is easier to imagine the end of the world than the end of capitalism, such a view portends conditions under which some not only imagine the end of the world but openly tout the brash accelerationist response—*bring it on*—because it is not their world that is imperiled; it is ours. Here, the mantra of the capitalist nihilist might well be *If the ice is gonna melt and the seas are gonna rise, at least I'll watch it all go down from the deck of my yacht!* So how might capitalist nihilism relate to, involve, or reveal the horror of police?

The centrality and impotence of police played out in high definition with the hurricane that struck the Carolinas in fall 2018. While assisting evacuation and rescue efforts, some local police also found time to vigorously defend Walmarts and dollar stores against looting and, even more outrageously, arrest some well-meaning volunteers for rescuing stranded cats and dogs without permits. Demonstrating their relative disregard for human life, at least human life in the category of criminal, the South Carolina Department of Corrections decided to "shelter in place"—in other words, abandon—thousands of prisoners housed in facilities smack-dab in the middle of mandatory evacuation zones. Tragically emblematic of that decision, in the same state, two women trapped inside a prison van that had been swept into floodwaters drowned, shackled and chained to their seats, while their guards sought refuge on the van's roof.[8] Paying heed to these and other examples, if we are to understand the 2018 hurricane season as a glimpse into our future in the Anthropocene, Capitalocene, or Cthulhucene[9]—whichever you prefer—we might quickly conclude that in police we'll find abandonment and death, and in the prison we'll find our tomb.

Enmity, War, God

If the limits and failings of police are as apparent as I suggest, then the question persists, Why must we collectively cling to what the police offer when they offer very little? Again, the simplest and perhaps best answer is fear: fear of others, fear of death, and fear of an unknown (or, rather, uncontrolled) future beg us to license the great violence committed on our behalf.[10] And it is the fear of an ever-present, though not always visible, enemy, as Mark Neocleous makes clear in *The Universal Adversary*, that forms the basis of the social contract and sovereign power. He writes:

> Fear of other humans drives us initially into the security and protection offered by the state, but the *ongoing* project of security is produced through an *imagination of a new Enemy* said to be an Enemy of all the members of that state and a threat to the very existence of the state itself.[11]

The state's quasi-religious power to conjure "things invisible" and "enemies fearsome" that Neocleous finds in Thomas Hobbes[12] mirrors what the late American political scientist Michael Rogin called political demonology—the conjuring of monsters by the inflation, stigmatization, and dehumanization of political foes.[13] As Carl Schmitt famously argues in *The Concept of the Political*, so exalted are the powers to name and demonize the enemy that they are the defining feature of the state and of the political itself:

> For as long as a people exists in the political sphere, this people must, even if only in the most extreme case—and whether this point has been reached has to be decided by it—determine by itself the distinction of friend and enemy. Therein resides the essence of its political existence. When it no longer possesses the capacity or the will to make this distinction, it ceases to exist politically.[14]

While the friend/enemy binary mirrors Manichean notions of good and evil, for Schmitt the political is distinguished by the *state of war*, fought not necessarily for "ideals or norms of justice" but always against a "real enemy."[15] In other words, once the distinction has been made and the line has been drawn, war follows.[16] Powerfully and succinctly summarizing Schmitt's position, Adam Kotsko adds that the political simply "deals with things worth killing and dying for," making it, thus, "the most important realm of human existence."[17]

Viewed through the crosshairs and pistol sights of enmity, police are less concerned with the why and more with the *who* of war. Granted the power to name the enemy, police operate as "petty sovereigns," to use Judith Butler's[18] language, free-floating agents with the discretion to invoke the law and, crucially, its violence as they see fit. As such, police must be understood not as servants of some mythical commonwealth but as sovereigns themselves, practitioners of, as Butler says, a "lawless and prerogatory power, a 'rogue' power par excellence."[19] Once clear of the minor hurdles of probable cause and reasonableness of command, their orders, desires, and predilections become law in action. Should a citizen/subject ignore or

challenge the police, they become enemy, the target of legally permitted violence—war.

Recalling John Locke's understanding of the prerogative or the
executive's discretionary power, Tyler Wall illustrates how the police
power, prefigured as an "ordinary" or "constant emergency power,"
was used to establish the legal architecture undergirding the Obama
administration's targeted-killing drone program. Wall refers to a
position paper authored by the then attorney general Eric Holder
that cited *Tennessee v. Garner* and the so-called "fleeing felon rule"
to argue that drone operators, like police, work under a state of ambiguous contingency and, hence, perpetual emergency, thereby ex-
empting their decisions to kill as pursuant to "national security." Perhaps mirroring the juridical maxim *enumeratio, ergo limitatio* (listing,
hence limiting), Wall suggests, "the very nature of the police encounter is such that no universal rules can ever really apply. If the
prerogative is limitless, this power is operative in the permissiveness
granted police: the law refuses to limit police discretion by literally
refusing to define it."[20] The emergency powers used by the president
to authorize "signature strikes" in the War on Terror, Wall finds in
the discretionary powers of the petty sovereigns—or, to use his term,
"everyday executives"—that patrol city streets.[21]

While this understanding of policing's emergency powers might
appear to be the purview of only its practitioners or stuffy legal theo-
rists, even the most esoteric bits of cop knowledge, as we have seen,
appear readily across the screens and texts of the police story, sitting in plain view, strewn like clues littering a crime scene. The 2011
police drama *Rampart*, for instance, offers a textbook explication of
Wall's "ordinary emergency." In the film's first minutes, viewers meet
Dave Brown (again, Woody Harrelson), a quintessentially bad cop
adjusting to the scrutiny brought on by the LAPD's Rampart scandal. When Brown's young trainee asks whether he is worried that
his old-school, "hard-charging" ways no longer fit with a department
rocked by scandal, he quips coldly, "Okay, listen, this is the most
important thing I've told you so far. Everything you learned at the
academy—bullshit. Illegal is just a sick bird. This is a military occupation, kid. Emergency law." Of course, as the film progresses,
Brown invokes his understanding of "emergency law" to justify all
manner of violence, including murder.[22]

Again, we must recall the familiar refrain "I feared for my life," which police use to authorize their violence, and the even more direct and crude form of political demonology Darren Wilson used to justify killing Michael Brown: "he had the most intense aggressive face. The only way I can describe it, *it looks like a demon*, that's how angry he looked."[23] In Brown's case, like Eric Garner's and countless others', it matters little that Wilson purportedly responded to reports of a petty property crime. Always already on war footing, operating under a self-imposed state of constant, ordinary emergency, the ontology of police is such that any threat must be considered an existential one. Of course, in the legacy, dare I say tradition, of U.S. police violence, the designation of enemy follows from and cannot be disentangled from the institution's racist origins, which were rooted and flourished in the poisoned soil of chattel slavery.[24]

And so we are forced to depart from Zygmunt Bauman's well-known understanding of social life populated by friends, enemies, and strangers.[25] In the epistemology of enmity and ontology of war employed by the "everyday executives" that occupy our streets, there is no third position—only friends and foes, allies and adversaries, angels and *demons*. From the police position of absolute enmity, we can perhaps better understand their seeming inexplicable and wanton violence. Sadly, for instance, in November 2018, Jemel Roberson was shot and killed by police responding to a disturbance call at Manny's Blue Room, a bar where he worked as a security guard. From accounts, Roberson, who was on duty and in uniform, was holding a combative patron on the ground while waiting for assistance, but police shot and killed him as soon as they arrived on scene. Calling the incident a tragic case of "friendly fire," Illinois's Midlothian Police Department initially refused to release the name of the shooter, who has since been cleared of any wrongdoing.[26] In a tragically similar set of circumstances, just two weeks after Midlothian police killed Roberson, a twenty-one-year-old man named Emantic "EJ" Bradford Jr. was shot and killed by Hoover, Alabama, police who were responding to a disturbance call at a shopping mall. According to reports, Bradford was simply a bystander to an altercation between mall patrons but was nevertheless shot three times in the back and killed. As with the Roberson matter, the police agent who killed Bradford was swiftly cleared of all charges.[27] While some police apologists are sure to cling to mitigating circumstances, or to dismiss both deaths as the unfortunate consequences of a supposedly dangerous profession, we must not overlook or forget that both Roberson and Bradford were Black.

This is the point Karen and Barbara Fields make in their book *Racecraft*, a term they use to describe the complex yet largely hidden collection of background forces that constitute race and racial differences and render the attendant practices of racism somehow rational.[28] Like the superstitious folk rituals and practices that make devotees of witchcraft believe the implausible and impossible, race, racial difference, and racial hierarchy are born of an equally pernicious set of superstitious beliefs and unscientific reasoning. Long since tasked with producing racial categories and patrolling the color line, policing is a bubbling cauldron, so to speak, of racecraft. Indeed, in the United States, police and crime are primary means by which liberal subjects come to know the supposed realities of race and racial difference and, importantly, act on them. In one particularly brutal instance, Fields and Fields recall the killing of Omar Edwards, a young Black NYPD officer who was mistaken for an armed suspect and shot and killed by a white colleague. Noting numerous similar incidents, they ask, "Why do black officers not mistake white officers for criminals and blaze away?" The answer, of course, is that while each of us has a skin color, not everyone's skin color is used as a stand-in for danger and criminality. The power of racecraft, as Barbara Fields explains elsewhere, transforms the action of the perpetrator into a characteristic of the target—*transferring one's action into another's being.*[29] Edwards lived and died as what his fellow cop thought of him: a threat. From the slave patrol, Jim Crow and the Klan, racially coded crime statistics, and eugenics to drug panics, gang sweeps, and stop and frisk, the police power has similarly constituted Blackness.

"War follows from enmity," Schmitt reminds, and war remains a possibility so long as the enemy remains viable.[30] Importantly, for our discussion here, Schmitt saw the primal and inconsolable fears of the enemy and the attendant state of war as not only defining the political but also birthing the security state's most vital institution, the police. In his reading of *Leviathan*, Schmitt writes:

> In the state of nature everyone can slay everyone else; everyone knows that everyone can slay everyone else; everyone is a foe

and a competitor of everyone else—this is the well-known *bellum omnium contra omnes* [war of all against all]. In the civil, stately condition, all citizens are secure in their physical existence; there reign peace, security, and order. This is a familiar definition of police. Modern state and modern police came into being simultaneously, and the most vital institution of this security state is the police. Astonishingly Hobbes appropriates as a characteristic of the condition of peace brought about by the police the formula of Francis Bacon of Verulam and speaks about man becoming god to man, *homo homini deus*, whereas in the state of nature man is a wolf to man. The terror of the state of nature drives anguished individuals to come together; their fear rises to an extreme; a spark of reason *(ratio)* flashes, and suddenly there stands in front of us a new god.

Who is this new god who brings peace and security to people tormented by anguish, who transforms wolves into citizens and through this miracle proves himself to be a god, obviously only a "mortal god," a *deus mortalis*, as Hobbes calls him?[31]

In the harrowing state of nature, where "man is wolf to man," the bringers of peace, security, and order become *god to man.*[32] It is precisely as the French poet and playwright Antonin Artaud once wrote: "*God does not exist, he withdraws, gets the fuck on out and leaves the cops to keep an eye on things.*"[33] Rather than diagnosing a personal preference or even political ideology, the widespread unwillingness to soberly confront just what the police are and what we ask them to do is rooted in our subjective experiences of living in and actively crafting this world-for-us. Collectively, we have not yet let the police go, because to do so would require that we let *this* world go. And so, we endorse, adopt, and reproduce an ontology where a never-ending war between good and evil is determined by savior, hero, God. Continuing on, I sketch an epistemology of enmity and ontology of war and zero in on policing's doctrinal core: the political theology of the thin blue line.

The Line Is Drawn

In order for the institution to shield itself from criticism and maintain political authority, it is crucial that liberal subjects side with and adopt the enemy of police as their own, engaging in or at least tacitly endorsing the resulting wars on crime, drugs, terror, and so on. Today, policing's enemies are named and marked in myriad ways, the least of which is the rhetoric of the thin blue line. Affixed to hats, T-shirts, stickers, flags, even inked into flesh, those who adopt the recognizable insignia apparently also see the police as righteous combatants in an ongoing struggle for civilization, thereby designating criminals, critics, and all those across the proverbial line as enemy.

While it has proliferated in the post-Ferguson era, the rhetoric of the thin blue line has its origins in the ancient mythology of the valiant men of war. In *Police: A Field Guide*, David Correia and Tyler Wall trace this history to Rudyard Kipling's poem "Tommy," which takes as its subject the "thin red line of 'eroes" in the Battle of Balaclava during the Crimean War. From the metaphorical line of a hopelessly outmatched, soon-to-be-slaughtered few, Correia and Wall locate the origins of liberalism's myth of police as the noble engineers of social order:

> The thin blue line claims that order and civilization can't exist without police, because police power is the very line—the border or boundary—dividing wickedness from the good life, morality from depravity, and the sacred from the profane. If there are no police, we are told, there will be no civilization, and life itself will devolve back to a Hobbesian state of nature, where life is nasty, brutish, and short. If we don't give our undying support to the cops, which is to say if we refuse the police definition of reality (that is, think for ourselves), mass violence and chaos will inevitably be the only result.[34]

By the time it appeared as the title of James Jones's 1962 World War II novel, the thin red line had long been colored blue, fitting the mythology of war onto U.S. police, with the implication that it is they who stand the line on our behalf. While he likely did not coin the phrase, as some suggest,[35] William H. Parker, who helmed the Los Angeles Police Department from 1950 to 1966, did much to solidify the mythology of the thin blue line in U.S. culture. As David Shaw gushed in the *Los Angeles Times* one month after the 1992 LA riots, under Parker's reign the LAPD "went from local disgrace to national fame—a crisp, militaristic 'thin blue line' (a phrase Parker coined) admired and emulated from coast to coast as it struggled valiantly to protect civilized society from godless communists, murderous thugs and the widespread dangers and decay of modern urban life."[36] An avowed white supremacist[37] and strident anticommunist, Parker organized the LAPD in accordance with his personal worldview, which saw the police as, in his words, "all that stood between the public and anarchy."[38] Parker's "public," of course, was a narrow swath of upper-class white supporters who shared his rigid nationalism and Christian conservatism. If, as Kotsko argues, political theology can be understood as theologically informed political action, the framing of politics in quasi-religious ways, or the study of transfers between the political and theological realms, we can understand Parker's LAPD as a wellspring of a particular form of political theology.[39] An unassailable sovereign authority for nearly two decades, licensed to use law, violence, and terror to remake the world as he saw fit, Parker was but one conduit for a distinct politics that dominated the Cold War–era United States.

Taking a cue from J. Edgar Hoover, who adeptly used Hollywood to embolden and protect the image of the FBI,[40] and with the help of his close friend Jack Webb, Parker used the TV cop's long-running show *Dragnet* as a propaganda arm of the LAPD. While *Dragnet* was meant to bolster police legitimacy among its white middle-class audience, the program, as Christopher Sharrett argues, was much more than a simple defense of the police, as it aimed to "define 'American values' and to separate the righteous not just from criminals but from all the misfits, oddities, and malcontents who pollute the American landscape."[41] *Dragnet* allowed Webb and, by extension, Parker to name and cathartically exorcise a litany of paranoid fears—the counterculture, queers, Black militants, communists—in the "anxious and angry tirades" of its flat-topped protagonist, Sergeant Joe Friday. As Mike Davis puts it in *City of Quartz*, "*Dragnet*'s Sergeant Friday precisely captured the Parkerized LAPD's quality of prudish alienation from a citizenry composed of fools, degenerates and psychopaths."[42]

By 1952, Parker's Public Information Division had launched its own weekly television program he named *The Thin Blue Line* to burnish the public's view of the LAPD and to set in celluloid and stone policing's position within the mythology of war. Unencumbered by the fictional gloss of *Dragnet*, Parker's *Thin Blue Line* purported "just the facts" of police work, again serving as a direct conduit for a reactionary politics aimed at "Blacks and Mexicans," "dopers," "hippies," "Commies," and anyone else who didn't fall in line with a rising order that would eventually birth the Reagan administration.[43] From *The Thin Blue Line* to the now widespread motto "protect and serve," Parker did much to position the police as modern-day crusader-knights defending the good and decent from a decadent and surrounding evil. Summarizing Parker's veneer in his book *Badges without Borders*, Stuart Schrader notes that the stern, serious, moralistic Parker's "hobbyhorse was standardization. Parkerism was proceduralism. The police procedural crime drama, a staple of US television, *was a Parker creation*. With de facto oversight of the 1950s television series *Dragnet*, Parker disseminated his vision of professional policing across the United States."[44] Without lapsing into the fool's-errand chase for the precise *effects* of media consumption, the far-rippling consequences of the police stories that Parker initiated cannot be overstated.

Bearing the undeniable weight of Parker's influence, the epistemology of enmity and the thin blue line feature prominently in the opening monologue of a latter-day saga of the LAPD, the popular cop drama *End of Watch*:

> I am the police, and I'm here to arrest you. You've broken the law. I did not write the law. I may even disagree with the law, but I will enforce it. No matter how you plead, cajole, beg, or attempt to stir my sympathies, nothing you do will stop me from placing you in a steel cage with gray bars. If you run away I will chase you. If you fight me I will fight back. If you shoot at me I will shoot back. By law I am unable to walk away. I am a consequence. I am the unpaid bill. I am fate with a badge and a gun. Behind my badge is a heart like yours. I bleed, I think, I love, and yes, I *can* be killed. And although I am but one man, I have thousands of brothers and sisters who are the same as me. They will lay down their lives for me, and I them. *We stand watch together. The thin blue line, protecting the prey from the predators, the good from the bad. We are the police.*[45]

Written by David Ayer—writer and/or director of a number of notable LAPD cop-hero dramas, including *Training Day, Street Kings, Sabotage,* and the straight-to-Netflix cop/monster fantasy *Bright*—the monologue performs the insidious but familiar trick of making police detached administrators, or perhaps bystanders, of laws they simply enforce. Indeed, in its depiction of a band of noble brothers and sisters "standing watch" on the thin blue line, protecting the prey from predators, good from bad, Ayer's authorial vision descends directly from the proceduralism of Parker, imagining police as faultless protectors, if not God's earthly designees.

As we will see, from the police of our imagination to the police on our streets, the mythology of the thin blue line powerfully characterizes an uncomplicated world thought by many to be neatly divided between friend and enemy. For instance, the National Border Patrol Council (NBPC), which is the largest labor union of the United States Border Patrol, produces a monthly podcast called *The Green Line.* The hosts, "active U.S. Border Patrol agents," claim the show "cuts through the politics, the rhetoric and the plain BS" and make "no apologies for their strong positions on border security."[46] Moving from blue line to green, each episode "broadcasting from the southern border" once opened with a sequence from the popular HBO series *Game of Thrones,* which also prominently features a wall.

Hear my words and bear witness to my vow. Night gathers, and now my watch begins. It shall not end until my death. I shall take no wife, hold no lands, father no children. I shall wear no crowns and win no glory. I shall live and die at my post. I am the sword in the darkness. I am the watcher on the walls. I am the shield that guards the realms of men. I pledge my life and honor to the Night's Watch, for this night and all the nights to come.[47]

For the uninitiated, in *Game of Thrones,* the Night's Watch stands guard over a massive ice wall that partitions the good and heroic "realms of men" from a vast zombie army. While it would be easy to write off the use of the monologue as a harmless pop culture reference, we must take them at their word and assume that the NBPC imagine themselves as noble protectors "keeping watch" on a similar wall, making up a "thin green line" that holds back an invading horde of uncivilized, subhuman, and, importantly, racialized enemies. As the clash between Border Patrol agents and the so-called "caravan" of Central American refugees at the Tijuana/San Diego border in November 2018 proves, "the line," whatever the color, is in fact the front line of an actual war, in which, like in all wars, the stakes are life and death.

Release the Beast!

Even more explicitly than films like 2012 that position a natural event as the catalyst of civilization's demise, the horror genre tends to depict the absence or impotence of police as a precondition for the murder and mayhem that unfolds. Consider, for instance, the established template of the slasher film. The terror-stricken flight of defenseless victims and the unshakable pursuit of a merciless killer tend to traverse some remote terrain—forest, desert, highway—almost always devoid of police. When police do appear, if they aren't the killers themselves, they rarely save the day, offering instead only momentary respite amid the blood and gore before they, too, meet a violent demise.

Taking this arrangement to spectacular, perhaps apocalyptic, ends, the premise of the popular horror film franchise *The Purge* rests on the engineered suspension of law, order, and police. The films imagine a near-future United States that has developed a novel, radical treatment for the excess urges thought to underlie most violence and crime: for twelve hours, one night each year, all crimes, including murder, are not only legal but encouraged as a cathartic expulsion of violent drives from the social body. Purge Night is meant also as a Malthusian culling of the lumpen poor, and members of the public are heartened to succumb to their basest desires, don terrifying carnivalesque masks and costumes, and "release the beast" by murdering undesirables or anyone else who may have offended them that year. Instituted by the New Founding Fathers, a neo-Fascist party swept into office in the midst of a second Great Depression, the yearly Purge is credited with eradicating crime and enabling full economic recovery. As if written by the zombie hand of long-dead political scientist James Q. Wilson, *The Purge* films not only remind that wicked people exist but insist that, once released from under the thumb of police, they quickly get up to wicked things. While not incredibly imaginative, the franchise is nevertheless a veritable public service announcement for the munificence of liberalism, making the horrifying descent into the state of nature an event to be overcome by cinematic heroes and, of course, banished the following morning with the return of the police.

In her widely read article "The Liberalism of Fear,"[48] Judith Shklar argues that the promise of liberalism is the freedom from fear of the violence and coercion of an unrestrained state. Yet, as Hobbes and Schmitt suggest and as *The Purge* depicts, liberalism gathers its coherence not by ensuring freedom from the tyranny of government but by emboldening the fear, terror, and horror of everyday life and then offering a slightly less horrifying alternative as remedy. This is the point Elisabeth Anker makes in her response to Shklar, "The Liberalism of Horror," in which she insists that horror, more than fear, is the animating affect of liberalism. For Anker, the horror genre reimagines the state of nature, replete with monsters that both diagnose the insecurities of the present order and, upon their defeat, reaffirms them. The films and their subsequent television spinoff, which carry the tagline "Release the beast!"—as if directly appropriating the Hobbesian mantra *homo homini lupus est*—envision a social order where sovereign power has not just receded but called forth and released "the beast," permitting man to once again become wolf to man.[49] As with the monster in police, here we are obliged to recall Jacques Derrida's *The Beast and the Sovereign*, in which he suggests that the beast, criminal, and sovereign share a "troubling resemblance," a "fascinating complicity," a "worrying familiarity," as they "seem to have in common their being-outside-the-law."[50] He writes,

> I believe that this troubling resemblance, this worrying super-position of these two beings-outside-the-law or "without laws" or "above the laws" that beast and sovereign both are when viewed from a certain angle—I believe that this resemblance explains and engenders a sort of hypnotic fascination or irresistible hallucination, which makes us see, project, perceive, as in a X-ray, the face of the beast under the features of the

sovereign; or conversely, if you prefer, it is as though, through the maw of the untamable beast, a figure of the sovereign were to appear.[51]

Placing Derrida's observations about the mutuality between beast and sovereign within the context of contemporary police violence, *The Purge* films not only imagine a lawless state of nature but, in their call to "release the beast," envision everyday subjects invested with the power of the police (sovereign, everyday executives)—able to act outside the law, releasing monstrous violence—in order to reaffirm existing social arrangements. Seemingly anticipating the films' premise as well, political theorist William Connolly likewise suggests that liberalism relies upon the looming horror of the state of nature and the fear of death to fashion proper political subjects, or at least keep them in line. He writes,

> The state of nature is shock therapy. It helps subjects get their priorities straight by teaching them what life would be like without sovereignty. It domesticates by eliciting the vicarious fear of violent death in those who have had not to confront it directly. And when one confronts the fear of early and violent death, one becomes willing to regulate oneself and accept external regulations that will secure life against its dangers. The fear of death pulls the self together. It induces subjects to accept civil society and it becomes an instrumentality of sovereign control in a civil society already installed. So while Hobbes seeks to dampen unruly lustful passions, he seeks to elicit and accentuate this one. It is a useful passion, useful to an ordering of the self and to peace and quiet in the social order.[52]

Substitute Connolly's "domesticates" with *pacifies* and we return precisely to the arrangement set out in the previous chapter, whereby the fear of violent death encourages political subjects to welcome the many inequities of the present order and the unremitting violence that undergirds it. That law and police can be and in fact are the only forces that will deliver society from disaster, disorder, chaos, and anarchy is one of the most carefully guarded and curated myths of liberal order. In fact, one recent survey not only diagnosed underlying commitments to absolutist rule but found that nearly 20 percent of the population admitted that they themselves would actively participate in the lethal violence of the Purge should they be released from the yoke of the law.[53] And because it benefits their position directly, it is the police themselves who are the most practiced in this sort of thinking.

Faced with a "budget shortfall crisis" due to "sharp declines in coal severance taxes," police in Eastern Kentucky advised their constituents to act as if *The Purge* had actually taken place. Responding to the shortfalls in early 2019, Martin County sheriff John Kirk, who polices an area of about 231 square miles and a population of twelve thousand, "temporarily ceased all law enforcement services provided by his office" and, expecting the worst, urged residents, "lock your doors, load your guns and get a biting barking dog."[54]

Even more dramatically, the website Law Enforcement Today publishes an ongoing opinion column under the nom de plume "Sgt. A. Merica," allowing cops from across the country to safely and publicly air their grievances. One particular essay, titled, "Ok, I'm Done. It's Time for the Purge," advocates for an actual purge, or at least a national police sick day—a "blue flu," as he calls it—to show the "hippies," "liberals," and "raging leftists" what life, even just a twelve-hour sliver, would be like without his kind. The anonymous author, a cop in the Northeast, writes,

Do these people not understand the role of police officers? That we are what allow them to sleep safely at night? That we protect them? Their children? . . .

"We'll show them," we say. "We'll all call out at the same time. THEN what will happen?" But . . . we don't. Because we all want to see the power of the blue flu, but at the same time we're all above it. We are here to be Sheepdogs, even if we do it in misery and count down the days to our retirement while doing it. We all secretly wish for *The Purge*, but we won't fight for it. We took an oath. We'll serve and protect. And as much as we might hate our neighbor and that socialist English teacher and that politician who identifies as a Native American . . . when the siren sounds and *The Purge* begins . . . we'll still be there to help. Just don't expect me to like you.[55]

It is important to pause and ask just what "Sgt. A. Merica's" understanding of police and social order suggests about human nature. Like those in the films, this cop apparently believes that law and police *allow* people to sleep safely at night, restraining the snarling beast that resides in each of us. For the author and, likely, others of his kind, who the police are, what they do, and what they want must never be questioned. We must do as they say and merely thank them for our lives and for forcing the surrounding wolves to act as men. Startling as it is, this worldview is not confined to the cynical editorial of one anonymous cop.

In 2014, members of the Miami-Dade Police Department used the same argument to warn of the dangers of cutting back on police resources amid contractual disputes with the city. Mimicking *The Purge* promotional materials, the police and their supporters distributed flyers warning that "During the upcoming Purge all law enforcement in Miami-Dade County will be suspended" and instructing, "Brace yourselves Miami-Dade County, as you are in for the ride of your lives . . . So, make sure you have an ample supply of water, popcorn and ammo!"[56]

Years before *The Purge* and the budget woes of Miami police, a similar campaign meant to elicit the fear and anxieties of a world without police sprang up in New York City. In 1975, a collective of police, fire department, and corrections workers calling itself the Council for Public Safety widely circulated a satirical travel guide titled *Welcome to Fear City: A Survival Guide for Visitors of the City of New York*. Bearing a menacing grim reaper skull, the pamphlet described the city as a place of violence and predation and warned, "the best advice we can give you is this: until things change, stay away from New York City if you can."[57] Ahead of public demonstrations targeting the then mayor Abraham Beame, the group took out a full-page ad in the *New York Times* to encourage fear and dissent. Under the headline "HOW MUCH IS YOUR LIFE WORTH? How about the life of your family . . . Your friends . . . Your neighbors?" the ad blamed the mayor for imperiling the lives of all New Yorkers by refusing to agree to the group's contract demands. Begging for participation and public support, it concluded, "Don't give the city up to muggers, rapists and arsonists! It's your city . . . it's

Amid contractual disputes with the city, the Miami-Dade Police Department parodies imagery from *The Purge*.

your life and safety. Attend this mass people's rally and help save a life . . . It could be yours."[58]

Though both were driven by contractual disputes, what is important to take from the Miami and New York examples is that from their vantage, and perhaps the vantage of all police, if not for their life-giving benevolence, civilization would quickly devolve into violence and debauchery. Key here is the term *all*, which is an unavoidable certainty of policing's Hobbesian ontology: just as they profess to "protect and serve," police are obliged to see *all* people as threats, enemies, and combatants in a war of chaos and disorder.

At this point, I should be clear in my assertion that the ascendency of this sort of worldview is not confined to cinematic fantasy or the screeds of a few misguided cops. Attorney General Bill Barr, at a ceremony honoring police in December 2019, reaffirmed the political theology of the thin blue line in clear, uncertain terms, stating, "Today, the American people have to focus on something else, which is the sacrifice and the service that is given by our law enforcement officers. And they have to start showing, more than they do, the respect and support that law enforcement deserve." He added that "if communities don't give that support and respect, they might find themselves without the police protection they need."[59] The force of Barr's statement is unsurprising given his long history of dutiful service in the Reagan and Bush administrations. Indeed, just a few short months after taking the office of attorney general under George H. W. Bush, Barr authored the now notorious report *The Case for More Incarceration*. Amid the still meteoric rise of mass imprisonment, Barr's argument was as you would expect: the United States was "incarcerating too few criminals, and the public [was] suffering as a result."[60]

In the years leading up to the "Reagan Revolution"—what Will Davies calls the era of "combative neoliberalism"[61]—politicians of both major U.S. parties used a particularly virulent form of political demonology to govern and restructure social life. In *Neoliberalism's Demons*, Kotsko convincingly argues that the parallels between God's demonic foes and the social order's most reviled and subjugated populations, articulated in a resurgent interest in the demonic and apocalyptic, offer a useful framework of understanding for the rise of neoliberalism.[62] Mirroring Neocleous's assertions in *The Universal Adversary* and the dialectic of Christianity discussed previously, Kotsko sees God's earthly authority as derived from a worthy opponent. Kotsko therefore understands political demonization, a key tactic of power, as a sort of moral entrapment: the act of "setting up someone for a fall," endowing them with just enough agency so as to render them blameworthy.[63]

Of course, the long and craggy trail of American politics is littered with the used-up carcasses of those unfortunates set up for a fall. As Rogin described years before Kotsko, these demons, "these monsters—the Indian cannibal, the black rapist, the papal whore of Babylon, the monster-hydra of the United States Bank, the demon rum, the bomb-throwing anarchist, the many-tentacled Communist conspiracy, the agents of international terrorism—are familiar figures in the dream-life that so often dominates American politics."[64] Whether targeting the Black Panthers and other dissidents, dodgy "welfare queens," or gang members and drug users of all kinds,

American criminal justice has for the last four decades been driven by the demonological energies of right-wing ideologues like Charles Murray, James Q. Wilson, and William Bennett and, equally, the center-right neoliberals that filled out the Clinton and Obama administrations. On the former, consider, for instance, how Bennett, a cabinet member and advisor to three Republican presidents, described in his book *The De-Valuing of America* a ride-along with Detroit police:

> The scene was familiar to almost every American who watches television: parts of an inner-city resembling what the philosopher Thomas Hobbes described as the state of nature where life is *"solitary, poor, nasty, brutish and short."*[65]

For Bennett, the "inner city" of the 1990s United States—or at least those places populated by those he did not recognize as fully human—realizes the Hobbesian war of all against all, thereby licensing the waiting violence of police. Of course, it was Bennett along with John DiIulio and John Walters who named the enemy with their demonological predictions of the rise of youthful "superpredators" and an attendant "crime bomb" set to decimate the mid-'90s United States. In their now fully discredited book *Body Count: Moral Poverty . . . and How to Win America's War against Crime and Drugs*, Bennett and his colleagues warn, "America's beleaguered cities are about to be victimized by a paradigm shattering wave of ultraviolent, morally vacuous young people some call 'the superpredators,'" a wholly "new generation of street criminals . . . the youngest, biggest, and baddest generation any society has ever known."[66] Important for our discussion here is that the antidote the authors prescribed for the underlying demonic rot of "moral poverty" supposedly giving rise to the superpredator, in addition to a healthy dose of authoritarian criminal justice, was the "widespread renewal of religious faith and the strengthening of religious institutions."[67]

While time would eventually prove their predictions laughably off the mark,[68] it would not be before they traversed the supposed chasm of left/right partisan politics to undergird the policies of the Clinton administration, offering ideological ballast for both "welfare reform" and the 1994 Violent Crime Control and Law Enforcement

Act. Touting the crime bill, Hillary Clinton, speaking to students at
Keene State College in 1996, adopted Bennett, DiIulio, and Walter's
language of predation:

> We're making some progress. Much of it is related to the initia-
> tive called "community policing." Because we have finally got-
> ten more police officers on the street. That was one of the goals
> that the president had when he pushed the crime bill that was
> passed in 1994 . . . But we also have to have an organized effort
> against gangs. Just as in a previous generation we had an orga-
> nized effort against the mob. We need to take these people on.
> They are often connected to big drug cartels; they are not just
> gangs of kids anymore. They are often the kinds of kids that
> are called superpredators—no conscience, no empathy. We can
> talk about why they ended up that way, but first, we have to
> bring them to heel.[69]

While seemingly unconcerned with the etiology of the mythical
beast, Clinton nevertheless coldly prioritized the administration's
plans to force the "superpredators'" obedience, "bring[ing] them to
heel" as one might an unruly dog. These words would rightly return
to haunt Clinton during her 2016 presidential bid, when Black Lives
Matter activists demanded an apology. While Clinton did issue an
apology, both Bernie Sanders and Donald Trump reminded voters
of her use of the racist term and her husband's disastrous crime bill
throughout the campaign, with Trump in late August 2016 tweeting, "How quickly people forget that Crooked Hillary called African-
American youth 'SUPER PREDATORS'—Has she apologized?"[70]

Trump, of course, should not have been first to cast that particular stone. Just a few years before "the rise of the superpredator," he
helped the public imagine bands of roving "wolf packs" of violent
young men across the nation's imagination with his unsought involvement in the so-called Central Park jogger case. Under headlines
like "Central Park Horror: Wolf Pack's Prey, Female Jogger Near
Death after Savage Attack by Roving Gang,"[71] police and their stenographers in the news media wrongly blamed five young Black and
Latino boys for the brutal rape and beating of a wealthy young white

woman, casting the specter of a lawless state of nature where "wilding" bands of predatory young men were loosed upon a defenseless city. From the initial reporting on the case:

> The youths who raped and savagely beat a young investment banker as she jogged in Central Park Wednesday night were part of a loosely organized gang of 32 schoolboys whose random, motiveless assaults terrorized at least eight other people over nearly two hours, senior police investigators said yesterday. Chief of Detectives Robert Colangelo, who said the attacks appeared unrelated to money, race, drugs or alcohol, said that some of the 20 youths brought into questioning had told investigators that the crime spree was the product of a pastime called "wilding."[72]

Particularly when paired with "wolf packs," a more apt descriptor for the state of nature could not have been devised. Though likely introduced by an ill-advised cop or member of the media, "wilding" quickly adhered to the popular lexicon as "the street term for robbing and torturing complete strangers for fun."[73] We should take care to note the language of savage animality foisted upon the racialized poor. As one city official describing a so-called "NY-Style Wilding Death" that occurred in Boston a year after the New York case stated, "You're talking about major-league wilding here. You're talking animal here, pure vicious."[74]

Though it took years, DNA evidence eventually helped to locate the actual attacker, but not before irrevocably altering the lives of the five wrongfully accused young boys. Trump ingloriously used the Central Park jogger case to insert himself into the realm of national cultural and, importantly, racial politics by taking out full-page advertisements in several New York City newspapers, stoking fear and outrage and urging widespread reprisal against street criminals, as the investigation unfolded. Under the banner "Bring The Death Penalty! Bring Back Our Police!" Trump summoned a highly racialized politics of enmity, envisaging an apocalyptic "breakdown" of social order, a lawless terrain deprived of the sheltering benevolence of police. From the advertisement:

What has happened to our City over the past ten years? What has happened to law and order, to the neighborhood cop we all trusted to safeguard our homes and families, the cop who had the power under the law to help us in times of danger, keep us safe from those who would prey on innocent lives to fulfill some distorted inner need. What has happened to the respect for authority, the fear of retribution by the courts, society and the police for those who break the law, who wantonly trespass on the rights of others? What has happened is the complete breakdown of life as we knew it . . . I recently watched a newscast trying to explain the "anger in these young men". I no longer want to understand their anger. I want them to be afraid.

How can our great society tolerate the continued brutalization of its citizens by crazed misfits? Criminals must be told that their CIVIL LIBERTIES END WHEN AN ATTACK ON OUR SAFETY BEGINS![75]

Like Clinton, Trump was not concerned with the social circumstances of violent young men—not the cause and certainly not the validity of their anger. Ever the reactionary, he simply endorsed brute reprisal, hoping to strike fear in the hearts of the "crazed misfits" plaguing his city. While it may be easy to view Trump's intervention into the case and his later law-and-order candidacy as the respective ends of a decades-long con, a cynically crafted strongman façade designed to appeal to the lowest forms of reactionary populism, it could also be that Trump's Hobbesian worldview is the most honest facet of his public persona. When describing his business philosophy in an interview with *People* magazine in 1981, Trump parroted the familiar belief that "Man is the most vicious of all animals, and life is a series of battles ending in victory or defeat. You just can't let people make a sucker out of you."[76]

Decades later, in his inaugural address, Trump reaffirmed his Hobbesian bona fides, assuming the mantle of sovereign while articulating a loathsome politics of *American carnage*:

But for too many of our citizens, a different reality exists: mothers and children trapped in poverty in our inner cities; rusted out factories scattered like tombstones across the landscape of our nation; an education system flush with cash, but which leaves our young and beautiful students deprived of all knowledge; and the crime and the gangs and the drugs that have stolen too many lives and robbed our country of so much unrealized potential. This American carnage stops right here and stops right now!

As he ticked the boxes of all the familiar right-wing talking points— the feminization of "inner-city" poverty, a corrupt education system, gangs and drugs—and linked the wars of the interior with the fight against "radical Islamic terrorism," promising to "unite the civilized world" and "eradicate [it] from the face of the earth," Trump anointed his followers God's chosen people. He concluded:

There should be no fear. We are protected and we will always be protected. We will be protected by the great men and women of our military and law enforcement. *And most importantly, we will be protected by God.*[77]

This is a sovereign statement par excellence, promising to banish the fear of violent death through the greater violence of "military and law enforcement," with Trump standing in as God's interlocutor. For Kotsko, Trump's rise bears all the hallmarks of combative neoliberalism, in which politics does the work of aligning friend and enemy through a "straight-forward apocalyptic narrative, where the self-identified righteous ones long for the battle with the forces of evil, in which God will win once and for all and his followers will be vindicated."[78] As we've seen, fear of violent death is a fundamental condition of Hobbesian ordering. And as the world has witnessed, Trump has proven himself a gifted political demonologist, skillfully riling his anxious base with a roster of fearsome threats— immigrants, Muslims, North Korea, Iran, MS-13, Democrats, socialists, globalists—each of which is positioned in diametric opposition to a mythical once-great America.

As the 2018 midterm elections drew to a close, Trump took this playbook to shameful new heights with a campaign advertisement distilling the worst of Reagan-era theatrics. Tweeted by Trump on Halloween, the ad features Luis Bracamontes—a Mexican national who, in 2014, killed two California sheriff's deputies—at a court hearing, shackled and surrounded by security, promising to "kill cops" and lamenting that he did not kill more. Overlaid by text asserting "Democrats let him into our country" and "Democrats let him stay," and closing with the question "Who else will Democrats let in?" projected onto footage of crowds pushing through barricades and fences, the ad cast the specter of an unhinged, remorseless cop killer onto the so-called "caravan" of desperate people running for their lives.[79] The openly racist and demonstrably false ad, drawn directly from the dirty-tricks playbook of Roger Ailes, Roger Stone, and Lee Atwater, engineers of the grotesque Willie Horton and "Revolving Door" ads that helped deliver Bush Sr. the presidency, suggested that despite his garish antics, Trump's administration was, in fact, in keeping with a long-established political strategy.[80]

A short time later, Trump tweeted a meme-style image of himself with the text "The Wall Is Coming" in the recognizable *Game of Thrones* font. Like police who operate in a constant state of "ordinary emergency," licensed to use violence as they see fit, Trump's declaration of a state of emergency in order to fund construction of his contentious southern border wall again demonstrates the reach and ubiquity of the executive's prerogative, invoked as it is by Trump to pacify his base and by everyday cops who justify their brutality under the maxim "I feared for my life."

Judge, Jury, Executioner

While Trump clearly wishes to install himself as a godlike sovereign authority, what of the *deus mortalis* of Hobbes and Schmitt? Returning to some of Hollywood's better-known end-of-the-world offerings, the position of police as savior, hero, God becomes all the more apparent. As mentioned previously, from the cops who figure prominently into both iterations of the foundational horror film *Dawn of the Dead* to Rick Grimes of *The Walking Dead*, the zombie apocalypse, with its hordes of shambling, killable enemies, proves the authoritarian personalities and violent acumen of police to be necessary skills for civilization's restart. It is also sometimes overlooked that the popular postapocalyptic film franchise *Mad Max* began as a *Death Wish*–style revenge flick with a cop as its hero. In the first film, released in 1979, the eponymous Max (Mel Gibson) is a highway patrol officer tripped into murderous rage when an anarchic biker gang murders his wife and infant son. With taglines like "When the gangs take over the highways, pray he's out there somewhere" and "The last law in a world gone out of control," the film's narrative emboldens the fear and savagery of a lawless Australian frontier and offers the violent retribution of an unhinged cop as antidote. As Calder Williams puts it, the *Mad Max* universe begins on the dusty outskirts of collapsing cities just giving way to the "anarchic dissolution into the Hobbesian state of nature. It's *homo homini lupus*—man is wolf to man—if wolves were interested in revenge plots and supercharged cars."[81] Not until subsequent films has the collapse fully set in, with Max assuming the role of a post-apocalyptic *High Plains Drifter*, the last vestiges of his former life as a lawman falling away with his disintegrating highway patrol jacket. Throughout all four films, Max nevertheless remains aligned against a clearly defined evil, taking the side of the good and virtuous in an effort to restore some semblance of the old order.

It should by now be quite obvious that what fantasy savior/heroes like Rick Grimes and Max Rockatansky share is their mastery of indiscriminate violence. Like the elite preppers Osnos interviewed for the *New Yorker*, it seems that in our contemporary eschatology, violence is God's, or mortal God's, preserve. Here the cop/heroes of the apocalyptic imaginary approximate the biblical *katechon*—a "restrainer" thought to hold back the onset of the apocalypse—standing against hordes of risen dead and roving bands of fuel-hungry highwaymen. Recognizing the fluidity between war power and police power, we can broaden our view and find yet more examples of the postapocalyptic savior figure in the Western imaginary. From Robert Neville in the various iterations of Richard Matheson's *I Am Legend* to Snake Plissken in John Carpenter's *Escape from New York*, the cop/soldier hero figure is a well-worn trope in the popular imagination of the end of the world, or at least the end of the world-for-us. As opposed to the messiah who marks the end of one world and delivers the new, police as katechon—like Grimes and Rockatansky, who violently cling to the withering traces of civilization—restrain social change and reproduce the miseries of the present order with blunt force.[82]

The comic-book future cop Judge Dredd is probably the best-fitting example of police as postapocalyptic katechon. In Dredd's world, war has decimated the United States and driven its surviving population into Mega-City One, a megalopolis that sprawls across most of the Eastern Seaboard. Joseph Dredd is one of many "Street Judges"—the literal embodiment of street justice—empowered to adjudicate crime instantaneously, acting in the moment as judge, jury, and, often, executioner. Prowling the streets on attack motor-cycles and strapped with "Lawgivers," pistols that fire a range of smart munitions, Judges are a dystopian distillation of Walter Benjamin's police violence, marking the very moment at which law breaks down with lethal finality. As Dredd's mantra "I am the law!" hammers home with brutal clarity, in the fantasy wasteland of Mega-City One, the sovereignty of police is unassailable.

In his analysis of the U.S. drone program, Chris Lloyd reads and employs *Judge Dredd* as a satirical attack on unrestrained po-lice power necessitated by the state of emergency.[83] In the tradition of Jacques Rancière, who argues that art can open space for radi-cal critique and "turn the spectator into a conscious agent of world transformation," Lloyd's "critical art" reading of *Judge Dredd* diagno-ses the U.S. drone program as symptom of a looming authoritarian state, enabled by the executive's prerogative. Citing the character's cocreator John Wagner, who insists *Judge Dredd* offers purposeful critique of authoritarian politics, Lloyd holds out hope for the radi-cal potentials of satirical art. Others, however, are not convinced. For instance, the self-described "Dreddoholic" and self-confessed fascist whom Martin Barker interviewed for his work on audience reception describes the image of a future police state ordered by in-stantaneous violence as "almost religious," viewing Dredd as a "hero in this world that hasn't got any."[84] For this fan enamored by the power to wash the messy and confusing world of human relations in an orderly contrast of black and white, Dredd, however violent and authoritarian, is the solution to myriad social ills. He explains:

> The thing I like about it so much is that he is so incorruptible, and even when he is corrupt, there is some sort of loophole in their legal system, you know, which makes him still the good guy. No matter what, he is still the good guy . . . I think it's

because the world, the world around us is not black and white anyway, Judge Dredd portrays it as black and white, but even if there's a grey area he suddenly makes it black and white to suit himself.[85]

Clearly, for this young fan, Dredd and other fantasy rogue cops like Rust Cohle, Jimmy McNulty, and Harry Callahan, who routinely exploit "loopholes" and break the law to enforce the law, embody the godlike power to cut through the contradictions of modern life with lethal certainty. Yet as Neocleous and Kotsko remind, police and God draw authority not simply from their constituents but from the fear of violent death marshalled by their adversaries.[86] As Hobbes writes in *Leviathan*, "The Multitude sufficient to confide in for our Security, is not determined by any certain number, but by comparison with the Enemy we feare . . ."[87]

In his book *Heroes: Mass Murder and Suicide*, Franco "Bifo" Berardi provocatively argues that acts of mass or "heroic" violence, specifically the spree killings common to the United States, should be understood as spasmatic, suicidal drives symptomatic of an unraveling and increasingly nihilistic age.[88] Set apart from serial killers who articulate their own sadistic drives, Berardi sees mass killers like Seung-Hui Cho at Virginia Tech, Dylan Klebold and Eric Harris at Columbine, and others as hoping to achieve a perverse hero status through the spectacle of violence, murder, and suicide. If these ultraviolent young men are engaged in some sort of poisoned hero's journey, as Berardi suggests, what can we make of the police who imagine themselves in diametric opposition? Like the comic-book superhero who gathers power and meaning in relation to their nemesis, police see themselves as heroes, meeting the violence of an increasingly nihilistic age with superior and righteous violence.

Appearing in the documentary film *Do Not Resist* as he delivers a seminar to a room full of cops, David Grossman heartens his audience to think of themselves as the "frontiersmen" of old, imploring them to meet the savagery of the city with the "superior violence," the "righteous violence" of the police power:

The policeman is the man of the city. Heard of the mountain man, the frontiersman? Nobody talks about frontiersmen anymore; we still talk about policemen. You are to your city, your county, your state what the frontiersman was to the frontier. You fight violence. What do you fight it with? Superior violence. Righteous violence, yeah? Violence is your tool, violence is your enemy, violence is the realm we operate in. You are men and women of violence. You must master it. Or it will destroy you, yeah?[89]

Touting himself as the "number-one police/military trainer in the United States" and author of books that are required reading at Quantico and numerous police academies, the former West Point instructor and founder of the grotesquely aptly named Killology Research Group delivers hundreds of "Bulletproof Warrior" and "Bulletproof Mind" seminars each year in collaboration with Calibre Press. While Grossman's influence on the police and military community is of little doubt, he did his work in relative obscurity until 2016, when the killing of Philando Castile was broadcast on Facebook Live. The killer, a Minnesota cop named Jeronimo Yanez, had been provided more than forty hours of Bulletproof and Street Survival Calibre seminars by his department in the two years prior to killing Castile.

From what has been made available to the public, it is clear that Grossman's trainings are steeped in the heroic mythology of the thin blue line. Indeed, a line scrawled across the top of a leaked "Bulletproof Warrior" training handout that reads "You are the thin line of heroes preserving the fabric of America during these dark and desperate times" could have been penned by William Parker, Jack Webb, David Ayer, or perhaps even Rudyard Kipling.[90] And, of course, we should not overlook the words "Bulletproof" and "Warrior," which seem to imply or endow police with the spectacular powers of a superhero.

From leaked training materials and snippets of video, it is clear that the seminars cultivate the hypervigilance of Wall's ordinary emergency. Operating from this sort of heightened war footing, police can never hesitate, even for an instant, when a threat is perceived. And, indeed, in the death of Philando Castile, we might grimly agree that the seminars accomplished their goal, as Yanez assumed the position of judge, jury, and executioner, killing the man

in his own car as he attempted to inform the officer that he was legally carrying a handgun. While this sort of threat orientation is
not unique to Calibre or Grossman, what is interesting for our discussion is the rationale and imagery Grossman uses to motivate his
audiences. In *Do Not Resist*, as he concludes a Bulletproof Warrior
training, Grossman offers the following:

> On your way home at night, park your vehicle on the overpass
> for just a minute. Step out of your vehicle for just a minute.
> Look out on your city. Look at your citizens going about their
> lives. And know deep in your gut! That today, at the risk of
> your life, you made their world a better place, whether they
> know it or not. Then walk up to that bridge rail, put your hands
> on that rail. Look out on your city and let your cape blow in the
> wind.[91]

Operating under a self-imposed perpetual emergency, encouraged to
see all they encounter as threats and to respond with "righteous" and
"superior" violence, it is no wonder that police imagine themselves as
heroes, saviors, gods in the eternal struggle between good and evil.
And while cops are the chief promoters of this sort of thinking, it
does not end with them. Beyond quotidian forms of police and military worship—boarding flights first, recognition at sporting events,
complimentary services and discounts, the obligatory "thank you for
your service"—several retailers and municipalities, for instance, offer
reserved "superhero-only parking" for police, military, and other first
responders, further codifying their mythical standing.[92]

Continuing with the simple method of paying attention to the
pronouncements of police and taking them at their word, we can easily locate the contours of this starkly Manichean worldview, which positions the police as not only the heroic line between good and evil but
the violent arbiters of the difference between the two. Popular among
both police and military is the practice of producing and trading
commemorative medallions bearing the insignia of a particular organization or event, known as "challenge coins." Of the hundreds
of challenge coins produced for and by members of the NYPD, the
one commemorating its notorious Street Crime Unit is quite revealing. Known as "the commandos of the NYPD," the notorious "City

A large supermarket chain offers "Super Hero Parking."

Wide Anti-Crime" unit was an aggressive plainclothes squad that, as described by the *New York Times* in 1999, was "dispatched into menacing neighborhoods each night to chase down rapists, muggers and dangerous fugitives, and above all, to get illegal guns off the streets."[93] In a forerunner of "stop and frisk" practices, the Street Crime Unit was well known for harassing residents of predominately nonwhite neighborhoods when several of its members shot and killed an unarmed Guinean immigrant named Amadou Diallo in 1999. Not long after, "City Wide Anti-Crime" was disbanded, but, following the American tradition of police reform, it was simply renamed and reorganized into smaller "borough-wide" units, where it continues today.[94]

Patterned after a detective's badge, black with raised white letters, the Street Crime Unit coin features a skull and crossbones just above the unit's famous revanchist motto, "We Own the Night." On its back is a quotation from Ernest Hemingway quite popular among police: "There is no hunting like the hunting of man and those who have hunted armed men long enough and liked it, never really care for anything else thereafter." Also taking the police at their word, in his discussion of the development of police "K-9" units, Wall suggests that the quote is best understood as "an honest admission of what they actually do: hunt, capture, cage, and often kill those subjects marked as fugitive, unruly, impolite."[95] Continuing on this point, Wall cites the French political theorist Honoré-Antoine Frégier, who in 1850 wrote that "It can be affirmed without fear of contradiction that police is the most solid basis of civilization."[96] With an explicit focus on the hunting power of police, realized in the police dog, Wall's point is that police not only defend civilization but are tasked with bringing it into being through the violence meted out under conditions of ordinary emergency and perpetual war. Here, the epistemology of the thin blue line marks the enemy and maps the ontological terrain of what Karl Marx and Friedrich Engels famously called "social war": "civil war" or "class war" fought to ensure property relations and bourgeoisie order.

Policing's epistemology of enmity and ontology of war appears even more starkly in another coin produced for or by the NYPD's "most decorated detective," Ralph Friedman.[97] Around the rim of this particular coin are Friedman's name and years of service, and at the top, bracketed by bullet holes, are the words "Justified 4X," which match the tattoo on his right trigger finger. At the coin's center, set against the stars and stripes, are pistols, handcuffs, and four human skulls meant to represent the four people Friedman killed in the line of duty—one of whom was mistaken for a burglar and killed in his own home.[98] As a glowing profile in the New York Post describes, Friedman was a veteran of some "15 gun battles" and shot at least "eight perps, including the four he killed." Wistfully recounting his time working out of the Forty-First Precinct Station House, made famous by the film Fort Apache, the Bronx (1981), the heavily tattooed Friedman casually insists "you had to be combat ready," endorsing, yet again, the belief that for police, enemies surround and their work is an all-out war.

Moving beyond the niche trade in challenge coins, the Marvel Comics character the Punisher and his iconic skull are now recognizable signifiers of the righteous violence of police power. Frank Castle, a.k.a. "the Punisher," first appeared in *The Amazing Spider-Man* #129 in early 1974 and was derived from the 1960s pulp series *The Executioner* and its title character. Castle, like his inspiration, is a Vietnam vet locked in an extralegal war with organized crime and "international terrorism." Appearing at the onset of the "tough on crime" era, he gained immediate popularity among readers as the embodiment of retaliatory rage, a no-nonsense antihero waging a literal war on crime without the encumbrances of due process afforded to undeserving street criminals. Of course, there is at least one NYPD challenge coin featuring the comic-book vigilante. Representing the New York/New Jersey Regional Fugitive Task Force, it features the Punisher dressed in battle garb, holding a smoking pistol in his left hand and, in the right, a SWAT-style bulletproof entry shield emblazoned with the task force's emblem. On the coin's back, another quotation popular among police, repeatedly and erroneously attributed to George Orwell: "Good people sleep peaceably in their beds at night only because rough men stand ready to do violence on their behalf."[99] As if channeling Rust Cohle's admission of being a "bad man" who "keeps other bad men from the door," the coin betrays a menacing worldview where might quite plainly makes right. Today, the armed-to-the-teeth lethal vigilantism of the Punisher proliferates among police, who after 2014 and the protests in Ferguson, Baltimore, and elsewhere have more openly touted an insular and antagonistic war footing. You will now find police and their fans sporting all manner of commercial memorabilia—T-shirts, hats, stickers, coins, mugs, and more—emblazoned with the Punisher's iconic skull, which also tends to incorporate the "thin blue line" as well.

The resurgence in popularity of the character and its associated iconography seems to have risen alongside the celebrity of former Navy SEAL Chris Kyle, who, as depicted in the Clint Eastwood–directed biopic *American Sniper*, wore the skull on his uniform and other equipment. In his book of the same name, Kyle describes how his platoon named themselves the Punishers before their 2006 deployment to Iraq. Insisting that "just because war is hell, doesn't

The Punisher skull overlaid with the thin blue line.

mean you can't have a little fun,"[100] Kyle explains the choice of the symbol:

> We all thought what the Punisher did was cool: He righted wrongs. He killed bad guys. He made wrongdoers fear him. That's what we were all about. So we adapted his symbol—a skull—and made it our own, with some modifications. We spray-painted it on our Hummers and body armor, and our

helmets and guns. And we spray-painted it on every building or wall we could. We wanted people to know, *We're here and we want to fuck with you.* It was our version of psyops. *You see us? We're the people kicking your ass. Fear us. Because we will kill you, motherfucker. You are bad. We are badder. We are bad-ass.*[101]

Endorsing ruthless violence and terror, Kyle's infantile admiration of a murderous comic-book character and his desire to use its logo to strike fear in the hearts of "wrongdoers" is reminiscent of Trump's fascistic desire to make street criminals "afraid." Even though one of the Punisher's creators, Gerry Conway, has explicitly stated that the character is not one to "admire or emulate," police, soldiers, and their supporters are nevertheless drawn to the fantasy of acting indiscriminately and, above all, violently. Invoking the tired myth of a lenient criminal justice system, one ardent fan and Department of Homeland Security employee explained he admired the Punisher because he "does to bad guys and girls what we sometimes wish we could legally do . . . Castle doesn't see shades of grey, which, unfortunately, the American justice system is littered with and which tends to slow down and sometimes even hinder victims of crime from getting the justice they deserve." Another fan, an ex-marine, similarly stated that he liked that the Punisher exhibits "No political correctness" and observes "no rules other than his own, he just does what needs to be done. Period."[102]

Rooted in a reactionary view of "political correctness" and of supposed moral decay, it may be that the Punisher is simply part of a long lineage of antiheroes like Dirty Harry Callahan and Paul Kersey of the recently resurrected *Death Wish* franchise, who administer street justice at the barrel of a gun. That so many grown men, ostensibly employed to defend, protect, and serve, fantasize about wielding a superhero's power to indiscriminately kill in order to deliver justice and "do what needs to be done" is more than troubling. This is particularly so given the murky, perhaps sinister origins of the comic-book superhero genre itself. Chris Gavaler makes the convincing and provocative argument that the roots of the genre can be traced to early twentieth-century genre fiction valorizing the mission of the Ku Klux Klan. Locating the birth of the American superhero in Thomas Dixon Jr.'s 1905 novel *The Clansman: An His-*

torical Romance of the Ku Klux Klan and its character "the Grand Dragon," Gavaler argues that despite the superhero's "evolution into a champion of the oppressed, it originated from an oppressive, racist impulse in American culture, and the formula codifies an ethics of vigilante extremism that still contradicts the superhero's social mission."[103] In his book *Sovereignty and Superheroes*, Neal Curtis departs somewhat from Gavaler, distinguishing the vigilantism of the Punisher from the "anomic sovereignty" of traditional characters such as Captain America who defend the rule of law even if they sometimes operate outside of it.[104] More sinister than rogues like McNulty, for Curtis, the Punisher is a distillation of a potent form of individualistic and retributive violence that operates independent of law, not only outside of it. Another cop attempting to explain the popularity of the character among police seemingly concurred, endorsing violence unrestrained by law and stating, "Some people want Superman, but then realize that it's a character like the Punisher that they actually need."[105]

Moving beyond expressing their fantasies of unrestrained lethality with stickers, coins, and T-shirts, several U.S. police departments have adopted the Punisher's skull and combined it with thin blue line iconography as official insignia. In early 2017, the Catlettsburg, Kentucky, police department caused a stir when it placed a large vinyl decal of the thin blue line Punisher skull and the text "Blue Lives Matter" on the hood of each of its eight patrol vehicles. Responding to criticism, the chief of the eight-officer department explained that he intended the decals to be a show of support for his officers, stating, "Our lives matter just as much as anybody's . . . I'm not racist or anything like that, I'm not trying to stir anything up like that. I consider it to be a 'warrior logo.' Just 'cause it has 'Blue Lives Matter' on the hood, all lives matter. That decal represents that we will take any means necessary to keep our community safe."[106] Like Chris Kyle and other self-described "badasses" and "warriors" set against some unnamed enemy, it is safe to assume that those departments that, like Catlettsburg, endorse the Punisher imagine their mission more closely aligned with "search and destroy" than "protect and serve." While the tiny department eventually succumbed to public pressure and abandoned its use of the insignia, other departments refuse to disavow the logo and its political meanings.

When the Solvay, New York, police department was criticized for its use of the thin blue line/Punisher skull, the department's chief, Allen Wood, issued a statement insisting that the symbol was the department's way of showing "citizens that we will stand between good and evil."

> The Thin Blue Line symbol shows that we also believe in the unity and support of Police nationwide. There is clearly a war on Police and the criminal element attempting to infiltrate and destroy our communities, lifestyles and quality of living requiring men and women willing to stand up to evil and protect the good of society . . . The symbol serves as a reminder that when called upon, no matter what the incident, we will stand between good and evil. The taxpaying citizens of Solvay, whom we proudly represent, understand our commitment and dedication and appreciate our effort to fight the evils that we encounter.[107]

Again, there is much to digest here, but it is clear that the Solvay chief, like the cops in Kentucky, sees his kind as heroic defenders of the good, guarding against some ambiguous evil "criminal element attempting to infiltrate and destroy" his community. As we have seen, not only do police imagine themselves as the boundary in a starkly Manichean world, but there is a sizable contingent among them who imagine themselves in heroic, if not fantastic, terms.

For a glimpse of yet one more facet of their heroic self-description, we return to the work of David Grossman and his colleagues at Calibre Press. Grossman, who makes it a practice to inscribe the books he sells at his trainings with lines like "Ecclesiastes 3:3: a time to kill, a time to heal,"[108] dedicates a portion of his presentations and a chapter of his coauthored book *On Combat: The Psychology and Physiology of Deadly Conflict in War and Peace* to the pesky Christian admonishment against violence. In the chapter "Thou Shalt Not Kill? The Judeo/Christian View of Killing," Grossman and Loren Christensen establish that, at least in their view, the correct translation of Exodus 20:13 from the original Hebrew is "You shall not *murder*."[109] The leaked Bulletproof Warrior training handout, in fact, offers more than a dozen biblical references to authorize the lethal violence of police, distinguishing it from murder. To further fortify this position, Grossman and Christensen point to the biblical figure Cornelius, likening him to today's "Professional Police Warriors." They write, "The first non-Jew we know of who became a Christian is Cornelius in Acts 10. He was a Roman centurion, a soldier, a police officer of the Roman Empire. Never once is it implied that it was inappropriate for him to be a warrior and still be at peace with God."[110]

Linking the Roman centurion to police and other "holy warriors" as Grossman and Christensen do here follows the popular trend among police, military, and right-leaning people of all kinds who appropriate the iconography of famed warrior classes. The Corinthian or Spartan helmet is an icon quite popular among police and self-described Second Amendment activists. When deployed by the latter, the helmet is often paired with the phrase *molon labe*, which roughly translates as "come and take them" and is attributed to the Spartan king Leonidas's refusal to surrender at the Battle of Thermopylae. When appropriated by police and their supporters, the helmet includes a vertical thin blue line, linking police to the heroism of an overmatched force like the three hundred at Thermopylae, who stood defiantly against an invading enemy. Such a view reaffirms the myth that the police are not only always in the right but are, importantly, under siege. As Wall writes, the thin blue line "is *always thin*, perpetually on the brink of being broken or obliterated by bestial hordes, if it were not for the valiant 'boys in blue' keeping darkness at bay. TBL marks less back-and-forth patrolling between norm and exception than it marks the police as always in constant crisis, under threat, inevitably insecure if ultimately triumphant."[111] Tying into this mythology is the belief that not only are police righteous, but their righteousness is ordained by Christian authority. For instance, police and their supporters seem particularly fond of a loosely translated version of Romans 13:4 that Grossman calls "probably the single most important verse for a warrior":[112]

> For he is God's servant for your good. But if you do wrong, be afraid, for he does not bear the sword in vain. For he is the servant of God. An avenger who carries out God's Wrath on the wrongdoer.

Appearing on T-shirts, stickers, and memes shared on police message boards, and invoked on websites like the Centurion Law Enforcement Ministry, the verse is sometimes boiled down to "we do not bear the sword in vain"—the suggestion clearly being that as "an avenger who carries out God's Wrath on the wrongdoer," the police officer is not only beyond reproach in their violence but in fact superior, righteous, *holy*. Upon closer inspection, however, the whole of Romans 13 offers a slightly different, or perhaps more complete, understanding of the Christian doctrine used to justify police violence. The whole verse, also widely shared in police circles, reads:

> Let everyone be subject to the governing authorities, for there is no authority except for which God has established. The authorities that exist have been established by God. Consequently, whoever rebels against the authority is rebelling against what God has instituted, and those who do so will bring judgment on themselves. For rulers hold no terror for those who do right, but for those who do wrong. Do you want to be free from fear of the one in authority? Then do what is wright and you will be commended. For the one authority is God's servant for your good. But if you do wrong, be afraid, for rulers do not bear the sword for no reason. They are God's servants, agents of wrath to bring punishment on the wrongdoer. Therefore it is necessary to submit to the authorities, not because of possible punishment, but also as a matter of conscience.

Mirroring Schmitt's *deus mortalis*, the verse equates the will of police to the will of God, anointing police violence in holy, bloody oil. In a collection of "365 Daily Devotions for Law Enforcement," the entry "Ready to Serve," which also invokes Romans 13, adds, "Heavenly Father, use me as a servant for those who do good and as your agent for those who do wrong. May I be just and fair in all I do today and forever. Amen."[113] Following the sentiments of Romans, it is clear that those who invoke it do so in order to reinforce and justify their actions, designating all those lawbreakers and wrongdoers great and small on the business end of the police power as enemies of God. Understanding the police first and foremost as political actors, their words and deeds again diagnose and reveal, in Kotsko's words, "theologically informed political action" and hence the lethal-ity of the political theology of the thin blue line. Here, white male Christian protectors "bear the sword" in the name of their kind and their kind alone.

Annihilation Is the Condition

In her book *Political Realism in Apocalyptic Times,* Alison McQueen describes how Hobbes, in order to counter the social upheaval brought on by the English Civil War, redeployed the power of antinomian apocalyptic imaginary in the service of sovereign power and civil peace, doing so by redirecting "the stunning visual and rhetorical resources of apocalypticism to secure belief in and obedience to the Leviathan state."[114] Centuries later, the Hobbesian brand of apoca-lypticism slithers on in race-baiting, fearmongering politicians who call forth demons from masses of the dispossessed and in the every-day executives who operate as street-level judge, jury, and executioner.

For a final example, one too stunning not to include in full here, we return to Law Enforcement Today's Sgt. A. Merica column and another editorial that details, with horrifying clarity, how police enlist the apocalyptic imaginary to place themselves at the cen-ter of a fabricated battle for civilization. The anonymous cop who authored "I Am Not Your Sheepdog. I Am the Wolf. And I Hunt Evil."—which just two months after publication had been read and shared more than sixty thousand times—makes no bones about it: America is at war. He writes:

> Every day, America sits on the brink. We teeter between good and evil. The Thin Blue Line isn't a fictional concept. It's real—and it's what separates society from anarchy. It's why you can go to work. Why your children can go to school. Why you can sleep in peace at night. Protecting the people . . . are the Sheepdog. They are our police. They are your protectors. They are the guardians of the castle and the people behind it. But I am not your Sheepdog. I do not guard the castle from direct attack. I do not seek to defend those whom it protects. No, I am the wolf. I am the one you don't want to know about. While the Sheepdog protect . . . I destroy. But I am YOUR wolf. I hunt

my prey—and my prey fears me. Those I hunt are those who would do you harm. Those who seek to destroy the castle and everyone behind it's [sic] walls. I am the one who stalks them. As they prepare to come for you . . . I pounce. I am not kind. I am not merciful. I take the fight out of them. Then I take them out of the fight. Their throat is my prize. Their end is my glory. I destroy evil . . . so it cannot destroy you. I am not your Sheepdog. I am your wolf. And you will never know my name.

For more than twenty-five years, I've served our country. I started in the military and moved my way up quickly. That's what happens when you are single and hellbent on destroying evil. I had no interest in starting a family. After just a few years in the military, I rose quickly and became part of a special operations group working in some of the most dangerous places in the world.

Here in America, we are spoiled. We take our fluffy pillows and lattes for granted. We close our eyes and sleep well because very good men are doing sometimes very bad things to very bad men to keep us safe.

But over the years, I watched the rules of engagement change. When serving our country, and then serving here in law enforcement, I watched as the hands of my brothers, sisters and I were tied.

September 11 happened because of failures here in America—not just because of evil. We lost countless lives because we drew a divide between our agencies. Politics and feelings got in the way of stopping evil. Red tape and a hierarchy of information ensured that destruction came to America.

It will come again. Political correctness has run amok. Evil has infiltrated our communities in the name of everyone being "offended". We are in trouble.

Luckily, there are still patriots like me who believe in destroying that evil. We will do what it takes to hold the thin blue line, even when it means we have to operate in the shadows.

I had no interest in having a family, but somewhere along the line that changed. I'm now a father of four. My wife and my children don't know what I do for work. My friends have no

idea. I'm part of an elite group of that tracks down and elimi-
nates that evil. *I do it for my children. I do it for my God. I do
it for my country. I do it for you. I am the wolf. And tonight, like
every night, I will hunt.*[115]

As unhinged and frightening as this sort of thinking is, it is not un-
common, and it also neatly illustrates this chapter's entire argument.
Whether or not "America sits on the brink" is not the issue. What
the author doesn't quite admit is that police want us on the brink,
need us on the brink. Fear, desperation, anger, and hostility: these
are the affective conditions of war. Liberal subjects will either find
a suitable target for blame—drug users, immigrants, the "politically
correct"—and join the side of the police or they will reject the police
and its callous violence and take the side of the other. There is no
third position; for police you are friend or foe. But this cop goes a bit
further. He does not pretend to be a detached administrator of the
law, a loyal sheepdog content to protect and serve. No, he is a violent
rogue, a punisher, possessing the will to do what is necessary to destroy evil. He is the *monster* in police.

"Taking out the enemy" for God and country, the words of this
wolf, cop, hunter, killer are eerily reminiscent of "For God and country, Geronimo," the racist, jingoistic phrase Navy SEALs used to
confirm the killing of Osama bin Laden. No doubt this cop, like ad-
mirers of the Punisher, fantasizes that he, too, is a special operator
in a clandestine war on the American homeland.[116] Whether or not
his account is true, what is important to consider is that the author
imagines it so (to say nothing of those who liked, shared, and com-
mented on the piece), placing himself and other gallant "patriots" on
the thin blue line and alongside *his* God in a war against evil.

At the end of the world, we are told, stand the police, holding
the fragile line between good and evil, civilization and savagery. So
long as the prevailing view of social order is premised on these simple binaries, those credited with upholding them will remain largely
beyond reproach. Read uncritically, the apocalyptic imaginary and
the thin blue line bear the same message, reminding fearful, anxious
subjects of the violent death that surely would await if not for the
sheltering benevolence of the police.

As many critics have argued, however, the speculative negativity of the apocalyptic imaginary can also operate radically, forcing a confrontation with the unthinkable.[117] Just as Thacker employs supernatural horror to reveal and undermine the Cartesian world-for-us, in *Combined and Uneven Apocalypse*, Calder Williams takes the apocalyptic as both his subject and theoretical instrument, using it to cut through "those universal notions that do not just describe 'how things are' but serve to prescribe and insist that 'this is how things must be.'"[118] In line with the ways Fisher sought to counter capitalist realism, Calder Williams suggests that such a view reveals the "undifferentiated," those things that have been hidden in plain sight all along but nevertheless occluded by the horizon of the thinkable. By "undifferentiated," he means

> all that we know very well yet regard as exceptional nightmares or accidents to be corrected with better, greener, more ethical management: hellish zones of the world, whole populations destroyed in famine and sickness, "humanitarian" military interventions, the basic and unincorporable fact of class antagonism, closer, closure of access to common resources, the rendering of mass culture more and more banal, shifting climate patterns and the "natural" disasters they bring about, the abandonment of working populations and those who cannot work in favor of policies determined only to starkly widen wealth gaps.[119]

Not unlike the enlightened catastrophism that closed the previous chapter, Calder Williams seeks the clarity necessary to apprehend the apocalypse that has long since arrived. In his use, the apocalyptic does not signal a destruction of the existing order but rather a revelation, a "lifting of the veil" aiming to bring about a *capitalist apocalypse* and the sort of postapocalyptic thinking that could resist the compulsion to repeat, the urge to rebuild the old order from its ashes.

This sort of apocalypticism hopes to escape the horizon of the thinkable determined by the prevailing order and to speculate, radically, about alternate histories and possible futures. As Fisher similarly wrote, "at a certain point, the unrelieved negativity of the dystopian drive trips over into a perversely utopian gesture, and annihilation becomes the condition of the radically new."[120] By arranging, or rather forcing, a confrontation with the horror of police, annihilation becomes the condition of the new, and the apocalyptic unfurls into the postapocalyptic, refusing cycles of crises and reform that so often characterize the police. Not only will police no longer serve as katechon, restraining progressive social change, but the apocalyptic envisions a new world not ordered by the violence of police and capital.

CHAPTER 3

RoboCop, or Modern Prometheus

> Analysts of AI caution us that it's not the prospect of being
> controlled or replaced by robots that ought to worry us.
> It's the idea of becoming robot-like ourselves in their midst.
> A fully automated society—be it luxuriously communist or
> greyly fascist—will yield automated human beings.
>
> —Peter Fleming, *The Worst Is Yet to Come:*
> *A Post-Capitalist Survival Guide*

Departing, for now, from the fiery dissolution of sovereign power
and liberal order, dystopian fictions like *The Handmaid's Tale* and
1984 help envision the enveloping terror of societies ordered by too
many, or maybe just the wrong kind of, police. These are futures
marked by barricades, checkpoints, and firing squads, the stifling
carceral power of techno-panoptic dragnets, and swarms of pitiless
killing machines. Tapping into the perennial optimism, or anti-
authoritarianism, of the young, this sort of dystopian future is a key
organizing premise among top-selling young-adult fiction. Represented by such series as *The Maze Runner*, where protagonists com-
pete in a Darwinian competition of social improvement; *Divergent*,
where the young are forced to assimilate into essentialist categories
under threat of exile; and innumerable others, the genre positions
the violence of social order above the subject in the form of an overwhelming, often technologically superior police state. Among the most
widely read is, of course, the *Hunger Games* trilogy. In these novels
and subsequent films, the future North American nation of Panem is
governed by the Capitol, which, through the threat of annihilation,

forces the citizens of its impoverished outlying provinces to offer their children to a brutal competition designed to theatrically perform and reproduce the city's inescapable martial grip. Here, the arcane bow and arrows of the series' hero, Katniss Everdeen, represent the revolutionary struggle against and eventual triumph over a technologically superior and seemingly invincible oppressor. With millions of volumes and tickets sold, the *Hunger Games* franchise, like its genre forerunners and contemporaries, offers a particularly fertile landscape upon which to contemplate and confront a heroic, if not murky future.

Writing on the 1980s resurgence of dystopian science fiction films featuring the human struggle against murderous robots and cyborgs, cultural critic Fred Glass suggested that the fascination and unease with technological progress was heightened by the political and social upheaval of the Reagan era. Despite Hollywood's unending predilections for heroic and happy endings, Glass saw films like *The Terminator* and *Blade Runner* continuing the tradition of technophobic "new bad futures," where Promethean offspring finally refuse their master's commands,[1] a trend later observed by Steffen Hantke and others in the post-9/11 Bush years.[2] At a time when search engines and smartphones place a universe of information at users' fingertips, self-driving cars take the road, and Kubrickian personal assistants like Siri and Alexa normalize human/AI interface, it may be that Glass's new bad future again waits just over the horizon.

Such a future is perhaps even more certain for those who see developments in automated warfare charting the course for what investigative journalist Nick Turse has forebodingly dubbed the "Terminator Planet."[3] Playing off James Cameron's influential *Terminator* franchise, Turse warns of a future where human freedom fighters are aligned against robotic "Hunter-Killers," and perhaps for good reason. In a 1969 speech to the Association of the United States Army, then chief of staff General William Westmoreland offered a future vision of a "battlefield array" of autonomous machines that would locate, track, and target the enemy, yielding "kill probabilities of near certainty."[4] Just four decades later, in an editorial for the *Guardian*, robotics professor Noel Sharkey proved Westmoreland's prescience, noting how the U.S. military had deployed its first armed battlefield robot in Iraq and warning that the world was carelessly "sleepwalking into a brave new world where robots decide who, where and when to kill."[5] Sharkey's assertion was further underlined by the Obama administration's targeted-killing program and associated *kill list*—infamously adjudicated on "terror Tuesdays"—which systematically directed semiautonomous, remotely piloted "signature strikes" against U.S. adversaries, even citizens, worldwide. In light of the U.S. military's ongoing efforts to upgrade its drone fleet with machines capable of "completely autonomous action, right down to targeting and combat," in many ways, as Turse puts it, the future Terminator Planet "is now."[6]

Driven, perhaps, by the same Promethean anxieties that animate science fiction, critics of the U.S. military drone program are quick to invoke the Foucauldian boomerang and warn of the arrival of similar robots for use in domestic policing. As the political geographer Ian Shaw observes, perhaps the most insidious development in automated warfare of the Vietnam era was that they were almost immediately put to work by police, in prisons and for purposes of border control. Here, Shaw refers specifically to the remote sensing technologies that fashioned a grid-like groundwork for Westmoreland's "battlefield array" of automated tracking and targeting used along the southern U.S. border.[7] Unsurprisingly, as of mid-2018, there were 910 local police, fire, and emergency departments licensed by the U.S. Federal Aviation Administration to operate "public safety drones."[8] While most of these machines—outside of the Predator drones operated by the Department of Homeland Security, U.S. Customs and Border Protection, and the Drug Enforcement Administration—are of the small "quadcopter" variety and not yet armed, the future of lethal police robots has long since arrived.[9]

The Rise of the Machines

On July 7, 2016, the Dallas Police Department ended its standoff with gunman Micah Johnson, killing him with a Remotec ANDROS Mark V-A1 bomb disposal robot loaded with plastic explosives. While the move was, like the use of drones, lauded by some for keeping the boys in blue out of harm's way, for others, Johnson's killing signaled the continued drift toward a dystopian future where lethal police machines are loosed upon the public under the sign of law and order. In the *Guardian*, one legal analyst warned that the Dallas case clearly demonstrated the pressing need for a legal framework to govern the lethality of the robot police force sure to arrive.[10] Despite the concerns raised by civil libertarians in Dallas and by radical police abolitionists like the Stop LAPD Spying Coalition, just a year later, the Los Angeles Police Department became the largest U.S. police force to deploy drones when it began testing the machines for SWAT team and search-and-rescue purposes.

Although debates over the use of drones and other unmanned machines in policing are of obvious urgency, fears of "killer robots" clearly extend beyond the narrow parameters of public policy and police ethics and can be read as symptomatic of anxieties stirred by the looming postcapitalist future. In some ways echoing the warnings of Turse's *Terminator Planet*, in *Four Futures: Life after Capitalism*,[11] Peter Frase sees the march toward fully automated production and the crisis of global climate change as charting the course of a number of contingent political and economic futures, the most harrowing of which he dubs *exterminism*. Frase envisions, in exterminism, a social system characterized by the outright elimination of superfluous populations, linking "endless war in the Middle East to black teenagers being shot down by police on the streets of American cities."[12] As the cleavage between the privileged elite and an increasingly downtrodden mass widens, Frase, like Mike Davis, sees automation and mass unemployment further exacerbating existing conditions of hierarchy and scarcity. Blurring the insights of both social science and speculative fiction, Frase's social science fiction looks to various cultural texts as roadmaps for his contingent futures. One such text, the 2013 science fiction film *Elysium*—in which lethally efficient robots police the impoverished dregs imprisoned on Earth's trash-strewn landscapes, toiling for an immortal elite looming above in a utopian space colony—maps a possible future where cyborgs and machines man the thin blue line, fabricating and securing a profoundly uneven social order. Like the two worlds of *Elysium*, Frase finds the symptoms of exterminism in a burgeoning global enclave society, where the rich live and travel between "tiny islands of wealth" (gated communities, secured high-rises, private islands, bunkers) "strewn around an ocean of misery."[13] Drawing on his filmic referents, he points, too, to a boomerang effect, suggest-

ing the lessons learned in the so-called War on Terror have returned
home as militarized police, deployed to cordon the world of the rich
from the world of the poor.[14]

While this chapter's approach is certainly compatible with Frase's
social science fiction, I am not as quick as are he and others to presume a boomerang effect, or to adopt a critique of police that focuses
solely on a blurring with or drift toward the military. The problem
with this sort of critique is that it rests on an ahistorical assumption
of a clear distinction between the goals of "crime control" for police
at home and of war for the military abroad.[15] As Anna Feigenbaum
argues, the critique of police militarization limits the aim of demilitarization to the removal of military practices and fails to recognize
the very colonial roots of police violence.[16] In addition to revoking
the fatigues, assault weapons, surplus military vehicles, and, now,
drones and robots increasingly associated with U.S. police, the "demilitarization" lot often advocate some form of community policing
as part of the corrective. Yet, as numerous critics have shown, the
community policing offered by reformers has its origins in the pacification and counterinsurgency programs the U.S. military developed
prior to and during the Vietnam War.[17] This is the "other war,"[18] or
"war by other means,"[19] advocated by the RAND Corporation—the
velvet glove ensconcing the iron fist, which seeks to pacify territories
and build markets either by winning the "hearts and minds" of unruly subjects or through their outright eradication. As one RAND
report plainly admitted, the U.S. military's pacification programs
now deployed in Iraq, Afghanistan, and elsewhere should be thought
of as an expanded variant of the "community policing technique that
emerged in the 1970s (encouraged in part by RAND research)."[20]
As Mark Neocleous thusly quips, "any serious analysis shows that
community policing is no less problematic and no less part of the
war power than a water cannon."[21]

And so, for a more thoroughgoing critique, we must always sup-
pose policing's martial origins—to *police* is to wage an internal war
under the auspices of "crime control," security, and law and order. It
is not so much that "endless war in the Middle East" and the killing
of Black youth on American streets are now linked by a through line
of police militarization, as Frase and others would have it, but rather
that distant battlefields of the "War on Terror" and city streets of

the myriad "Wars on" drugs, gangs, and so on were always different settings of the same project—stitched together by the noxious threads of war power and police power. By placing both police and military on a continuum of state violence and obliterating any artificial distinction between the two, we are better equipped to see both as constitutive of a single project set in pursuit of liberal order and thus the always unequal world-for-us.[22]

If the critique of police militarization is a theoretical and political dead end, what, then, of dystopian "new bad futures" where machines and men are loosed by the state to stalk human revolutionaries? Taking a cue from Frase, Fisher, Evan Calder Williams, and, of course, Thacker, we turn again to the landscapes of horror fiction for some direction. With the publication of Mary Shelley's *Frankenstein; or, The Modern Prometheus* in 1818, a new tradition in both horror and science fiction emerges, with monsters born not only of premodern superstition but also of the intentionality of human cunning and hubris.[23] Birthing arguably the most "famous monster of the last two centuries," Shelley's patchwork wretch initiates the line running through Glass's new bad future and Turse's Terminator Planet, offering useful insight with which to confront the anxieties surrounding policing's increasingly apparent monstrous face.[24]

While it offers rich grounds for psychoanalytic, feminist, queer, and critical race readings, *Frankenstein* has long been a key metaphorical framework with which to contemplate troubling developments in science, medicine, and technology and to explore the "increasingly blurry boundaries and distinctions between what we label human and nonhuman/the natural and the unnatural."[25] As Daniel Dinello puts it, Shelley's technophobic vision provides "a powerful anti-science diatribe that still reverberates as a quintessential parable of the dangers unleashed by technological creation and irresponsible scientists."[26] Similarly, if not more plainly, science fiction giant Isaac Asimov blamed Shelley for initiating a decidedly dystopian view of scientific progress, a "Frankenstein Complex" in which "hordes of clanking murderous robots, reproduced story after story," overrun the cultural imaginary.[27]

The anxieties Shelley articulated two centuries ago have, of course, not abated with time, nor have they been confined to the pages and screens of fantasy. Take, for instance, the wide-awake horrors materialized by the Defense Advanced Research Projects Agency (DARPA) contractor Boston Dynamics. In 2018, the company made news when it posted a video to YouTube of Spot, a "nimble robot" designed to work in offices and homes, able to handle delicate objects and navigate stairs. Like the lurching alterity of its predecessor, BigDog, which was developed by DARPA as a mechanical pack animal, the brief clip of Spot slowly raising a single snake-like appendage to casually open a door drew gasps from curious viewers, who offered the satirical motto "Boston Dynamics, where dreams become nightmares" and, referring to *The Terminator*, "this is how it starts #Skynet."[28] On another video of Boston Dynamics' most advanced (public) prototype, Atlas, a viewer similarly remarked, "I'm looking at Atlas thinking, 'how come it doesn't have hands?' Then I realized, it's because his hands are going to be guns."[29] Observations such as these register the unease, perhaps terror, generated by our robotic progeny, with *The Terminator*, starring Arnold Schwarzenegger as the eponymous robotic assassin, being a particularly popular contemporary referent for Shelley's manufactured nemesis. Invoking the terrifying pursuit scenes of slasher films like *Friday the 13th* and *Halloween*, the Terminator methodically remains locked on its target, just steps behind. As one of the first film's protagonists pleads, "You still don't get it, do you? He'll find her! That's what he does. That's all he does! You can't stop him! He'll wade through you, reach down her throat, and pull her fuckin' heart out!"[30] In his patented Lacanian-Marxian fashion, Slavoj Žižek suggests that the horror of the Terminator and robots more generally derives not only from their unassailable killing power and utter physical superiority to their human analogues, but also from their relentless, single-minded efficiency and adherence to task. As he puts it, the horror of the cyborg or robot emerges not from its Promethean potentials, but from its being the perfect "embodiment of the drive, devoid of desire." The Terminator functions precisely as intended, "even when all that remains of him is a metallic, legless skeleton": he "persists in his demand and pursues his victim with no trace of compromise or hesitation."[31] The machine's indifference to human desire is powerfully communicated when, in the film, the Terminator coldly lays waste to an entire precinct of hopelessly outmatched LAPD personnel—quite plainly obliterating liberalism's dream of law, order, and *security*—without batting an artificial eye.

If Schwarzenegger's overmuscled body and scant dialogue sufficiently invoke the alterity of a pitiless robotic monster, what, then, can we make of the sequel's villain, which conspicuously takes the form of police? In an interesting turn of happenstance, an Angeleno named George Holliday shot footage from his apartment's balcony of the *Terminator 2* crew as they filmed a scene on a stretch of LA freeway. A few weeks later, Holliday would train his camera on the same freeway and shoot the now famous footage of LAPD agents savagely beating Rodney King. As Cameron likes to point out, the footage that would later seed the '92 LA riots actually contains two segments: the first featuring his Terminator/Cop/Monster and the second his everyday analogues.[32]

It is certainly no coincidence that the LAPD played the villain in both segments, as Cameron explains:

> The *Terminator* films are not really about the human race getting killed off by future machines. They're about us losing touch with our own humanity and becoming machines, which allows us to kill and brutalize each other. Cops think of all non-cops as less than they are, stupid, weak and evil. They dehumanize the people they are sworn to protect and desensitize themselves in order to do that job.[33]

Made through the figure of the police as much as the machine, Cameron's caution against the drift toward a cold mechanistic indifference is reminiscent of another warning offered by science fiction luminary Philip K. Dick in his now famous speech "The Android and The Human," given at the Vancouver Science Fiction Convention in the winter of 1972. Dick names the loss of humanity decried by Cameron *androidization*, a kind of subjectification, a beating down of the human until it is little more than a tool, performing the whims of its masters, whoever or whatever they might be. Dick explains:

> Becoming what I call, for lack of a better term, an android, means as I said, to allow oneself to become a means, or to be

Terminator 2 villain T-1000 (Robert Patrick) takes the form of an LAPD officer.

pounded down, manipulated, made into a means without one's knowledge or consent—the results are the same. But you cannot turn a human into an android if that human is going to break laws every chance he gets. Androidization requires obedience. And most of all, predictability. It is precisely when a given person's response to any situation can be predicted with scientific accuracy that the gates are open for the wholesale production of the android life form. What good is a flashlight if the bulb lights up only now and then when you press the button? Any machine must always work, to be reliable. The android, like any other machine must perform on cue.[34]

Eerily forecasting the manufacture of the neoliberal "*homo economicus*,"[35] Dick's androidization is useful for our purposes, offering a particularly fruitful avenue for challenging and reconceptualizing the theoretical and political dead ends of the critique of police militarization. Rather than seeking to reform police by returning them into some mythical premilitarized state, Dick's androidization encourages us to consider how cops themselves are subjects assembled and produced, becoming instruments of violence, of embodied drive, that perform on command. From such a vantage, police are not somehow corrupted by technology or tactic but instead themselves components of a broader technological architecture designed and assembled for specific tasks. Moving from Shelley to *RoboCop*, the remainder of this chapter offers a few ways to think about the relationship between police and police technology—phenomenological embodiment, transcendental materialism, and vital materialism— that avoid the traps of technological determinism. The aim, then, is to place the anxieties surrounding police militarization in the context of broader concerns and questions of social and technological progress and to focus on the mechanized, inhuman alterity of the police of the present and the "new bad future" long since arrived.

The Iron Fist Is a Robot's Hand

In 1975, Tony Platt and his colleagues at the nascent but soon-to-be-shuttered University of California, Berkeley, criminology program published *The Iron Fist and the Velvet Glove*,[36] offering activists and radical academics new ways to analyze, critique, and resist mounting police repression. While the authors, along with radicals like George Jackson and James Baldwin, were among the first to warn of police militarization, the epigraph of their chapter on police technology— "let us not forget there is always someone behind each technological device,"[37] attributed to Ernesto Che Guevara—suggests that they were already weary of the technological determinism that had come to characterize the topic. Nevertheless, under the sign of the iron fist, they outline a number of concerning developments in police technologies: information systems, identification techniques, command and control, surveillance systems, and weaponry.

Charting the breakneck speed of technological advance and the inevitability of "full computerization of police information," Platt and his colleagues showed how the National Crime Information Center (NCIC), for instance, had grown from a database of fewer than half a million entries of wanted persons and stolen cars at its inception in 1967 to a nationwide network of computer terminals supporting more than 130,000 daily queries of some 4.9 million records just a decade later. (Today the NCIC has twenty-one files and sixteen million active records and is accessed millions of times each day.)[38] From the analysis of speech patterns to the collection of trace evidence to the digitization and storage of fingerprint records, the authors warned that developments in "identification techniques" and the field of forensics would also be a boon for police power. As with developments in computerization and identification, which dramatically increased investigative capacities of police, innovations in "command and control" allowed police units to be directed toward calls and "hot spots" with martial efficiency. Taking an inventory of police weaponry, the authors undercut the supposed novelty of the present moment, citing studies that, even then, documented the profound racial disparity in "suspects fired on" and killed by police. Lastly, Platt and colleagues touched upon the growing prevalence of aerial surveillance, which, at the time, consisted mostly of small airplanes and helicopters. Marking police helicopters as the wave of the future, they described a Los Angeles County helicopter unit, the Sky Knight program, designed to aid in chases and "civil disturbances," which dramatically advanced nighttime operations with infrared systems and spotlights called Nightsuns. A similar program of the NYPD linked helicopters to an "electronic war room" via onboard closed-circuit television broadcasts, offering command and control a veritable eye in the sky. Of course, that "eye in the sky" vantage would soon become an entertainment commodity, normalized by news media coverage of California police chases, which first trucked into the public's imagination with O. J. Simpson's white Ford Bronco.

Making little distinction between everyday crime control activities and the spying, harassment, and subterfuge of the FBI's Counter Intelligence Program (COINTELPRO), the authors stake out a stridently abolitionist position against a disquieting vision of future police. While their unflinching critique of how police operated in the mid-1970s proved even more prescient as the Reagan, Bush, and Clinton years unfolded, the practices of contemporary police perhaps more closely resemble one of Dick's short stories than they do *The Iron Fist and the Velvet Glove*. Under the auspices of "smart policing," "intelligence-led policing," and, more commonly, "predictive policing" (predpol), the command and control infrastructure of major U.S. police departments is increasingly reliant on machine-learning-based big data analysis. Nowhere in the United States is this more evident than in Los Angeles, where the LAPD has heavily invested in predpol. Appropriating a mathematic model initially designed to predict earthquake aftershock clusters (Epidemic Type Aftershock Sequences, or ETAS)[39], LAPD's version of predpol draws three key data points—crime type, location, time—from a living database of police calls for service to calculate and identify 500×500-foot hotspots used to direct police resources into the future.[40] As critics have long argued, using historical data to make predictions about the future invariably produces a feedback loop, whereby the "hot spots" identified are among those spaces already overpoliced. Andrew Ferguson, author of *The Rise of Big Data Policing*, succinctly puts it this way: "algorithms and big data models, simply take in inputs, crunch them up to create outputs. So, if your inputs are biased, your outputs are going to be biased."[41] One of the clearest and most troubling examples of the biased inputs in the poisoned well of big data is the Microsoft AI chat bot named Tay. Launched on Twitter on March 23, 2016, it used existing tweets to learn and duplicate human communication practices; in less than twenty-four hours, Tay was tweeting its hatred of feminism, admiration of Adolf Hitler, and support for a southern U.S. border wall.[42]

Drilling down even further, the LAPD in 2009 implemented the Los Angeles Strategic Extraction and Restoration (LASER) program, targeting "repeat offenders" as a "medical doctor uses modern technology to remove tumors." With hot spots, community, "quality of life," and "broken windows" policing as foundational philosophies, LASER integrated big data analytics with other surveillance platforms, such as geocoded automated license plate readers (ALPRs) provided by billionaire Peter Thiel's Palantir Technologies (named after a magical "far-seeing" crystal ball that appears in J. R. R. Tolkien's *Lord of the Rings* novels) to identify, track, and ultimately incapacitate a population of "chronic offenders."[43] Harkening to the Reagan-era obsession with "career criminals,"[44] LASER and programs like it work as a self-fulfilling prophecy, hiding what amounts to the selective incapacitation arm of the LAPD's broader counter-insurgency strategy under the supposed value-free objectivity of algorithms and huge data sets.

Like the Precrime unit of Dick's *The Minority Report* (1956), now realized by the likes of Microsoft, Google, and Palantir, the lethal assemblage of computing, surveillance, and killing power predicted by *The Iron Fist and the Velvet Glove* has appeared most notably on the screens and pages of U.S. popular culture. For instance, the 1983 hit *Blue Thunder*, cowritten by Dan O'Bannon (*Alien*, *The Return of the Living Dead*, *Total Recall*), features an aptly named LAPD helicopter equipped with all manner of sophisticated surveillance equipment and weaponry meant to put down the kind of "civil disturbances" that had marred Los Angeles decades prior. Underlining the technophobic message that some tools, technologies, and powers are too great for man to possess, the helicopter's pilot, a burned-out Vietnam War veteran played by Roy Scheider (also a heroic cop in *Jaws*), thwarts a plot to use the machine in a coup d'état and then promptly destroys it by landing it in the path of a speeding freight train. *Blue Thunder* (and its ill-fated television spin-off) is but one example of several popular programs that paired sophisticated machine-characters with the familiar rogue cop and set in pursuit of law and order. The television series *Airwolf* (1984–87) likewise draws on many of the same themes as *Blue Thunder*, pitting the crew of a cutting-edge stealth helicopter against a parade of Cold War–era villains. Like its airborne contemporaries, the short-lived series *Street Hawk* (1985) again marries the marvels of machine, in this case a tactical motorcycle, with the crime-fighting desires of man. *Street Hawk*'s opening sequence provides an exemplar of the narrative and theme employed by similar programs, the pairing of man and machine:

> This is Jesse Mach, an ex-motorcycle cop, injured in the line of duty. Now a police troubleshooter, he's been recruited for a top-secret government mission to ride Street Hawk—an all-terrain attack motorcycle designed to fight urban crime, capable of incredible speeds up to three hundred miles an hour, and immense firepower. Only one man, federal agent Norman Tuttle, knows Jesse Mach's true identity. The man . . . the machine . . . Street Hawk.[45]

Like in *Blue Thunder*, a technological panacea, in this case a jet-powered attack motorcycle, is envisioned as antidote to the rising anxieties surrounding civil unrest and "urban crime." Important for all of these programs and quite apparent in the monologue above is that the pairing of "the man" and "the machine" ultimately produces a single figure—*Blue Thunder, Airwolf, Street Hawk*. As with the terrible unity of *monster and police*, aided by "the latest in technology," the police power assumes the form of and emerges as a singular hunting and killing *machine*.

Of course, the longest-running and, hence, best-known of the early-1980s man/machine singularities is NBC's *Knight Rider* (1982–86), which aligns a conscious, artificially intelligent 1982 Pontiac Firebird named KITT and its ex-cop partner/pilot against a veritable who's-who of corny bad guys. However predictable, the perpetual reimagination of the *Knight Rider* franchise (*Knight Rider 2000, Knight Rider 2010, Team Knight Rider*, etc.) and the impending rebirth of *Blue Thunder* as a lethal police drone prove the formula's resilience. While each of these programs offered a speculative vision of a spectacular future where the pairing of man and machine formed a particularly potent and tidy avenue to crime control, their everyday analogues proved markedly less sophisticated and, indeed, far more horrifying. On May 13, 1985, in a standoff with the Black liberation primitivist group MOVE, Philadelphia Police dropped a pair of FBI-supplied one-pound bombs on the group's home from a Bell helicopter, killing eleven people, five of whom were children, sparking a fire that ultimately destroyed sixty-five homes. While hardly the technologically sophisticated vision offered by *Blue Thunder* or *Airwolf*, the MOVE bombing nevertheless demonstrated the nuts-and-bolts lethality of policing's airpower. On the thirtieth anniversary of the bombing, Mumia Abu-Jamal, who, as a Philadelphia journalist, had covered MOVE's ongoing clash with police, remarked on the whitewashing of the event:

> Why should we care what happened on May 13, 1985? . . . I'll tell you why. Because what happened then is a harbinger of what's happening now, all across America. I don't mean bombing people, not yet, that is. I mean the visceral hatreds and violent contempt once held for MOVE is now visited upon average people, not just radicals and revolutionaries like MOVE. In May 1985, police officials justified the vicious attacks on MOVE children by saying they too were combatants. In Ferguson, Missouri,

as police and National Guard confronted citizens, guess how cops described them in their own files? Enemies. Enemy combatants, anyone? Then look at twelve-year-old Tamir Rice of Cleveland. Boys, men, girls, women, it doesn't matter. When many people stood in silence, or worse, in bitter acquiescence, to the bombing, shooting, and carnage of May 13, 1985, upon MOVE, they opened the door to the ugliness of today's police terrorism from coast to coast. There is a direct line from then to now: May 13th, 1985, led to the eerie *RoboCop* present.[46]

Referring to the 1980s science fiction film franchise, the "eerie *RoboCop* present" of which Abu-Jamal speaks has, of course, always been here. Like the masters of capital who hope to trim the fat by replacing flesh-and-blood workers with rigid analogues, automated cops have long been a dream of developers and police futurists. Consider, for instance, the May 1924 issue of *Science and Invention* magazine, which featured plans for a future "Radio Police Automaton"[47]— appearing just four years after Karel Čapek's play *R.U.R.* (1920) popularized the term *robot* and a few years before the film *Metropolis* (1927) introduced viewers to "artificial humans" en masse. It seems as soon as the robot entered the cultural imaginary, it was imagined as a cop and outfitted with a badge and gun. Clearly designed with labor disputes and political policing in mind, the article describes how the radio-controlled automata, equipped with telegraphones, loudspeakers, tear-gas tanks, and spinning lead balls on flexible leads to approximate "police clubs in action," would have "no superior for fighting mobs or for war purposes."[48]

While this particular robocop seems never to have escaped the pages of *Science and Invention*, the dream of police automata lives on. In the mid-1980s, the Orlando, Florida, police department developed a public service robot named OP2 to deliver public service programming to area schoolchildren, for instance.[49] Today, driven by the desire to reduce labor costs and generate proprietary data, private manufacturers like the Silicon Valley tech firm Knightscope are quickening the arrival of "autonomous security robots." As the sales copy for one of the company's products reads, "There's no need to spend hours on those boring and monotonous patrols. You'll

In 1924, *Science and Invention* magazine offers a speculative design for a Radio Police Automaton, or "mechanical cop," complete with tank tread, tear gas, and spinning "police clubs in action."

find the K3 patrolling the interiors of businesses like sporting arenas, shopping malls, and warehouses. Big technology. Small package."[50] The company combines a range of technologies in stationary or roving machines—think five-foot-tall, four-hundred-pound Roombas—designed to collect data as they roam private property. As Stacy Stephens, the former cop who cofounded Knightscope in 2013 following the mass murder at Sandy Hook Elementary school, explains, "the math of only 700,000 plus sworn men and women protecting our streets . . . doesn't pencil" (we can't pay for all the cops we need), so he and his partners developed machines that would work as so-called force multipliers while also perpetually generating the necessary "actionable intelligence," or data (capital), needed by police and other private security providers to drive predpol and programs like LASER.[51] Each Knightscope machine uses a bundle of sensors, including GPS triangulation and a lidar system that produces a "three dimensional map every 20 milliseconds" to generate reams of data and an incredibly accurate depiction of space, all of which is saved and stored in Knightscope's proprietary cloud system. Of course, in addition to the autonomous collection of geospatial data, the machines can be outfitted with license plate readers, weapons detection systems, thermal imaging, video surveillance, facial recognition, and any other application making up contemporary surveillant assemblages.

Even in a country that already employs nearly one million police, it seems there is still a desire for more, even a market for robotic "force multipliers." In San Francisco, the local ASPCA employed a Knightscope robot in hopes of deterring "graffiti, car break-ins and homeless encampments" around the facility. According to an ASPCA spokesperson, the machines appeared to be working—and at seven dollars an hour, a price much less than a human security guard. Still, not all were sold on the prospects of a robotic security force. As one local resident who encountered a Knightscope machine while on a walk with her dog wrote, "This robot was a total invasion of our space on the public sidewalk, and we were shocked that the SPCA of all places would be so insensitive to both the rights of pedestrians and the needs of the often traumatized dogs that typically fill that particular sidewalk."[52] Despite the unease, Knightscope shows no signs of changing its business model. According to the company's marketing materials, in its short history, Knightscope machines have "helped law enforcement issue an arrest warrant for a sexual predator," "helped a security guard catch a thief in a retail establishment," and "assisted a corporation in tracking down a vandal."[53] Perfectly encapsulated by its motto, "The future is here and Knightscope will help you secure it," the company is one of many to capitalize on commoditized security with the help of robot adjuncts.

Most of the products presently offered by security companies like Knightscope are simply that: products meant to augment or in some cases replace human labor. This follows the common-sense logic of the robot, a term that comes from *robota* in Čapek's native Czech and refers to servitude or forced labor—a slave.[54] Likewise, police robots like the Remotec ANDROS Mark V-A1 presently operate as duplicate, adjunct, and prosthetic to the police power.[55] This is perhaps best represented by the "robot cop" currently at work on the streets of Dubai. Essentially a human-shaped, interactive mobile kiosk, the unit allows citizens to interact with police through an onboard touch screen while also collecting data through GPS and facial recognition sensors. This is not simply a technological fix for labor shortfalls; Dubai hopes to replace a quarter of its flesh-and-blood police by 2030.[56] Overgrown Roombas aside, whether it's the "Skunk Riot Control Copter" that showered freedom fighters in Gaza with pepper spray and tear gas[57] or the "robo-guards" that patrolled the 2018 Winter Olympics and now patrol South Korean prisons, by and large, the machines deployed by public and private police remain mostly under human control. Yet, as *Wired* noted in its coverage of Knightscope, even if a company wants to retain full human control of its machines, it is only a matter of time before another company decides differently and imparts its machines with much more autonomy. Meaning that, much like the U.S. military's plans for a fully autonomous AI-driven drone fleet, a future where fully autonomous police are loosed on city streets to search for wanted persons and patterns in crime is presently left to the whims of the market.[58]

Recalling the utility of Frase's social science fiction, we need only dip into the filmic imagination to register the fully autonomous progeny of today's "security robots." Combining the unremitting murderous drive of Cameron's Terminators with the shuddering alterity of Boston Dynamics' "dogs," the "Metalhead" episode of the Netflix future-shock series *Black Mirror* portends the horror of a rather plausible autonomous hunter-killer. In the episode, set in a post-collapse future, three scavengers break into a warehouse in search of some unnamed item. Finding it, they also awaken a small dog-like security robot still dutifully guarding the grounds and contents of the long-abandoned warehouse. As the dog clinically dispatches each of the three scavengers and viewers learn that they were only after a teddy bear meant to comfort a dying child, the episode grimly underlines the horror not of killer machines run amok but of those that coldly act precisely as intended.

Again, the horror of the drive offers a powerful riposte to liberal critiques of police militarization. While accounts and images of battle-clad police agents bearing down on unarmed protestors in Ferguson, Missouri, in 2014 may have for some revealed policing's monstrous face, we must locate the horror of police not in the fatigues, assault weapons, or armored vehicles ushered in by the Pentagon's 1033 program but rather in the forces of androidization that transform "once living men," as Dick put it, into instruments bound by institutional codes, commands, and directives and the broader architecture of racial capitalism.[59]

The robotic adherence to task—drive devoid of desire—shared by killer dogs of the future and police of the present is evidenced by how police frame "the job" in response to both praise and criticism. For instance, when a twenty-nine-year-old Uzbek named Sayfullo Saipov drove a rented truck onto a bike path in Lower Manhattan in late 2017, killing eight and wounding a dozen more, the NYPD agent credited with ending the attack offered the familiar refrain that just as "thousands of officers do every day," he and his colleagues were "just doing our job."[60] But when faced with scrutiny, police and their supporters tend to invoke the same rhetorical defense, stating they were "just doing their job" and that critics should "let them do their job."[61] While it is reasonable to read adherence to one's job as either false modesty or a "cop-out,"[62] what if we take police seriously—perhaps literally? Through the figure of the robot, inhuman labor designed for a particular task, might we similarly understand the flesh-and-blood beings occupying the position of police as robotic automata, cybernetic organisms, bound to the "job" by the strictures of command and code?[63]

Postmodern Prometheus

Equipped with Dick's androidization and Žižek's horror of the drive,[64] we arrive at perhaps the most immediately recognizable representation of policing's rigid inhumanity: *RoboCop*, a film about a cop/cyborg/hero named Alex Murphy who delivers a crime-torn future Detroit from runaway street crime and the ruthless profiteering of multinational security and defense contractor Omni Consumer Products (OCP). Directed by Paul Verhoeven and released to surprise acclaim in 1987, the first film was followed by two sequels, a handful of animated and live-action television spin-offs, and a 2014 remake, with another on the way. Held against *Blade Runner's* dystopian Mike Hammer, RoboCop is more a cyberpunk Dirty Harry who dispatches unlucky street punks with his space-age hand cannon.

In the mini documentary *Flesh + Steel: The Making of RoboCop*, co-screenwriter Edward Neumeier, as if channeling Glass's "new bad future," explains that he, Verhoeven, and the film's other producers hoped to use the popularity of films like *The Terminator* as a satirical vehicle to push back against the gross self-interest of the Reagan era:

> *RoboCop* to me is essentially a satire. It's a satire of the '80s, some people say it's a satire of Reaganomics. But it's a satire of that era when everybody's getting rich and everybody in business were being tough. Businessmen were reading Asian martial arts books to learn how to be better businessmen and they were calling each other killers and they were talking about hostile takeovers.[65]

In apparent agreement, critics lauded the film for its humorous but dark depiction of corporate colonization and cheap violence. In the decades since its release, the first film has attained cult status and remains a foreboding but increasingly popular referent for all manner of abhorrent policing. When reporting on the uprising in Ferguson, the event that introduced "police militarization" to the American public, journalist Glenn Greenwald wrote:

As is true for most issues of excessive and abusive policing, police militarization is overwhelmingly and disproportionately directed at minorities and poor communities, ensuring that the problem largely festers in the dark. Americans are now so accustomed to seeing police officers decked in camouflage and Robocop-style costumes, riding in armored vehicles and carrying automatic weapons first introduced during the U.S. occupation of Baghdad, that it has become normalized.[66]

Also commenting on the SWAT teams, riot cops, and armored police vehicles deployed in Ferguson, a journalist similarly lamented that U.S. police had "gone from beat cop to RoboCop, from guardian to warrior," recapitulating the tired trope of a once-benevolent police somehow corrupted by technology and tactic.[67] Part of the disquiet generated by the "robocops" that have barged into public discourse in recent years is the belief held by some that these battle-clad "warrior cops" mark a decided turn toward a wholly authoritarian and dystopian future. That SWAT teams and contemporary "riot control" tactics were developed expressly to repress 1960s civil rights movements, first the United Farm Workers in Delano, California, and later the Black Panthers in Los Angeles, is a fact apparently lost on incredulous liberals but definitely not on the poor and minority communities long under their boots. Like today's SWAT teams and riot squads, *RoboCop* must be understood not as some wrong-turn future but a glimpse of the horrifying present, always visible, should we care to look.

RoboCop ratcheted up the violence of the police story at precisely the time that violence in Detroit and cities across the United States was also rising under auspices of the Reaganite war on drugs. Three decades on, the U.S. state still dutifully writes its own social science fiction in preparation for the wars to come. Citing numerous studies and a particularly colorful Pentagon training video, *Megacities: Urban Future, the Emerging Complexity*, obtained by journalists via Freedom of Information Act requests, Nick Turse illustrates the "world of Robert Kaplan-esque urban hellscapes," an anarchic pastiche of *Escape from New York* and *RoboCop*, *Warriors* and *Divergent*, envisioned by the U.S. military. In the future imagined and planned for by the Pentagon, the city breeds and harbors leaderless gangs of enemy combatants, while Guy Fawkes–masked hackers take the fight online. This harrowing future, the narrator asserts, is one "that the masters of war never foresaw"—outside the fantasy of science fiction, that is.[68]

Mirroring the Pentagon's vision of future war, the original films and the recent remake imagine RoboCop and its OCP brethren, like the wobbling bipedal cannon ED-209, as machines "programmed for urban pacification." The 2014 film, in fact, conspicuously opens with U.S. military personnel and OCP robots and drones on counter-insurgency operations in war-torn Tehran, a highly prized target of Pentagon hawks. Employing the same risk-averse pragmatism used to prop up the U.S. drone program, a political talk-show host (Samuel L. Jackson) makes the case for a robotic police force:

> What if I told you that even the worst neighborhood in America could be made completely safe? And what if I told you that this could be accomplished without risking the life of one single law enforcement officer? How do I know this? Because it's happening right now in every country in the world but this one.[69]

In both versions, having seen its marketing efforts dashed by un-cooperative politicians and a technophobic public, OCP looks to op-portunistically seize the middle ground between fully autonomous robot police and their inferior human analogues by creating a cy-borg cop with a human face. After his murder by a local gang, OCP scientists resurrect Murphy, augmenting his damaged flesh with tita-nium prosthetics and integrating his nervous system with the latest cybernetics. With his human agency overwritten by three unbreak-able "Prime Directives," codes reminiscent of Asimov's Three Laws—serve the public trust, protect the innocent, uphold the law—Murphy is, at first, little more than the *robota* of Čapek's imagination, a drone launched for a particular set of tasks. As one slimy OCP executive in the first film snaps, "He doesn't have a name, he's got a program. *He's product.*"[70]

Following Shelley, then, RoboCop might be better understood as *Frankencop*, a grotesque amalgamation of advanced science, corpo-rate greed, and good old-fashioned police violence.[71] "Naïve, quixotic in his belief that the role of the police is to protect the citizenry," as

Jackie Wang writes in her book *Carceral Capitalism*, RoboCop "represents a certain idea of the police that circulates as a public fact."[72] Less menacing than a killer dog or Terminator, RoboCop embodies both sides of the community policing or counterinsurgency coin: capable of unassailable violence through superior technology and firepower but also of winning "hearts and minds" by peddling policing's ideal type, a lethal Andy Taylor for postmodern times. It should come as little surprise, then, that Peter Weller, who played RoboCop in the first two films, appeared in a number of Reagan-era "Just Say No" public service advertisements while the RoboCop character, like McGruff the Crime Dog, appeared on behalf of police and the establishment at countless public events. All of this neatly maps onto the "copaganda" efforts of actual police, who bring their tactical vehicles for "show and tell" at community events and give talks to children in schools about drugs and policework.

Not only does *RoboCop* offer a vision of future police organized around white, middle-class anxieties, but as automated labor the character provides perhaps the only plausible vision of an incorruptible cop—a machine bound by equally incorruptible firmware. As the film's other screenwriter, Michael Miner, suggests:

> When people have faith that the streets are policed by incorruptible individuals—which, in a way, RoboCop was—it renews a sense of community, and I think that's also where the film sort of touched people's unconscious, because they felt there was somebody out there who was not corruptible.[73]

RoboCop, of course, becomes less of a product, struggles against his programming, and eventually remembers his name.[74] As such, this particular cyborg, the "illegitimate offspring of militarism and patriarchal capitalism," as Donna Haraway famously put it, fulfills its Promethean promise, proving unfaithful to its origins and rendering its OCP fathers essentially inessential.[75] As opposed to the Terminator, which is bound to its task and utterly devoid of desire, Robocop is both a dead man and lifeless machine. Caught between two deaths, Murphy moves from a driven machine to a being of desire and is eventually resubjectified as his previous life comes back to him.[76] In a "wonderful revolutionary flourish," adds producer Jon

Davison, "the created turns on the creator just like the Frankenstein myth, but in this case on the side of law and order, which is kind of reactionary in a way."[77] Even though he eventually refuses his OCP masters, RoboCop's primary directives, as Wang correctly reminds, include a fourth, classified directive (no fucking with your creator) that overrides the other three.[78] So, while RoboCop might replay Shelley's Promethean fantasy of social rebellion by saying no to his creators, the machine entwined with the lingering remnants of Alex Murphy nevertheless endeavors to serve social order and "fight crime." No matter the familiar struggle between man and machine/monster, no matter how heroic, even utopian an incorruptible future police it might portend, RoboCop is and always will be a *cop* in service not simply of its creators but of law and liberal order.[79]

Fascism for Liberals

RoboCop, then, as Davison admits, "is really just fascism for liberals." Which is to say that, like *Elysium*, the films envision a rapidly approaching—or, rather, long since arrived—future, where machines reaffirm the unavoidable inequalities of liberal social order, doing so in "the most violent way imaginable."[80] Foreshadowing the resignation of Fisher's capitalist realism, Miner adds that this sort of future is inextricably entangled with a world-for-us ontology that views the police as a necessary evil of capitalist order.

> Now we have a more [OCP villain] Dick Jones vision of law en-
> forcement, a militarism in which no secret gets out, which is
> really troubling when you think about it. But America deserves
> that—it's a land of private property, where everything has to be
> owned, serial numbered, protected and controlled. We're ad-
> dicted to a pretty bad drug called capitalism, and until we get
> over that we're gonna need police in the way that they are.[81]

Given Miner's capitalist realist resignation, it is hardly a coincidence that *RoboCop*'s producers selected Detroit, a city long marked
as ground zero of U.S. economic collapse, as the testing ground
for, as the film's tagline advertises, "the future of law enforcement."
Just as the deadly airpower of *Blue Thunder*, a fantasy antidote to

"civil disorder," was realized by the Philadelphia Police Department's bombing of MOVE, *RoboCop* offers a thinly veiled representation of the actual "law and order" politics emerging in the 1980s in response to the racialized specter of urban crime and disorder. As if casually endorsing the necessity of violent police repression to support a world-for-us, Neumeier also suggests that, not unlike his cinematic progeny, U.S. police "look just like peacekeeping troops . . . because that's what the cities are demanding now."[82]

While its creators meant for *RoboCop* to be a satirical riposte to Reagan-era inhumanity, three decades on, theoretically informed critics like Wang also see the films as more than kitschy pop cultural mockery and instead a rather accurate reflection of "the future of law enforcement." Wang writes,

> What is the future of law enforcement? RoboCop is it. It is the place where the violence and coercion of prisons and police meet soft counterinsurgency. On the one hand, the militarization of the police. On the other, cybernetic forms of control. The old Detroit of RoboCop, devastated by the effects of Reaganomics, becomes the corporation's testing ground for technologies of war.[83]

Like the warnings of *The Iron Fist and the Velvet Glove* nearly five decades ago, such a view accurately depicts how policing's technologies of violence circulate between the colony and the metropole. Again, the mistakes, as I see them, are to assume a distant future and to prop up an artificial barrier between war and police and to recoil in "it can't happen here" disbelief at the sight of riot cops and tear gas on U.S. streets.

Again, much of this incredulous reformist handwringing is driven by well-meaning liberal critics, who adopt a sort of straight-line determinism, fetishizing the tools—weapons, uniforms, modes of conveyance—with which the police equip themselves. The logic being that, once outfitted, police agents who were previously democratically accountable and aimed to "protect and serve" become somehow compelled to behave in a more warlike fashion. Just a cursory review of policing's martial origins, from Robert Peel in Ireland to the slave patrols and night watches of the American colonies, "police science" forerunner August Vollmer's instruction in pacification during the Spanish–American War, the counterinsurgency programs of Vietnam, Iraq, and Afghanistan, and right on through to the antigang, anti-immigrant, and protest-policing regimes of the present, proves the hope for the return, or even the arrival, of "de-militarized" police to be misguided. As police historian Stuart Schrader similarly argues,

> We should be skeptical of calls for police reform, particularly when accompanied by cries that *this* (militarization) should not happen *here*. A close look at the history of US policing reveals that the line between foreign and domestic has long been blurry. Shipping home tactics and technologies from overseas theaters of imperial engagement has been a typical mode of police reform in the United States. When policing on American streets comes into crisis, law-enforcement leaders look overseas for answers. What transpired in Ferguson is itself a manifestation of reform.[84]

Nevertheless, calls to roll back and "demilitarize" are front and center in contemporary debates over the future of U.S. policing. For instance, criminal justice professor Peter Kraska has relied upon this sort of technological determinism in his ongoing critique of police militarization, likening it to the relations between hammer and nail. In a public lecture titled "All We See Are Nails: Using Militarism as a Problem-Solving Strategy," he explains,

> My overall and rather simple idea this evening is that militarism has been, and is increasingly today, the hammer that views and sometimes actively constructs many of our problems and difficulties as nails worthy of pounding. Put differently, militarism has become the apex lens or the theoretical filter underpinning our government's approach to drugs, crime, civil unrest, and terrorism.[85]

Again, to avoid any confusion, my assertion is that, rather than being equipped with a hammer, the police *are* and always have been the hammer. The uncomplicated determinism of Kraska and others is, of course, at odds with long-standing and varied deliberations concerning the human relationship with tools and technology. A century and a half ago, English novelist Samuel Butler in his novel *Erewhon* (1872) offered a remarkably astute and prescient observation about the body's ability to act through technology. Somehow anticipating contemporary posthumanist theory, he writes:

> A machine is merely a supplemental limb; this is the be all and end all of machinery. We do not use our own limbs other than as machines; and a leg is only a much better wooden leg than any one can manufacture . . . In fact, machines are to be regarded as the mode of development by which human organism is now especially advancing, every past invention being an addition to the resources of the human body.[86]

In the years after Butler, a variety of thinkers have remarked on the body's ability to link to, merge with, or operate through tools and technology. A common observation, for instance, is that when driving a car, the operator's nervous system seemingly grafts onto the vehicle, allowing the driver to instinctually judge distances from the car in a manner similar to how one might judge distances from one's own body. Steering, braking, accelerating, signaling become sense extensions, linking the operator through the vehicle's components to the surrounding terrain and environment.[87] Observations such as these, like those of early phenomenologists Edmund Husserl, Martin Heidegger, and Maurice Merleau-Ponty, wholly upend the technological determinism of police somehow corrupted by technology.

In the traditional reading of Heidegger's famous tool-analysis, for instance, objects are only understood through their relationship to human use. As opposed to his teacher Edmund Husserl's assertion that objects must first be understood as they are present before the mind, Heidegger argued that the hammer is mostly taken for granted, so long as it feels and operates as anticipated, and only when it is broken does the user more closely grasp its objective qualities. Providing the foundation for what is now widely understood as the phenomenology of embodiment, the observations of Husserl, Heidegger, and Merleau-Ponty clarify the epistemological distinction between subjective and objective qualities of things, as well as the ontological distinction between subjective and objective being.[88]

Michael Polanyi's notion of *dwelling in technology* likewise understands the tool as an extension of the body. As he wrote in 1958, "the way we use a hammer or a blind man uses his stick, shows in fact that in both cases we shift outwards the points at which we make contact with the things we observe as objects outside ourselves."[89] Even today, those working in the field of robotics find that the programming and training of artificial intelligence is best and perhaps only accomplished through machines' direct interaction with their environments. That is to say, the robots and robocops of the future will not be preprogrammed with set instructions authoring their movements in a given environment and instead will program themselves in real time, through direct interactions with their particular surroundings. Pushing this thinking even further still, advanced work in the field of social robotics employs principles of phenomenological embodiment to teach robots to use tools and navigate complex environments by extending their sensors outside their physical bodies, to the surrounding environment and the tools themselves.[90]

If the blind man's stick or the carpenter's hammer becomes an embodied extension of the self, as phenomenologists suggest, what then can we make of the uncomplicated suggestion that the violence of so-called militarized police simply results from the police having a hammer and seeing everything else as a nail? Rather than facilitating or even eliciting a particular behavior, as some might have it, we might better understand objects such as the policeman's gun as, paraphrasing Bruno Latour,[91] always already invested with human labor and, as such, artifacts of human extension, containment, and manipulation simultaneously.[92]

As Haraway sets out in her massively influential "Cyborg Manifesto," at its core, the notion of the cyborg challenges understandings of nature and humanity as a discrete, independent phenomenon somehow poisoned by technology. Obliterating the boundaries of the human, as does Haraway, in turn obliterates the notion that the police agent might be corrupted by a particular tool or mode of conveyance. Rather, we might arrive at a more sustained critique of police by beginning with the assumption that their tools are simply an extension of their already existing essence—the police power—the sovereign prerogative of legally sanctioned violence.[93] Like Haraway's cyborg, embodiment of this sort is fundamental to RoboCop and hence the social science fiction projection of future police.

A key aesthetic feature of all the RoboCop films is the manner in which, when confronted by a threat, RoboCop's targeting visor drops over his eyes and his weapon automatically juts forth from a compartment in his thigh. Drawing on the low-slung holster and quick draw of 1950s spaghetti westerns and the sound of a racking shotgun in contemporary action films, the dropping visor and auto-holster are signature features of this futuristic cop. Yet, as an OmniCorp tactician remarks in the 2014 remake, it's not so much the gun that matters but the *hand*:

> OMNICORP DRONE TACTICIAN: If you sense you need a weapon or are threatened, your visor goes down and the system makes the weapon available. You've got to remember, it's not the weapons that count, it's who is handling them, or in your case *what*.

While this film departs somewhat from the originals, making the subtle point of sparing Murphy's right gun hand, leaving it and his face the remaining traces of human flesh, all of the films lay bare the perils of attempting to separate the gun from the hand—tool from being. Describing what he calls the *prosthetics of law*, Joseph Pugliese similarly suggests that all state agents, in his case U.S. military drone operators, are always already inscribed with the technics of law.[94] Which is to say, the tools of war, such as the Predator and Reaper, dislocated by thousands of miles, must be understood as "phantom members" grafted onto their operators through the knotted powers of technology and law. As with RoboCop's embodied pistol housed within his titanium thigh, a number of tools—gun, Taser, chemical agents, club—are always ready-to-hand, to use Heidegger's language, grafted onto the cop through the technics of law. This is to say nothing, of course, of the myriad killing tools waiting inside the patrol car, at the station, or in the jail and prison. The point is that just as with the operator and the drone, these technologies of violence are not just normalized but embodied tools, grafted onto the figure of the policeman, fashioning a legally appointed and authorized unit, a *killing machine*. In the posthumanist social science fiction of *RoboCop*, the flesh-and-blood cop and his titanium armor, cybernetic operating system, futuristic sidearms, and lethal "data spike" are all components of the same machine and, as such, a unitary embodiment of the police power—*always already militarized*. By extension, we might simply conclude that in the world of everyday cops, the gun as embodiment or prosthetic is not separate from the hand. Such a recognition begins to shift the reformist concern from contemporary policing's "militarized" components and from questions of aesthetics to the underlying commands, codes, and drives that always reside within the police themselves. After all, the vast majority of police violence is accomplished not by the battle-clad "warrior cop" but by "Officer Friendly" on routine patrol.

In the remake, when detailing the development and tuning of Murphy's targeting and weapons systems, an exchange between RoboCop's creator, Dennett Norton (Gary Oldman), and the conniving OmniCorp CEO (Michael Keaton) offers a glimpse at the transcendence of embodiment, to the point where the machine "takes control."

> DR. DENNETT NORTON: The machine assesses the threat and acts, that's it—two steps. Now watch Alex: The software assesses the threat, just like a robot, and it sends the information to the brain. Alex's brain receives the information and decides what to do with it based on his emotional and cognitive abilities like any man would. Then the brain relates this to the AI module and, ah . . .

> OCP CEO: Right, yeah, a *year* later.

> DR. DENNETT NORTON: You wanted a man inside a machine, and that's what you've got. But the human element will always be present. Fear, instinct, bias, compassion—they will always interfere with the system.

> OCP CEO: Okay, but—damn it, I've got to give the American people something they can root for, something aspirational, right? . . . We, you and I, have got a release date. And we've got to make it okay . . . Dr. Norton, how is he doing this?

> DR. DENNETT NORTON: His software is faster, his hardware is stronger, he's a better machine.

OCP CEO: But you said humans hesitate?

DR. DENNETT NORTON: Only when they're making decisions.

OCP CEO: So, he's not making decisions?

DR. DENNETT NORTON: Well, yes and no. In his everyday life, man rules over machine. Alex makes his own decisions. Now when he engages in battle, the visor comes down and the software takes over. The machine does everything. Alex is a passenger, just along for the ride.

The excerpt demonstrates how, as in the original films, the visor marks the point of androidization, where "the software takes over" and Alex Murphy withdraws into RoboCop, moving from a man with a human face to a cold, lethal machine. For some, the same sort of aesthetic transformation is apparent in the workings of actual cops who hide behind the protective anonymity of the riot helmet's visor. Depicting RoboCop rising from a patrol car, visor down, under the tagline "part man, part machine, all cop," the original film's poster does, admittedly, bear some resemblance to the proliferating images of battle-clad riot cops, such as those found on the cover of Radley Balko's widely read *Rise of the Warrior Cop*.[95] The point is that for those whose critique of police begins and ends with militarization, policing's monstrous power only emerges in the instant when its human face recedes behind the visor, club, and shield.

However, focusing on this particular symptom, I suspect obsessive critics of police militarization hide an even darker motive, aiming to rescue "nonmilitarized" police from under the thumb of public criticism. As Kraska alleged in an interview, in the process of militarization, "SWAT had gone from an entity that was all about saving lives in real dire circumstances to prosecuting the Drug War inside people's residences."[96] The distorted history Kraska invokes holds that SWAT was engineered for legitimate "emergency situations" rather than race and class oppression and could therefore be legitimate again with measured reform. The reformist vision shared by many a critic in kind leaves the core police project—institutionalized violence and terror—hidden and mostly unchallenged.

Returning to the visor and mask, this is the point Žižek makes in his writing on French burka bans. Asking why burka-covered faces have stirred so much anxiety, he suggests that an encounter with a covered face reminds us that we really cannot know Others at all. The burka, mask, visor, SWAT balaclava force a confrontation with that which lies behind the subject's public veneer, the unrecognizable "Other-Thing," the Neighbor that we know but do not or cannot *know*. Covering the face, he writes, "obliterates a protective shield, so that the unrecognizable, Other-Thing stares us directly in the face."[97] Put to the question of the armored cop, all the consternation ginned up by their alien gear may in fact give away that what lies under their smiling mask of community outreach, friendly slogans, and claims to duty is, in fact, far worse. To put it plainly, clearly there is something in the visor, shield, mask that is horrifying—it could be robocop or a riot cop, but in the end, it is just the cop. The scene continues:

> OCP CEO: But if the machine is in control, then how is Murphy accountable? Who is pulling the trigger?
>
> DR. DENNETT NORTON: When the machine fights, the system releases signals into Alex's brain, making him think he's doing what our computers are actually doing. I mean, Alex believes right now he's in control, but he's not—it's the illusion of free will.
>
> OCP CEO: So you've circumvented the law by creating a machine that thinks it's a man, but that's illegal.
>
> DR. DENNETT NORTON: No, it's a machine that thinks it's Alex Murphy, and in my book, that's legal.

Questions of accountability, the illusion or obliteration of free will, and the view of Murphy as a "passenger, just along for the ride" all inch closer to Dick's androidization and an understanding of the figure of the cop as the product of a particular form of cultural and political power. As if parroting Heidegger's discussion of a hammer as opposed to a broken hammer, Dick compares the transformed subject to a flashlight, an object that is worthless unless it performs on command. But Dick's androidization extends beyond phenomenological embodiment of tools and warns of the processes that make a human being into an actual tool. Again, as he put it, "the android, like any other machine, must perform on cue."[98] As we will see in the following chapter, failing to perform on cue—to act violently and, at times, lethally—calls individual cops' and policing's entire reason for being into question.

Misery Made Me a Fiend

Not far from the operations that fashioned RoboCop out of Alex Murphy's trashed carcass, Dick warns of historical forces that render a human little more than an instrument. Again, quoting from his speech at length:

> I would like then to ask this: what is it, in our behavior, that we can call specifically human? That is special to us as a living species? And what is it that, at least up to now, we can consign as merely machine behavior, or, by extension, insect behavior, or reflex behavior? And I would include, in this, the kind of pseudo-human behavior exhibited by what were once living men—creatures who have, in ways I wish to discuss next, become instruments, means, rather than ends, and hence to me analogs of machines in the *bad* sense, in the sense that although biological life continues, metabolism goes on, the soul—for lack of a better term—is no longer there or at least no longer active. And such does exist in our world—it always did, but the production of such inauthentic human activity has become a science of government and such-like agencies, now. The reduction of humans to mere use—men made into machines, serving a purpose which although "good" in an abstract sense has, for its accomplishment, employed what I regard as the greatest evil imaginable: the placing on what was a free man who laughed and cried and made mistakes and wandered off into foolishness and play a restriction that limits him, despite what he may imagine or think, to the fulfilling of an aim outside of his own personal—however puny—destiny. As if, so to speak, history has made him into its instrument. History, and men skilled in— and trained in—the use of manipulative techniques, equipped with devices, ideologically oriented, themselves, in such a way that the use of these devices strikes them as a necessary or at least desirable method of bringing about some ultimately desired goal.

Moving beyond sense extension or simple ideology, Dick's androidization points toward a transformative process whereby "once living men" *become* something else entirely. Such a transformation is readily apparent to police themselves, who see actual robocops among their ranks and in their own reflections. As an entry in the "favorite cop nicknames" blog on the popular website Police1 illustrates, "Robocop" is part of everyday vernacular used by police to describe a particular type of cop, a subject of drive:

> ROBOCOP: Know an especially aggressive rookie? This nickname may stick to officers who are "stereotyped as strictly enforcing laws and rules without any regard for fairness, extenuating circumstances or explanations from those subject to the enforcement." Yes, it originates from the 1987 science-fiction movie.[99]

While the tag might signal flaws in the makeup of some particularly rigid and unseasoned rookies, we should not dismiss it outright as harmless fraternal jocularity, as clearly, for some, the violent drives of RoboCop are coveted indeed.

Take the case of William "Robocop" Melendez,[100] a veteran of the Detroit Police Department and two smaller departments in neighboring Highland Park and Inkster, Michigan, who, by local accounts, earned the nickname for his notoriously "aggressive policing."[101] Though he was finally banished from policing in 2017 for the brutal 2015 beating of a Black man named Floyd Dent, over the course of his career Melendez had been the subject of more than a dozen formal complaints alleging theft, extortion, wrongful arrest, excessive force, falsified reports, and planted evidence. He had also, unsurprisingly, escaped punishment for killing two unarmed Detroiters in 1996 and 2003. In the first instance, the family of Lou Adkins, whom Melendez and his partner Dominic Gonzales shot more than eleven times following a traffic stop, was awarded just over $1 million. In the 2003 killing, the City of Detroit awarded the family of Ernest Crutchfield II more than $50,000 in a wrongful death civil suit. The verdict in the Dent case—which included a $1.4 million judgment for the plaintiff and a thirteen-month prison sentence for Melendez—was secured by dashcam footage of the attack and text

William "Robocop" Melendez suited in tactical gear, and the *Detroit Free Press* reports on the Melendez case.

messages from another officer on the scene, which confirmed the pair's cruel satisfaction with "beating up niggers."[102] All told, it appears the already cash-strapped cities that chose to deploy this particular machine paid nearly $4 million to atone for his decades-long rampage.[103] Not unlike Catholic priests shuttled from assignment to assignment just ahead of abuse allegations, Melendez cycled from department to department, exploiting a common practice that allows cops to obtain new employment after being fired or resigning.[104]

When asked about the "Robocop" moniker, Melendez's former supervisor approvingly gushed, "If you've seen him, he is in outstanding physical condition and is probably built like the Hulk."[105] Melendez, who stood more than six feet two inches and weighed more than 245 pounds, was, in fact, the hulking embodiment of an institutional culture that prizes Schwarzenegger's iconic physique and, as John Hoberman writes in his book *Dopers in Uniform*, keeps the use of anabolic steroids a widely held open secret.[106]

As with the filmic RoboCop's weapons and titanium armor, Melendez's badge, insignia, uniform, Kevlar vest, duty belt, and body merge and form the corporeal embodiment of the police power. "Who better to sell the fantasy of safety, security, and self-control than a cop?" asks Kenneth Saltman, pointing to Ronnie Coleman, one of the most dominant professional bodybuilders of all time, whose day job was, predictably, as a cop. Like so many other bodybuilders, cops, and bodybuilder/cops, Coleman could not attain his desired physique without the help of illegal drugs. Nevertheless, Coleman reached, Saltman continues, "the height of civilization by becoming robo-cop, part human, part synthetic, he is a super law enforcer who embodies the achievements of science."[107] Taking Coleman and Melendez as extreme examples, we might therefore consider how the body *and* mind are remade in the process of *becoming* police. Here, I am not merely pointing to the power of total institutions to socialize new recruits into obediently performing police duties. Rather, returning to our previous discussion of the ways humans solicit the trap of their own subjectivity, we can understand cops like Melendez not simply as "bad apples" or the unfortunate outcomes of the rotten barrel of militarization but as active agents who have, under their own volition, transformed themselves, become cyborg, become android, become *RoboCop*.

With his famous dictum "spirit is a bone," Georg W. F. Hegel expels the problems of mind-body dualism, pointing instead to the material concretion of the immaterial: the spirit that resides in one's bones. As sociologists and anthropologists have similarly observed, rather than simple stylistic choice, decoration, or symbolism, cultural and political power is quite literally written into the flesh upon birth.[108] All of this is to suggest that the production of the cop involves more than education, socialization, acculturation, or interpellation. Drawing on Žižek's model of subjectivity and developments in contemporary neuroscience, Adrian Johnston offers a transcendental materialist model of subjectivity that emphasizes the inherent adaptability of humans and the plasticity of the brain itself.[109] Presupposing the dialectic between material and ideal, Johnston eschews notions of a preexisting moral presence at the core of human subjectivity and instead advances an understanding of a pliable core that responds to its material and ideological environments with equal accord.

As Steve Hall, the first to apply Johnston's ideas to the study of crime and violence, describes, "transcendental materialism conceives of the body as a true neurological and subsymbolic 'thing,'" actively produced and reproduced through the force of unconscious drives, desires, experiences, and the need for a coherent symbolic order. Real and Ideal, he writes, "combine in dialectical tension to create a third realm of structural dynamism that we call [transcendental] 'subjectivity.' Established politico-economic and socio-cultural systems get the type of subjectivity they need, which in turn willingly and actively participate as powerful actors in the reproduction of the system. Those who seem to fit the system's needs and perform well in its institutions will achieve power and influence authorized by the majority."[110] Offering a bridge between structure and agency, materialism and idealism, Johnston's model allows us to include the body and mind in our efforts to understand the development of a hypermasculine, ultraviolent cop like William "Robocop" Melendez.[111]

For those like Melendez called to work in policing, the symbolic order they draw upon is built upon the legitimacy of liberal legal order (rule of law, impartial criminal punishments, etc.) and the social order it serves. The activities of policing, its cultural and political environment, extend beyond the "indoctrination" of the total institution and provides the subject the tools necessary to actively shape their own subjectivity. As Simon Winlow, who also engages Johnston's work, writes, the symbolic order unique to the inner world of policing itself holds powerful sway over one's subjectivity.

> Rather than a fundamental force residing at the core of our being, there simply exists a void, or the absence of a thing . . . The subject solicits a symbolic order to escape the terror of the Real. Once the symbolic order is in place, meaning can be ascribed to the phenomena. The subject, keen to keep the terrors of the unsymbolisable Real at bay, enters the symbolic order and submits to its meanings, customs and rules. When the subject has faith in its symbolic order, constitutive lack at the core of its being is effectively "filled up" with a symbolic substance that shapes desire.[112]

We might read the transformation of Melendez's body and behavior for clues, not only to his inner cop-fantasy life but to the transformative power of policing's broader symbolic order. As we will see, the fabrication of his own body, his racist violence, and his wanton illegality must also be understood as authorized by both the symbolic order of police and the broader imperatives of racial capitalism. And so, with the mechanistic violence of robocops like Melendez in mind, we might alter Hegel's famous dictum and say that no longer is the spirit a bone; the spirit is, in fact, a *metal*.

Through the process of becoming robocops, or rather Frankencops, Melendez and others take their place in the "armed formation comprised of people," as Adam Greenfield puts it, "whose pumped-up bodies, fragile psyches, and febrile politics are fundamentally unsuited to maintaining the peace of the twenty-first-century United States."[113] Greenfield's observations map neatly onto the figure of what Anna Feigenbaum and Daniel Weissman have called the "vulnerable warrior." That their duties invariably place them in harm's way, under constant threat of attack and in a state of ordinary emergency, is perhaps the most widespread and pernicious of all police myths. The exaggerated vulnerability of the "warrior cop" underlines, among other things, the irrepressible "I feared for my life," "him or me" mantra, the bad-faith justification for all manner of violence, coercion, and brutality. Following insights from transcendental materialism, however, we move one step further and consider how the ideologies of "warrior cop" and "vulnerable body" operate dialectically and map mutually reinforcing ontological circuitry, necessitating the transformation of mind and body into a cop, a distinct political subject—a killing *machine*.[114] From this vantage, Melendez's "Terminator" physique, embodiment of police weaponry, robotic inhumanity, and near quarter-century career of violence and disrepute are not mere by-products of a noxious institutional culture. Instead, they mark the transformation of a man into an actual machine, designed and produced for a particular set of tasks.[115]

Of course, it is not my actual intention to impute the political subjectivity of Melendez, or anyone else, for that matter, through a superficial reading of secondary source material. My aim, rather, is to offer a speculative model to account for the production of hypermasculine, hypermilitarized "warrior cops" that does not reaffirm the simple rotten-barrel model of police deviance. Continuing in that spirit, we can look to not only Melendez's deeds, which are many, but also his words. Given the opportunity to speak on his own behalf at his sentencing hearing for the crimes he committed against Floyd Dent, instead of offering an apology to his victim, community, and profession, Melendez chose instead to read aloud a version of the poem "The Final Inspection."

> The policeman stood and faced his God, which must always
>   come to pass.
> He hoped his shoes were shining, just as brightly as his
>   brass.
> "Step forward now, policeman. How shall I deal with you?
> Have you always turned the other cheek? To My church have
>   you been true?"
>
> The policeman squared his shoulders and said,
> "No, Lord, I guess I ain't,
> because those of us who carry badges
> can't always be a saint.
>
> I've had to work most Sundays,
> and at times my talk was rough,

and sometimes I've been violent,
because the streets are awfully tough.

But I never took a penny
that wasn't mine to keep . . .
though I worked a lot of overtime
when the bills got just too steep.

And I never passed a cry for help,
though at times I shook with fear.
And sometimes, God forgive me,
I've wept unmanly tears.

I know I don't deserve a place
among the people here.
They never wanted me around
except to calm their fear.

If you've a place for me here,
Lord, it needn't be so grand.
I never expected or had too much,
but if you don't . . . I'll understand."

There was silence all around the throne
where the saints had often trod.
As the policeman waited quietly,
for the judgment of his God.

"Step forward now, policeman,
you've borne your burdens well.
Come walk a beat on Heaven's streets,
you've done your time in hell."[116]

As if scripted by Shelley's pen, the monster speaks, lashing out at
the mob that has brought him to justice. Admitting only the sins of
casual violence, "rough talk," and "unmanly tears," Melendez shame-
lessly claims heavenly reward for suffering the thankless "hell" of
police work, somehow invoking the monster's refrain, "I was benevolent and good; misery made me a fiend."

That Melendez—a man who killed two people and brutalized
many more—could, at his own sentencing for beating a Black man

bloody, so easily assume the position of victim provides a glimpse of his subjective core. While we cannot know whether he entered policing "benevolent and good," the "Robocop" moniker and all that it implies are, in fact, suggestive of some sort of becoming. It is, however, important to be clear that such an understanding of becoming must not be reserved for only the most horrific outliers like William Melendez. Indeed, the model of subjectivity offered by transcendental materialism accounts for policing's routine and spectacular violence with equal accord. Moving forward with this and Dick's androidization, it is perhaps, then, a useful exercise to consider how all police agents operate as parts of a broader system, network, *machine*.

The Ghost in the Machine

Admittedly, it is rather unoriginal to compare U.S. criminal justice to a machine, even as it "processes" millions of "cases"—a cold euphemism for lives and deaths—each year. Yet if we are to understand all cops, not just those who have risen to the level of robocop, as mechanistic subjects, or androids in Dick's language, we must also consider the ways in which each cop fits within policing's broader systemic architecture.

In "The Android and the Human," Dick refers his audience to "The Pedestrian," a short story by Ray Bradbury published in 1951. Set one hundred two years into the future, it imagines a city where, not completely unlike today, the vacuous programming of television keeps nearly all mesmerized residents glued to their glowing screens indoors at night. This is a wholly technocratic future that has lost the use for men of letters like Leonard Mead, a solitary man whose lone joy is his nightly stroll on his city's empty streets. A joy, that is, until his path crosses that of an autonomous police car—the last police car, in fact, for a crime-free city of three million. An eerie foreshadowing of Knightscope's security robots or Dubai's kiosk cop, the disembodied voice emanating from the car refuses to believe that Mead or anyone else would enjoy aimlessly walking at night and, despite much pleading, forces him into its interior, into a "little black jail with bars," and wheels him away to the Psychiatric Center for Research on Regressive Tendencies.[117] Inspired by his own late-1940s encounter with the LAPD, an experience that also birthed

Fahrenheit 451, Bradbury's is no more a warning of runaway technologies than it is a cautionary tale against policing's rigid inhumanity.

Decades later, Dick finds in Bradbury's automated police car inspiration for his own future vision of androidization. Warning of the dehumanizing power of routinized postwar consumer culture, he laments, "even the most base schemes of human beings are preferable to the most exalted tropisms of machines." Recognizing that "even police cars are expendable, can be replaced," he further cautions:

> It is the person inside who, when gone, cannot be duplicated, at any price. Even if we do not like him we cannot do without him. And once gone, he will never come back. And then, too, if he is made into an android, he will never come back, never be again human.

Clearly no fan of police, Dick nevertheless wishes to keep a human, however flawed, at the patrol car's helm. Here, I will depart from Dick and those fixated on policing's martial drift and suggest that concern and criticism should always remain on the power that underlies and animates the machine, whether it comprises flesh and blood or steel. Indeed, a "technological veil covers the brute presence and the operation of the class interest in the [machine]," as Herbert Marcuse insisted. "Is it still necessary to state that not technology, not technique, not the machine are the engineers of repression, but the presence, in them, of the masters who determine their number, their life span, their power, their place in life, and the need for them?"[118] As we have seen, whether grafted onto or taken into the body, implicated in an active process of subjectification or, as is the case with "The Pedestrian," at work within a wholly non-human object, the police power is immutable and, indeed, downright horrifying.

In his book *The Concept of Mind* (1949), the philosopher Gilbert Ryle undermines the ascendancy of Cartesian mind-body dualism with the memorable and descriptive phrase "the ghost in the machine." Ryle's point is that for Cartesians, the mind and the body each operate independently of the other, thereby likening human subjectivity to a mystical force trapped inside a flesh-draped contraption. Since Ryle, the ghost in the machine has become a popular device in horror and science fiction, notably deployed by Stephen King, by Arthur C. Clarke, and in the popular manga and anime franchise *Ghost in the Shell* to describe a magical, sometimes unruly force alive within an inanimate vessel. It seems to me that Bradbury's autonomous cop car, the fantasy RoboCop, and his flesh-and-blood namesakes are each animated, or rather haunted, by the same ghost: the police power. This, again, is a conclusion also drawn by Walter Benjamin, who described the waiting violence of police as "formless, like its nowhere tangible, all-pervasive, ghostly presence in the life of civilized states."[119]

Moving from a human with embodied mechanical parts to a human made into a machine, our third and final position is one where the ghostly presence of the police power haunts an assemblage composed of both the human and the nonhuman.[120] Following the vital materialism of Jane Bennett's influential *Vibrant Matter*,[121] we can consider how human and nonhuman objects—in this case, all things police—are invested with what she calls "thing-power." Extending the thought of Gilles Deleuze and Félix Guattari, Bennett suggests that when bodies unite as assemblage, thing-power courses through and animates the whole. Radically decentering the human, Bennett sees agency less as the product of human will, emerging, rather, from an endless range of human and nonhuman collaborators, or actants, to use Latour's language.[122] What we think of as individual agency, she suggests, is more aptly "distributed across an ontologically heterogeneous field, rather than being a capacity localized in a human body or in a collective produced (only) by human efforts."[123] Accordingly, we might understand the police power as thing-power distributed across an assemblage of the historical, legal, and physical architecture of all things "police." From this vantage, policing, however militarized, cannot be reduced to the behavior of actors with equipment and instead must be understood in terms of a living and autonomous network, system, assemblage—*machine*.

Recall, again, the iconic T-1000 Terminator of the franchise's second film, *Terminator 2: Judgment Day*. Resembling mercury or molten aluminum but composed of a network of "mimetic nanorobotics," the T-1000 is nothing if not a lethal assemblage animated by thing-power. Though able to assume any form, in *Terminator 2*, the villain nevertheless always returns to that of an LAPD officer. As a social science fiction rendering of Bennett's vital materialism, the shape-shifting T-1000 represents myriad actants—most of all the murderous cop—animated by thing-power, or, rather, the police power. Here the point is not the forms that the actants assume but the underlying power and drive that unites them all.

Also recall that the violence and corruption of William "Robocop" Melendez was prolonged for decades as he was shuttled between duties and departments. Like Melendez, so many other cops—such as Timothy Loehmann, who killed twelve-year-old Tamir Rice after having been forced to resign from his previous department for lacking emotional stability, or Michael Rosfeld, a seven-year journeyman also forced to resign amid brutality allegations who later killed an unarmed seventeen-year-old boy named Antwon Rose just hours after being sworn in at his new post—benefit from the same enablement. From the vantage of vital materialism's flat ontology, Melendez, Loehmann, Rosfeld, and others of their sort are not "bad cops" who have conveniently escaped discipline but actants plugged into a normally functioning machine. It cannot be overstated that internal discipline and reform are built-in components of policing's broader systemic architecture. Like a computer network that searches out and destroys its own viruses and repairs its own code, the trial, expulsion, and incarceration of crooked cops, even when long overdue, as was the case with Melendez, makes policing appear autotrophic, self-correcting, and accountable. Like the Terminator or *Black Mirror*'s relentless metalhead dog, the horrifying *machine* operates precisely as intended. And while for some, the riot-gear-clad "warrior cop" or a fully autonomous "killer robot" might reveal policing's monstrous face, Bennett's vital materialism returns us to the vast and volatile mix of language, law, policy, theory, badges, boots, gasoline, helmets, radio transmissions, cars, clubs, computers, weaponry, architecture, and human and nonhuman bodies, fashioning a recombinant monster/corpse, stitched together and (re)animated by thing-power—*police power*. Assembled, animated, and unleashed, its creator long ago announced, *"It is alive!"*

Dick once explained that what inspired and fused all his work was the question *Who is human and who only appears, or masquerades, as human?*[124] Questions of authenticity and humanity do, indeed, unite Dick's corpus, from the counterfeit memories of "We Can

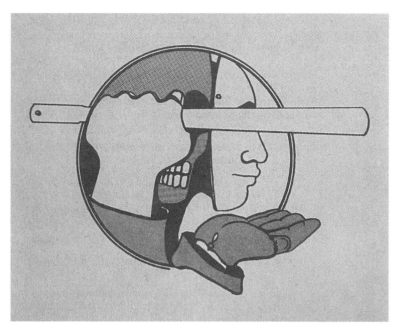

Created by the well-known radical Chicano illustrator Malaquias Montoya, the title page of *The Iron Fist and the Velvet Glove* depicts a monstrous face hidden behind the figment humanity of police.

Remember It for You Wholesale" to the more-human-than-human replicants of *Do Androids Dream of Electric Sheep?*[125] Yet at the peak of his sadly undervalued career, he seemingly failed to fix the optics of his grand theme to the time in which he lived. Halfway through "The Android and the Human," Dick openly muses, "The totalitarian society envisioned by George Orwell in 1984 should have arrived by now. The electronic gadgets are here. The government is here, ready to do what Orwell anticipated. So, the power exists, the motive, and the electronic hardware. But these mean nothing, because, progressively more and more so, no one is listening."[126] The suggestion, if I am reading it correctly, is that androidized complacency had rendered Orwellian authoritarianism unnecessary. Yet right when Dick was giving this speech, not far from where he lived, Tony Platt and his conspirators at the Berkeley School of Criminology were indeed listening and fast at work on the *Iron Fist and the Velvet Glove*.

For critical criminologists writing in 1975, like the "ghetto children" who instinctively drew "monsters with badges," Orwell's "boot stamping on a human face" future vision was grimly apparent in their own lived present. The aim for radical critique, then, it seems to me, is to alert all, even the most perceptive and far-seeing prophets, to the future that has long since arrived. Continuing with the discussion of police subjectivity in the next chapter, I further investigate the familiar refrain "I feared for my life" and consider the figure of the frightened, horrified police.

CHAPTER 4

Monsters Are Real

Maintaining order is the main activity of an order that
has already failed.

—The Invisible Committee, *Now*

In 1956, Evan Hunter, writing as Ed McBain, published *Cop Hater*,
the first of his 87th Precinct series. McBain, who would become
synonymous with postwar police procedurals, had taken a cue from
Dragnet, his favorite show, and would begin each of the series' fifty-
five books with the now-familiar disclaimer "The city in these pages
is imaginary. . . ." But in the "ripped from the headlines" style that
he helped popularize, the subject that filled out the book's pages
was, of course, always a bit more than pulp-fiction fantasy, zeroing
in as it did on fears that persist today. In *Cop Hater*, set in a thinly
veiled New York City, a searing heat wave is heightened by a "cop
hater" who, in a seemingly haphazard fashion, ambushes and exe-
cutes unwitting cops. Following McBain's sparse procedural arc, the
book's narrative is stitched together by the mundane details of detection and the grind of police work—collecting and inspecting evidence, chasing down leads, knocking on and kicking in doors, making and clearing suspects—until, at last, the dutiful cops get their
man. Neither a madman nor a pinko with a grudge, the titular *hater*
is simply a patsy seduced into murder by the conniving wife of one
of his victims. And while the book's payoff is the conjectural trail
bringing the cops to the killers, the balmy tensions of a city gripped
by an assault on law and order fill out its affective core. To attack the
police, as one cop explains, is to attack society itself:

If you read the newspapers, and if you start believing them, you'll know that cops hate cop killers. That's the law of the jungle, that's the law of survival. The newspapers are full of crap if they think any revenge motive is attached. We can't let a cop be killed because a cop is a symbol of law and order. If you take away that symbol, you get animals in the streets. We've got enough animals in the streets now.[1]

Invoking the Darwinian jungle, McBain makes clear that not only do cops hate cop killers, they fear a world not dependent on their own violence. Just as the thin blue line is said to mark the craggy fault between civilization and savagery, in the universe of the 87th Precinct, cop killing marks a rupture in an otherwise pristine social order (the world-for-some-of-us). Nearly forty years later, another artist took up the subject of cop hating—or, rather, cop killing—to advertise and aggravate this rupture.

In March 1992, less than a month before Los Angeles exploded in rage following the acquittal of the cops who trounced Rodney King, Tracy Lauren Marrow, better known as Ice-T, and his Body Count bandmates released their self-titled debut album and the single "Cop Killer." From the album's opening skit ("Smoked Pork") to its end, urban poverty, racism, and, importantly, violence committed by and against police are central themes, the last of which is heavily underlined by the introductory monologue of "Cop Killer":

This next record is dedicated to some personal friends of mine, the LAPD. For every cop that has ever taken advantage of somebody, beat 'em down or hurt 'em because they got long hair, listen to the wrong kind of music, wrong color, whatever they thought was the reason to do it, for every one of those fucking police, I'd like to take a pig out here in this parking lot and shoot 'em in their motherfucking face.[2]

As Ice-T's contemporaries NWA had learned just a few years prior, police and much of the American public would not stand by approvingly as artists, particularly Black rappers, openly defied their authority. Quickly, a host of high-profile politicians and police weighed in. Not wanting to be outdone by his Democratic challenger, Bill

Clinton, who had his own performative tussle going with rapper Sister Souljah, President George H. W. Bush took "Cop Killer" head-on. As had been the case with the murder of NYPD rookie cop Edward Byrne—Bush often used the dead cop's badge as a theatrical prop during speeches—"Cop Killer" provided the incumbent a powerful instrument with which to mobilize racist anger, placing Black people on one side and the police on the other.[3] On the campaign trail, speaking at the New York headquarters of the DEA, Bush challenged Clinton's tough-on-crime bona fides and called Body Count "sick," promising to "stand against those who use films, or records, or television or video games to glorify killing law enforcement officers."[4]

From the president on down to local beat cops, the self-appointed arbiters of moral decency aligned against their new "gangsta rap" adversaries. In an essay titled "The Music of Murder" published in the newsletter of the Academy of Criminal Justice Sciences (ACJS), the then president of the National Association of Chiefs of Police, Dennis R. Martin, wrongly linked "Cop Killer" to at least two police shootings and blamed the "primitive" music for inflaming racial tensions across the country. As Martin would have it, an attack on police is an attack not only on civil peace but also on the bedrock of liberal capitalist social order, the "right" to private property:

> With growing lawlessness and violence in our society, every American is at risk of losing his property and his life to criminals. Police officers risk their lives daily to preserve peace and property rights for all Americans. The officers deserve protection from abusive speech when that abuse imperils not only their ability to protect citizens, but also their ability to protect their very lives.[5]

Given the tack and tenor of those who, like Martin, spoke on behalf of other cops, it was evident that their beef was not only with the music but with the musicians and the particular communities they signified. In their response to Martin, criminologists Mark Hamm and Jeff Ferrell rightly noted that from nineteenth-century murder ballads to Depression-era tunes extolling gangsters like Pretty Boy Floyd to Eric Clapton's bloodless cover of Bob Marley's "I Shot the

Sheriff," violence against police had long been a relatively innocuous and accepted subject of popular music.[6] In an interview with *Rolling Stone*, Ice-T said as much, adding that the reason he had received so much criticism was that he and other rappers provided a useful foil—an adversary—to align against. He explains:

> They're yelling about a record that came out in March, and just yesterday the cops were killing people out in the street. They're under the gun, and the best defense is a good offense, so what they've done is taken Americans' minds and said "Look at this record, look at how people are treating us." But why all this noise? Why all the protest about a record that speaks about killing cops and not protest against the cops killing kids out there in the streets?[7]

Here, then, we might conclude that the theatrics of the "'Cop Killer' controversy," as it was called, simply provided a new, highly visible, and easily reviled adversary with which to fortify the thin blue line at a time of mounting crisis.

Drawing closer to the present but remaining in Los Angeles, in early 2013, an actual cop killer stepped out from the city's bustle and gripped the nation's imagination. That February, a former LAPD cop named Christopher Dorner declared a campaign of "unconventional and asymmetrical warfare" on his former employer after he reported his training officer for abusing a prisoner and was fired. Described by ABC News as "playing out with all the intensity of a Hollywood action thriller, *LA Confidential* meets *Cape Fear*," Dorner's war on the LAPD, which lasted ten days and claimed five lives, including his own, briefly turned hunter to hunted, predator to fearful prey.[8] Before it ended with Dorner's dead body amid the charred ruins of a cabin at Big Bear Lake, two innocent women were also violently swept up in the manhunt and nearly killed. Four days into Dorner's war, Margie Carranza and her seventy-one-year-old mother, Emma Hernandez, were on their daily newspaper delivery route when their truck (blue) was mistaken for Dorner's (gray) by frenzied LAPD officers on the hunt. Allegedly misreading the truck's slow crawl for Dorner's tactical advance and the sound of tossed newspapers hitting the pavement for gunfire, eight tightly wound patrol officers fired more than one hundred rounds into Carranza's vehicle, hitting Hernandez twice in the back and wounding Carranza with flying debris. Nearly three years later, the LAPD and the city's attorneys resolved the matter, replacing the truck and awarding the women $4.2 million. It was also resolved that the responding officers had acted in good faith and would not be held criminally liable.

The "officer-involved shooting" report released by the Los Angeles County district attorney cited case law setting out the "reasonableness of self-defense" and "reasonableness of force to detain a fleeing felon" to defend their actions.[9] In the former, attorneys stated that "the fears of a reasonable man" authorize him to "act upon those fears . . . and slay his assailant," while in the latter, they insisted that the manhunt had instilled a general "fear of death and great bodily injury" in all police, thereby justifying their overreactions. Elaborating both points, the report stated:

> The circumstances immediately prior to, and during, the shooting put each of the officers into a situation in which they were required to *make split-second judgments under an incredibly heightened emotional state.* There is no question that each of the officers' judgment was clouded by the circumstances surrounding Dorner and the environment on Redbeam. *The fear of Dorner was understandable and justified.* There is no evidence to suggest that the officers did not honestly believe that Dorner was in the vehicle, nor is there evidence to suggest the officers did not honestly believe they were being fired upon.[10]

Ultimately, the police and their defenders fell back to the familiar defense, the "heightened emotional states" of officers that "feared for their lives." In this case, firing 103 rounds at two innocent and utterly defenseless women was deemed "understandable and justified." As this and countless other examples attest, police need simply mention their own fear in order to excuse their wanton knee-jerk violence. We are obliged to recall, for instance, that in his trial for the murder of Walter Scott, Michael Slager of the North Charleston Police Department *testilied*[11] that he was in "total fear" of the unarmed man and that he "did as he was trained" and "fired until the threat was stopped." Video footage, of course, contradicted Slager's account, proving he shot Scott multiple times in the back as he attempted to flee.[12] While it may be easy to cynically dismiss Slager's claims of "total fear" as a stock police defense—something akin to pleading the fifth—what if we take his claim and those of other police seriously? *What if the police are actually afraid?*

The Gift of Fear

In his widely read self-help book *The Gift of Fear*, "security guru to the stars" Gavin de Becker calls police the masters of the "technology of intuition" and "perhaps the greatest experts at day-to-day high-stakes predictions."[13] For de Becker, the technology of intuition—a stew of war stories, pop psychology, gut feelings, and, most importantly, *fear*—is a mystical reservoir of signs and signals somehow severed from the worst of human prejudices, an objective instrument, operating in the moment independent of history and culture. His "gift of fear" shares obvious affinities with the Bulletproof Warrior curricula of Dave Grossman and the Killology Research Group. In fact, writing in the foreword to Grossman and Loren Christensen's *On Combat*, de Becker draws clear links between the two:

> We have a brain that was field-tested millions of years ago in the wild. I call it the wild brain to distinguish it from the logic brain so many people revere. The logic brain can't do much for you when the situation becomes critical. The logic brain is plodding and unoriginal . . . The logic brain has strict boundaries and always it wants to obey, but the wild brain obeys nothing, conforms to nothing, answers to nobody, and will do whatever it takes. It is unfettered by emotion, politics, politeness, and as illogical as the wild brain may sometime seem, it is, in the natural order of things completely logical. It doesn't care to convince us of anything by using logic. In fact, during combat, the wild brain doesn't give a damn what we think.[14]

Like for the Killologists, for de Becker, staying safe means succumbing to our basest fear-drenched instincts, trusting a primordial "wild brain" unfettered by emotion, politics, or politeness (and by emotion, he likely means empathy, certainly not fear). Where de Becker uses fear to hone the tools of intuition, Grossman's Killology aims to keep it from interfering with the "psychological arousal," muscle memory, and reflexes that "enable and restrain killing." The systems of thinking de Becker, Grossman, and their ilk tout rest on an understanding of the world as a dangerous place, where stakes are high and the price of inaction, or slow *reaction*, is death. As we have seen, this mixture of cartoonish masculinity, racism, nationalism, and Manichean eschatology combines as a virulent ontology of war, where "the only thing that stops a bad guy with a gun is a good guy with a gun."[15]

Taking the killing of Philando Castile as one tragic example, however, we know all too well the outcome of this gift of fear. Cops certainly fear death, as do we all. Whether their fear is heightened by training or by the existential threats of their jobs makes no difference, or shouldn't. The problem, as I see it, is that the police exploit our shared fear of death for political ends, tearfully invoking their desire to "go home to their families" at the end of their shifts (don't we all?) and playing upon the fears of a worried public to shield themselves from criticism and resist honest self-inspection.

Reflecting on his fifteen-year career, former Baltimore cop Larry Smith challenged the myth of police as the "good guys with guns" who "run toward danger," suggesting instead that the training he and his fellows received foregrounded, first and foremost, fear.[16] Despite well-known (or at least readily available) evidence demonstrating, year after year, that policing is a relatively safe occupation, it is routinely held up as a life-and-death affair. For some context, according to the U.S. government's own data, among the top ten riskiest job categories recorded by the Bureau of Labor Statistics—logging; aviation; oil, gas, and mining; roofing; refuse and recycling; structural iron and steel working; truck driving; farming; firefighting; power-line engineering—policing is conspicuously absent. In fact, the death rate of 111 per 100,000 people who work in the logging industry, the riskiest profession in 2018, towers over the rate of 13.7 for police.[17] All of this, of course, contradicts the validity of the fearful "firing until the threat is stopped" war footing on which police willingly place, or imagine, themselves. What is more, if we closely examine the manner in which police die, their "ordinary emergency" mantra unravels further. Of the 835 police that died on duty from 2014 to 2018, about one-third (248) died in the hail of gunfire that

Hollywood typically imagines. Far more commonly, traffic accidents, heart attacks, and "duty-related illnesses" claim the lives of U.S. police. Nevertheless, as Smith admits, because of the "us versus them" ontology that police nurture, under auspices of "self-defense and remaining alert," cops are taught "to fear even the average citizen—to beware that someone will take your gun and use it on you, to be on alert for ambushes, to be ready to fix yourself up if shot so you can keep going."[18] As we have seen, all of this places the police at the center of an uncomplicated hero's journey in which they fight evil on our behalf. Yet evidence shows that rather than "fixing themselves up" so they can again "run to the sound of gunfire," police quite often do precisely the opposite.

In the aftermath of the mass shooting at Marjory Stoneman Douglas High School in Parkland, Florida, courts again pondered the legal duty of police to protect the public at risk of their own safety after it was learned that police present at the school that day failed to confront shooter Nikolas Cruz. One cop, Scot Peterson, was particularly reviled after video emerged showing him hiding at a distance as Cruz killed seventeen people and wounded seventeen more. Max Schachter, father of one of the murdered students, blamed Peterson for permitting the slaughter, stating, "He's no police officer, no law enforcement officer. Anybody with a badge would have done something. He did nothing. I hope he rots in hell."[19] In a suit brought against the school district, Broward Sheriff's Office, and several individuals, including Peterson, U.S. District Judge Beth Bloom upheld previous rulings finding that police in fact bear no legal obligation whatsoever to defend the public.[20] This ruling follows a 2005 Supreme Court case in which police in Castle Rock, Colorado, failed to enforce a no-contact order against a man who abducted and later murdered his three children.[21] As later with the Parkland case, the court ruled that since the killer was not in state custody (i.e., an escaped prisoner) the police could not be held liable for their inaction.

In another instance, one seemingly borrowed from the script of a cheap slasher film, two NYPD agents came under fire for failing to escort emergency medical technicians into a Brooklyn apartment where a man had attacked two young women with an axe and where a four-year-old girl presumably still slept. After one of the bloodied women escaped to call the police, the two responding cops refused to assist other emergency workers, claiming the apartment complex was outside their jurisdiction and, while the child was still apparently in danger, notified dispatch that the call was complete. Despite repeated calls for assistance, EMTs were unable to render aid for nearly two hours, and when they finally made entry alone, they found a woman nearly decapitated.[22]

All of this is not to say that the human beings who work as police always shirk their duties and never risk their safety in service of others—of course not. Again, my point is this: Despite what we are taught to believe, we must face the horrifying fact that the police offer no real protection. Even when positioned to do so, police are under no legal obligation to save the proverbial cat from the tree. Quite often, in fact, they just turn and walk away.

Reading their stock claims of fear alongside cases like Parkland, Castle Rock, and Brooklyn, it seems that police have the best of both worlds, able to invoke the gift of fear to excuse both overreaction and inaction. This contradiction, revealing yet again that police are not the faithful protectors they claim to be, lies at the heart of our shuddering ontological schism, the horror of police. Until now, the horrifying faces revealed by this vastation—the villainous rogue, the monstrous sovereign, the lethal automaton—have been our abiding concern. Yet, as the above examples attest, perhaps there is more to policing's violent, authoritarian, fascistic tendencies than constant coercion and brute force from above. Perhaps it is necessary to ask *What do police fear?*

Fundamental Anxieties

Based on the wide-ranging examples that opened this chapter (pulp fiction, popular music, the actions and inactions of actual police), it would seem that police and fear are hopelessly entangled. This should come as no surprise given the theme of this book. Fear, particularly fear of the unknown—recalling the famous first lines of H. P. Lovecraft's essay "Supernatural Horror in Literature"—is the oldest and strongest emotion of mankind.[23] David Correia and Tyler Wall see "the fear of not knowing or the fear of the unknown" as driving the police as well. This is the "fundamental state anxiety" underlining a range of actions, they suggest, from knee-jerk shoot-first violence to the algorithms and massive data sets of predictive policing.[24]

For Thomas Ligotti, humans are perpetually haunted by what we do not know, or what we know and wish to not.[25] These two onto-logical positions are tied in an unsolvable knot by the ceaseless fear of death. As for knowing that we will die, he writes, "our ignorance is absolute, now and forever. We can only fear death without know-ing anything about what we fear. Some people can short-circuit their jitters about public speaking by exposing themselves to it re-peatedly. But no mortal can overcome the fear of death with prac-tice. You can only put it out of your mind for the nonce, pathetically non-victorious over your fear and still unwitting of the feared inevi-tability."[26] Backing up the pessimistic musings of horror writers is a raft of compelling empirical evidence that places the pathetic non-victory over fear of death at the center of human action. Following the cultural anthropologist Ernest Becker's influential *The Denial of Death*,[27] social psychologists working in "terror management theory" find the fear of death at the center of a range of socially noxious attitudes and actions. One well-known experimental study found that sentencing judges in criminal courts rendered more se-vere sentences when confronted with their own mortality. Similar studies generally find participants more apt to lash out at outsiders and cling to in-group dogma when faced with an existential threat.[28] Of course, one need only recall the rush to nationalistic war in the days, weeks, and months following September 11, 2001, to reckon the perspective's merit. It is perhaps a safe assumption that the tragic consequences of the hypervigilant shoot-first threat orientation nur-tured by police departments across the country are aggravated, if not driven, by the immovable fear of death.

Echoing some of the themes set out in chapter 2, Corey Robin notes that grand political thinkers from Thucydides, Aristotle, and Machiavelli to Michel de Montaigne and, of course, "the master theorist of fear," Thomas Hobbes, placed the fear of death at the cen-ter of their respective projects.[29] Again, contra Judith Shklar's belief that freedom from fear is the necessary precondition of liberal de-mocracy, Robin points to a vast collection of thinkers who name fear as a necessary catalyst of both politics and human agency. From the motivating uneasiness of John Locke's moral psychology to Edmund Burke's prodding, delightful horror, these patron saints of liberalism and conservatism see fear not as the opposite of freedom but as the necessary condition of modern subjectivity. Mark Neocleous also engages Burke, albeit more broadly, to diagnose and unpack the ways that he, like Hobbes with *Behemoth*, elaborated fear through the monstrous to name, describe, undermine, and attack the nascent proletariat during the French Revolution. Elaborating this position in his book *The Monstrous and the Dead*, Neocleous inverts the familiar Machiavellian arrangement of a tyrant who rules through fear and asks his readers to consider the tyrant not only as terrifying but also as *terrified*. If one reads *Mein Kampf* this way, he writes, "one notices something rather odd: Hitler is really quite scared . . . Germany and everything German is under attack . . . the nation, the fatherland, authority of the law, school, religion: 'there was absolutely nothing which was not drawn through the mud of a terrifying depth.'"[30] Just as the Nazi jurist Carl Schmitt provided insight into the ways that security, order, and police are imagined and justified by the state and population at large, following Neocleous, we can look to Adolf Hitler, a fearful and highly consequential tyrant, for insight into the actions and inactions of police. From this position, the violence of the petty sovereign is read not only as the instantiation of horror but also as a symptom of horror itself. When read through the barbarism of disorder and order set out in the previous chapters, we might conclude that for police, horror emerges from the shuddering recognition of their own vulnerabilities and likewise from the recognition of their own absolute enemy. Continuing on, we concern ourselves not only with the horror of police but with the actions and inactions of the *horrified* police as well.

Monsters Are Real

In October 2014, speaking to a group of ranking police officials at the annual conference of the International Association of Chiefs of Police, then FBI director James Comey ran down a list of challenges that he and the FBI were prepared, or preparing, to meet. Unsurprisingly, Comey's speech named the metastasizing "cancer" of terrorism, warning of those bent on violence able to "go dark" and evade police through technological means. But the theme of the speech and clearly the subject on Comey's mind was not the violence of but violence committed against police. Using "tour" tellingly to describe a cop's typical shift, Comey recounted the "last tour" and death of Pennsylvania state trooper Bryon Dickson. As if reading from the pages of one of McBain's novels, he described how a real-life cop hater armed with a sniper rifle "hunted" and "ambushed" Dickson and his fellow troopers, "shooting them from a hide for no reason." The killer, Eric Frein, whom local news media described as a "self-taught survivalist with a grudge against cops," had hoped the attack would spark some sort of revolution.[31] Generalizing Frein's attack to the whole of police work, Comey takes up the adjacent controversy surrounding "so-called warrior cops" and "the militarization of police" and calls forth the monster:

> First, I think it's very important to remind our fellow citizens that we all tell a lie to our children. I have five children, and all five of them have woken up during the night afraid of monsters, and I have lied to them and told them that monsters aren't real. "Go back to sleep, monsters aren't real." Monsters are real. Monsters are barricaded inside apartments, waiting for law enforcement to respond, so they can fire rounds that will pierce a ballistic vest. Monsters are real. Monsters are equipped with horrific equipment designed to harm innocent people—good men like Trooper Dickson in Pennsylvania. That is the reality we face in law enforcement.[32]

If monsters are, in fact, real, as Comey insists, then we must count police among them. Police, as we have seen, are masters of deception, hiding their own monstrosity behind threats external to themselves and the communities they represent. One of the ways police accomplish this is by elaborating their own personal concerns, fears, and vulnerabilities. Police memorials, parades, "humanizing the badge," "back the blue," and any number of similar copaganda efforts all seek to rally support around the police, trading in sentimental human-interest stories and staged videos of cops playing basketball or dancing with nonwhite children.

Despite evidence dampening claims of policing's inherent dangers, Comey seizes upon and stirs the fear of violent death. Without lapsing into questions of media effects, sympathy for police is ginned up by news media coverage when police do meet violent ends. In one such incident, following the killing of NYPD officers Rafael Ramos and Wenjian Liu in late 2014, the defiant slogan "Blue Lives Matter" solidified as a formal countermovement to the rising Black Lives Matter movement. Just five months after their deaths, President Obama signed the Rafael Ramos and Wenjian Liu National Blue Alert Act of 2015—to establish a nationwide communication network to share information about threats to police—surrounded by members of the slain officers' families. At a time when he had come under fire for limiting the Pentagon's 1033 "police militarization" program, the Blue Alert Act was an important symbolic gesture of support. Lost in the thanatopolitical spectacle surrounding Ramos and Liu was that the shooter, Ismaaiyl Brinsley, had murdered his former girlfriend, Shaneka Thompson, before traveling from Baltimore to Brooklyn, killing Ramos and Liu and then himself. Four lives lost, not two. Nevertheless, the act headlined a throng of similar state legislation aimed at safeguarding police, such as the "Blue Lives Matter" laws first passed in Louisiana and later in Kentucky and Mississippi, which broadened state hate crime provisions to include police. Legislators in Arizona went even further with their "Blue Lives" provision, covering all "peace officers" (cops and prison guards) whether on duty or off.

Three decades before the murders of Ramos and Liu, another dead New York cop was used to bolster a rising political order. As Justin Turner's astute reading of the 1988 murder of Edward Byrne details, violence against police provides a useful avenue for sloganeering and retaliatory violence. In his words, "socio-communal grief, memorialization, and the concrete policing practices which they underpin" fashion a thanatopolitical order rendering some people and communities enemy.[33] In the case of Byrne, a rookie cop murdered by members of a Queens drug gang, vitriolic calls from the NYPD as well as George H. W. Bush and Rudy Giuliani to "take back the streets" fit perfectly within a rising order-maintenance and broken-windows policing campaign that ramped up violence against poor people across the city under the banner of "quality of life."

As Black Lives Matter rose to national prominence, alongside it and the various iterations of "Blue Lives" emerged another counter-movement or narrative, heralding a violent insurrection, a so-called, "war on cops." One of the leading proponents of this narrative, for-mer Milwaukee County sheriff David Clarke, gained notoriety as a vocal and, notably, Black critic of Barack Obama. Days after Micah Johnson killed five Dallas cops, Clarke took to Fox News to link the attack to Black Lives Matter:

> Stand up to Black Lives Matter. Show you don't kowtow to the liberal pressure exacted to achieve their political goals on the backs of the suffering of black Americans due to crime and the dissolution of their communities. It is the hard road to sow in our culture where the right thing is shamed and the wrong thing is held up, but as a law enforcement officer I can tell you this is the time for choosing: law and order, justice, the American way or anarchy, division, hate, and authoritarian-ism. Black Lives Matter has shown their hand in Dallas: they choose the latter.[34]

Elevating the group to mythic standing, for Clarke, Black Lives Mat-ter is the harbinger of death, bringer of "anarchy, division, hate, and authoritarianism" and the end of the "American way," which, of course, is another way of saying the world-for-us. Yet even before Clarke and other conservative pundits began focusing on Black Lives Matter, the war on cops was part of a broader narrative advanced by prominent right-wing think tanks and activist groups, meant to posi-tion the police as targets and victims of "left-wing attacks." Continu-ing in the Red-baiting tradition of the John Birch Society, Manhat-tan Institute affiliate Heather MacDonald has pushed a stridently pro-cop agenda since the 1990s, writing two books and dozens of ar-ticles decrying liberal challenges to law and order. In the first pages of her aptly titled *The War on Cops: How the New Attack on Law and Order Makes Everyone Less Safe*, she chides:

> Fueling the rise in crime in places like Baltimore and Milwau-kee is a multipronged attack on law enforcement. Since late summer 2014, a protest movement known as Black Lives Mat-ter has convulsed the nation. Triggered by a series of highly

publicized deaths of black males at the hands of police, the Black Lives Matter movement holds that police officers are the greatest threat facing young black men today. That belief has spawned riots, "die-ins," and the assassination of police officers.[35]

MacDonald, like Clarke, sees Black Lives Matter not as a symptom of inequality but as the vanguard of a coming war and an attack on social order itself. For instance, when, in *The War on Cops*, MacDonald describes the killings of Ramos and Liu as "assassinations" and the first shots in an "attack on civilization," she helps to imagine and solidify the vocation of police as a unique identity, perhaps subject position, worthy of not only respect but sympathy.[36]

In their essay on the Brinsley case, Nijah Cunningham and Tiana Reid describe "Blue Lives Matter" as a reactionary incantation uttered by those across the political spectrum, helping to raise the fearful apparition of "blue life" in order to counter challenges to police authority. Once Brinsley's identity dissolved into the monstrous category of *cop killer*, they argue, he and, by extension, Black Lives Matter became representative of the broader and incalculable threat of Black political solidarity. Positioned against the Black Lives Matter movement, the reactionary claim "Blue Lives Matter" performs a double move, conjuring a faceless enemy from a crowd of supposed "cop haters" while simultaneously disowning and rendering invisible the violence and terror that police bring into being. As a moral claim and performance of vulnerability, the reactionary slogan translates nearly any action into an attack on a fictional blue life, transforming protest into violence, collectivity and solidarity into riots, and self-defense into resisting arrest.[37]

Before Black Lives Matter gave a new monstrous face to Black political solidarity, other monsters had shuddered and provoked the police into new violent forms. As Comey reveals in his next stanza:

Second: Because of that reality—because monsters are real, and too often equipped with firepower to outgun those of us in law enforcement—we need a range of weapons and equipment to respond and protect our fellow citizens and protect ourselves. We need to respond appropriately at the drunk-driver scene, at the car-stop scene, at the mass-casualty event, and we need to be able to respond to killers with assault weapons and body armor. That equipment is never meant for offense. It is meant to give our officers the best possible chance to survive; it is meant to help us bring bad people to justice, and protect good people.[38]

Beyond the more practical implications of his fear of being out-gunned, we must read Comey's "real monsters" through the Schmitt-ian politics of enmity, an ontological position also staked out in his memoir, *A Higher Loyalty*. Viewing police and prosecutors as sover-eign in a world absent any absolute moral authority, Comey justifies his decision to aggressively prosecute television personality Martha Stewart for insider trading, Comey writes:

> There was once a time when most people worried about going to hell if they violated an oath taken in the name of God. That divine deterrence has slipped away from our modern cultures. In its place, people must fear going to jail. They must fear their lives being turned upside down. They must fear their pictures splashed on newspapers and websites. People must fear hav-ing their name forever associated with a criminal act if we are to have a nation with the rule of law. Martha Stewart lied, blatantly, in the justice system. To protect the institution of justice, and reinforce a culture of truth-telling, she had to be prosecuted. I am very confident that, should the circumstances arise, Martha Stewart would not lie to federal investigators again.[39]

For Comey, fear is clearly key to good order. The prosecution of Stewart, or any prosecution for that matter, performs a political theological ritual of deterrence—"a sacrifice to an absent God," as Patrick Blanchfield put it.[40] Part of his job as a spokesperson for police, apparently, is to invoke the monster and instill fear. But re-calling Neocleous and the complementary findings of terror man-agement theory, we must not overlook or understate how the au-thoritarian tyrant's own fear drives him to act. In the case of Comey, one of the nation's top cops, his fearful and retributive political the-ology underlies and maps onto a virulent politics of reaction that has long animated police.

It is widely agreed that what we know today as SWAT units grew in direct response to the so-called civil unrest of the 1960s, forming first in Delano, California, to suppress the United Farm Workers. Fears of being "outmatched" and "outgunned" during the Watts rebellion allowed Daryl Gates to argue for the mobilization of a "Special Weapons Attack Team."[41] While SWAT-type units have existed in larger departments for decades—for instance, the NYPD's Emergency Service Unit, or "Machine Gun Squad," began in the 1920s—because of several high-profile deployments, it is Gates who is usually credited with their advent. In 1969, SWAT faced off with its monstrous adversary in a highly publicized shoot-out between the LAPD and members of the Black Panther Party. Recalling the incident, Gates reminisced, "It was the first time we got to show off."[42] Five years later, he and the LAPD would again "show off" on live national television, this time trading thousands of rounds with members of the Symbionese Liberation Army. Following the lead of his mentor William Parker, Gates capitalized on the public's apparent fascination with shoot-outs between squads of supercops and gangs of criminals and revolutionaries, authorizing and assisting in the production of the aptly named *S.W.A.T.* television series that debuted a year after the battle with the SLA. All of this is not to point to some definitive starting point of a particular form of policing, or to endorse Comey's idea that "monsters" must be met accordingly. Indeed, for police, fears of being outgunned precede Gates and certainly Comey. So while it is clear the fabrication of a monstrous enemy has long been necessary to scale up policing's capacities for violence, we must not endorse a particular turning point, or even attempt to map a teleology of militarization, because to do so would be to disown policing's settler-colonial origins.

While the Panthers and the SLA were politically fearsome adversaries to align against, police and their supporters continue to point to a late-1990s bank robbery as evidence that monsters are, in fact, real. On February 28, 1997, just after 9 a.m., Larry Phillips Jr. and Emil Mătăsăreanu entered a Bank of America branch in North Hollywood intent on robbery. By chance, two passing LAPD patrol officers spotted the two as they entered, sounded the alarm, and lay in wait for the pair to reemerge. No doubt influenced by the famous shoot-out scene in the film *Heat*, Phillips and Mătăsăreanu, who each carried automatic weapons and thousands of rounds of ammunition and wore sophisticated body armor, came out of the bank guns blazing. From the *Los Angeles Times'* initial coverage:

> In warlike pursuit captured on live TV, dozens of police officers tracked down and killed two heavily armed bank robbers in North Hollywood on Friday in the face of blistering automatic-weapons fire. Ten officers were wounded, including six in a spectacular eruption of firepower that draped a shroud of fear over a vast residential area of the eastern San Fernando Valley. Three civilians were also hit by gunfire in a confrontation that recalled the apocalyptic 1974 gun battle between police and the Symbionese Liberation Army, the Maoist kidnappers of heiress Patty Hearst, in South-Central Los Angeles.[43]

On the *Times* front page, a headline describing one of the robbers as a "Huge Monster in Black" and another more succinctly advertising "Guns, Hostages and Terror" narrated the "warlike," "apocalyptic" event that, despite thousands of rounds expended and several serious injuries, miraculously left only Phillips and Mătăsăreanu dead.[44] In many ways, the shoot-out was a win for the LAPD, as the live coverage showed their hopelessly overmatched ranks standing courageously under fire. As the *Times* noted, from Rodney King to "surrendering the intersection of Florence and Normandie to a violent mob during the 1992 riots, the often-unforgiving eye of the video camera, on this day, showed the LAPD to be courageous, swift and decisive."[45] Providing, in real time, terrifying evidence of policing's monstrous adversaries and, by extension, adversaries of all law-abiding subjects of liberal social order and "the enemies of all mankind," in Neocleous's words, years later, the North Hollywood shoot-out is still invoked by police from California to Kansas as reason enough to be armed to the teeth.[46]

Rejecting the simple argument that police must be equipped for any contingency—militarized—such as that offered by Comey, the politics of security that give form to the police power shine through. For everyday people awash in modernity's ambient fear, Phillips and Mătăsăreanu, like the Panthers and the SLA, Frein and Brinsley, demonstrate in spectacular fashion that monsters are, in fact, "real" and thereby rationalize and perpetually authorize the waiting violence of the police in its multitudes. Lost, of course, in the tidy dialectic between the monster and police are questions of history and political economy, of racial division and terror, that must be considered if we are to take seriously the complaints of the Panthers and the SLA and even the more transparent motivations of young men who choose to rob banks. As we have seen, police give short shrift to questions of causality and history, choosing instead to live in the moment, reacting quickly to "meet violence with violence." Just as they successfully argued the necessity of SWAT to deal with civil rights activists, armed cops on patrol with "long rifles" after North Hollywood, and more recently pushed for and obtained hate crime protections, police are animated and armored by their adversaries, real or imagined. So while we might easily connect the reactionary patterns of police to fear, this doesn't quite satisfy the question "*What* do they fear?" Toward an answer to this stubborn question we must again closely scrutinize the police at work.

Fear the Walking Dead

On August 19, 2014, ten days after Darren Wilson killed Michael Brown, a St. Louis cop shot and killed another young Black man named Kajieme Powell. Like Brown, Powell was initially confronted for allegedly shoplifting from a local market. Twenty-three seconds later, police shot and killed the twenty-five-year-old, mentally ill Powell for "furtive movements" or allegedly advancing toward them with a knife. Though footage of the shooting is not clear on this point, it does usefully document an interesting, if not odd, police practice: *handcuffing the dead.* As the man who recorded Powell's death describes the moments just after he fell, lifeless, to the ground:

> They just killed this man, he's dead. They're putting him in cuffs, he's dead. Oh my god, they just killed this man, he didn't have a gun on him, now they're cuffing him. He's already dead. He's already dead. They're cuffing him, they're cuffing, I've got everything on camera.[47]

For onlookers at the scene, as well as casual observers of U.S. police, handcuffing the dead might seem like overkill laid atop overkill. More critically, however, that police are taught to treat even a corpse as a threat to be secured is emblematic of how fear animates the police power. Of Powell's death and police killings in general, journalist Ezra Klein contritely wrote, "It is easy to criticize . . . It is easy to forget that police get scared. It is easy not to ask yourself what you might have done if you had a gun and a man came at you with a knife."[48] On this point I agree with Klein—of course it is easy to criticize after the fact—but criticism is necessary if any sort of dysfunctional system like police is to improve. I also wholly agree that police get scared—as we have seen, police are, indeed, taught to embrace and harness fear. Not only is fear essential to their day-to-day practices, but fear of crime, fear of others, fear of the unknown scaffold policing's entire reason for being.

University of Missouri–St. Louis criminology professor David Klinger, a former LAPD cop who in recent years has been a frequent contributor to national news media coverage of police violence, given his proximity to Ferguson, rationalized in an essay for *Police Chief* magazine (published by IACP) the practice of handcuffing "downed suspects." He writes:

> Handcuff all downed suspects. Some officers might feel that it is not nice to handcuff suspects that have been shot, and others might believe that it is unnecessary to cuff all suspects because some are "obviously" dead. Counted among the suspects shot during incidents that officers reported during the VALOR interviews were some who appeared to be dead—for example, from multiple rifle rounds to the head—but who were still alive. As noted in the introduction, some human beings have a remarkable capacity to survive gunshot wounds. Fortunately, none of the thoughtdead offenders managed to injure any officers interviewed, but the fact that they were still alive meant that they maintained the capacity to do so. The capacity of downed suspects is hindered substantially when they are cuffed. No matter how severely injured they might be, therefore, all downed suspects should be handcuffed.[49]

In sanitized copspeak, Klinger's simple and seemingly rational argument is this: all "suspects," even those "downed" by police bullets, are a threat until carted off in body bags. Klinger—also author of *Into the Kill Zone: A Cop's Eye View of Deadly Force*, a case study of police killing, including his own quasi-ethnographic account of killing a "criminal named Edward Randolph"—has spent his career asking, "What goes through police officers' minds when they are involved in shootings? How does facing deadly force affect what they see, hear, and feel?"[50] Such questions, as Correia and Wall suggest, invariably rationalize and justify police violence, performing a linguistic sleight of hand, transforming killing another human being into "deadly force."[51] While Klinger's essay and his broader body of work remain faithful to the usual bloodless "better safe than sorry" precautionary principle that structures much of police practice, it is hard to read his advice without also imagining a scene from *The Walking Dead* or any other horror film where a "thoughtdead" corpse imperils the living. Just as with those who fight the avaricious "biters" of zombie fantasy, police are taught to never let down their guard, to fire until the threat is stopped, to "handcuff downed suspects" and *fear the dead as they do the living.*

The zombie has, in the years since the 2009 crash, become *"the monster of our time."*[52] Transposed onto a swelling lumpen mass, the zombie has transcended pop cultural cliché, becoming the literal description for the ways many cops view those in their charge. One project that compiled a searchable database of questionable social media posts of U.S. police documents several instances where cops discursively zombify the public. For instance, one video of a man acting erratically, captioned "When it's time to get tased" with the hashtags #brainondrugs and #zombie, was shared by an Arlington, Texas, cop.[53] Venting about the week he'd had, another cop posted an image of a man kneeling in prayer and the text "Dear Lord, please let there be a zombie apocalypse so I can start shooting all these motherfuckers in the face."[54]

In the most widely covered case of a 2012 spate of so-called "zombie crimes," a Black man named Rudy Eugene, later dubbed the "Miami Zombie" by the thoughtless news media, moved from man to monster after his brutal attack on a homeless man named Ronald

Poppo. In March of that year, Eugene, for reasons still unknown, attacked Poppo, "plucking out" the man's eyes and biting away large chunks of his face, before being shot dead by police.[55] Following established practices, police and media attributed the attack to drugs and a nascent family of synthetic stimulants known colloquially as "bath salts." On nothing more than a hunch, a Miami Police spokesperson riled an anxious public with claims that the drug turned "normal people into monsters" with "superhuman strength and no ability to feel pain."[56] (Autopsy later disproved the bath salts link.) Stretching back more than a century, this sort of drug-driven zombification is a tried-and-true technique police and their supporters use to license all manner of cruelty and violence. More than one hundred years ago, a *New York Times* article authored by a well-known physician warned of Black people transformed into menacing "fiends," granted "superhuman strength" by cocaine. Reproducing an account from North Carolina in which a deputy's standard revolver was not powerful enough to "put down" an enraged "negro cocaine fiend," the fear of being bested by former slaves licensed larger-caliber firearms and a higher degree of violence for police across the South.[57] In 1980, police and their stenographers in the news media warned, without irony, of a rash of supposed "zombie murders" brought on by the drug PCP.[58] And, of course, the late '80s and early '90s were marred by "inhuman" or "superhuman" violence attributed first to crack cocaine and later to methamphetamines. In each of these instances and others, fear of zombified drug users effectively excused and, in some instances, scaled up policing's capacities for violence.[59]

In the case of the so-called Miami Zombie, however violent the attack, it is important to note that Eugene was not only unarmed but naked when police killed him in a flurry of gunfire, apparently so panicked that they also shot his victim twice. Following the attack, there were no protests or demonstrations, no hearings, no discussion of use-of-force policies or "less than lethal" technologies, and virtually no reflection on the fact that police had killed a naked, unarmed man. In this instance, Eugene powerfully characterizes the phrase "naked before the state," embodying a grim, zombified rendering of Giorgio Agamben's *bare life*.[60] Following these and countless other examples, zombies are not just a tongue-in-cheek referent for mindless consumerism but also diagnose the oft-hidden violence of police and social order. Zombification, accordingly, must be understood as part of an active process, the "production of non-production," in Josh Clover's words, most visible along race and gender lines.[61]

Noted zombiephile Max Brooks—whose three wildly popular books on the subject he parlayed into a fellowship at West Point's Modern War Institute—now prepares the next generation of "war fighters" for the crises of the future. Brooks finds zombies the perfect sigil for the end times, signifying as they do "broad social collapse, when anyone—a policeman, a nurse, a friend—can turn into a force of evil."[62] Like Brooks, the U.S. Department of Defense and Centers for Disease Control, private security contractors, local militia groups, and police firearms instructors all use the zombie as a stand-in for a monstrous universal adversary.[63] This should give us pause. Not only is this dehumanizing trope widely recognized and used by official agencies, but it diagnoses a form of sociality in which human life is increasingly defined as excessive, surplus, and therefore *cheap*.[64]

In *Universal Adversary*, Neocleous suggests that what underlies and explains the zombies' resilience as a popular culture referent is the fear of contagion, of social bodies "touching" and linking together, the spreading of ideas and ideology.[65] A persistent fear of contagion, he suggests, spans and links the early-modern fears of rising masses of "masterless men and women," "the swinish multitude of the eighteenth and nineteenth centuries," to "the zombie multitudes" of the present.[66] Rather than simply a killable monster, the surplus, cheap life of the zombie proves more analytically fruitful as stand-in for the outbreak and insurrection, of disorderly, unruly political collectivity. To fear zombies' contagion is to fear the crowd, mob, and riot.

We know well the conditions. Housing, health care, and food costs climb as wages stagnate. In 2017, the combined annual salary of the richest 0.1 percent of the U.S. population was nearly two hundred times that of the poorest 90 percent. Average CEO pay that year was more than 350 times that of the average worker. Three white men—Warren Buffett, Jeff Bezos, and Bill Gates—held more personal wealth than nearly three-quarters of the United States combined.[67] Elsewhere in the world, it is much worse. Oligarchs, financiers, and multinational corporations drive a savage economic order that, when combined with global climate change, looks more like the two worlds of *Elysium*: paradise for some, hell on earth for the rest. In the now decade-long slow climb away from the economic crash—marked by war, famine, mass displacement, retrenchment politics, resurgent fascism, and ethno-nationalism—police are increasingly called upon to stand between the keepers of the old order and the pitchforks, or, in Dennis Büscher-Ulbrich's explicitly Marxist phrasing, the "growing global surplus proletariat of dispossessed, immiserated, and commonly racialized (non-)workers 'no longer directly necessary for the self-valorization of capital.'"[68] Spit out by the political and economic order, the churn of accumulation and the production of nonproduction, angry people are gathering together and getting angrier.[69]

Formed in their opposition, police have long feared the revolutionary potentials and sheer power of the crowd.[70] In 1971, sociologist Rodney Stark published *Police Riots*, a study undertaken amid protests and riots when, as he puts it, "police were often at their worst."[71] As a student of police researcher Jerome Skolnick at the UC Berkeley Center for the Study of Law and Society, Stark had worked on the National Commission on the Causes and Prevention of Violence, empowered by the Johnson administration after the assassinations of Martin Luther King and Robert Kennedy. Despite what he documents in the book, Stark unequivocally states his is not "anti-police" work and those who adopt such "vulgar nonsense" oppose society itself. Nevertheless, he finds that much of the police violence he documented resulted from mismanagement, hypervigilance, knee-jerk reaction, and, ultimately, fear. Asking his readers to "consider how little we have now come to expect of the police and how greatly we have come to share their obsession with their own safety,"[72] he writes:

> Unfortunately, the police typically place their safety first and in recent years we have come to accept this priority. Thus, policemen in Berkeley fired shotguns into crowds of students because they felt imperiled by scattered rock and bottle throwing despite the fact that the police were wearing bullet-proof "flak" jackets, hard helmets, and face masks. Thus Guardsmen at Kent State shot down students with rifle fire in the face of puny and petty threats to their safety. Thus, highway patrolmen at

Jackson State riddled a dormitory because of the threat to their safety inherent in taunts and curses. Thus, police commando squads bust into Black Panther headquarters in the dark of night to serve insignificant warrants. And so it goes.[73]

And so it goes, indeed. Decades and countless clashes between police and protestors have passed since Stark's time, with little change. From Occupy demonstrators pepper sprayed by UC Davis cops to the spectacle of battle-clad cops descending on unarmed people at Ferguson, Baltimore, Standing Rock, and elsewhere, police continue to strike first and meet the dissent of the crowd with violence. As Richard Gilman-Opalsky writes, from antebellum slave revolts to the "race riots of the twentieth century, from Springfield, Illinois, in 1908 to Watts, Los Angeles, in 1965, to current insurrections in Ferguson 2014 and Baltimore 2015 . . . there is always some part of the event that expresses disaffections carried over from the previous ones."[74] Uprisings of recent years should not be viewed as isolated incidents but, instead, part of an ongoing struggle against police violence and terror.

Police have always stood in diametric opposition to the crowd. With the collapse of feudalism in Europe, police power rose in tandem with and mutually constitutive of a proto–working class, producing and corralling it at once.[75] In the United States, fear of revolutionary collectivity marks the birth of the institution itself. First formed in the early 1700s, the slave patrol, progenitor of U.S. police, emerged not only to catch escaped slaves but also to seek out and extinguish the embers of rebellion.[76] The Paris Commune, which characterized proto-Nazi Gustave Le Bon's "era of crowds," likewise posed a direct challenge to the nascent bourgeois order and necessitated a police of crowds in return.[77] Around the turn of the twentieth century, antilabor, anticommunist police units, or Red Squads, as they were then called, sprang up in industrial centers across the United States, backed by moneyed interests.[78] Clashes such as those with labor organizers at Haymarket Square helped to solidify the power of the Chicago Police Department,[79] while the brutality of the private Coal and Iron Police led to the establishment of the first "state police" in Pennsylvania under the banner of reform.[80] Driven by fears of a so-called "black messiah," J. Edgar Hoover's FBI formed

COINTELPRO (the Counter Intelligence Program) in the earliest years of the Cold War to "'disrupt' groups and 'neutralize' individuals deemed to be threats to domestic security."[81] COINTELPRO proved incredibly effective, using disinformation to sow discord within the Panthers and adjacent revolutionary groups like the Student Nonviolent Coordinating Committee, Socialist Workers Party, Students for a Democratic Society, and women's liberation movement.[82] While the FBI is alleged to have also sought to disrupt right-wing groups like the KKK, leftist groups were the clear targets of COINTELPRO, with the Panthers, as Kristian Williams puts it, "being the most targeted organization of the late 1960s and perhaps the most targeted organization of all American history."[83] Bringing counterinsurgency war to the Panthers, COINTELPRO, in cooperation with the Chicago Police Department, culminated in the 1969 assassination of chapter leader Fred Hampton.[84] The seemingly extreme measures taken against the Panthers, as James Baldwin wrote in 1972, were in fact anything but:

> Nothing more thoroughly reveals the actual intentions of this country, domestically and globally, than the ferocity of the repression, the storm of fire and blood which the Panthers have been forced to undergo merely for declaring themselves as men—men who want "land, bread, housing, education, clothing, justice, and peace." The Panthers thus became the native Vietcong, the ghetto became the village in which the Vietcong were hidden, and in the ensuing search-and-destroy operations, everyone in the village became suspect.[85]

Though congressional hearings supposedly brought COINTELPRO to an end in 1971, Baldwin's "storm of fire and blood" continues under other names.[86] In the years since 9/11, the FBI and major police agencies have worked together to track, infiltrate, and subvert suspect communities.[87] Creating what it called "mosque crawlers," the NYPD Critical Response Command infiltrated more than one hundred mosques, tracked every Pakistani taxi driver in the city, and even sent undercover officers on a whitewater-rafting trip with Muslim students from the City College of New York.[88]

A leaked FBI report also seems to confirm Hoover's continued legacy. Authored by its Counterterrorism Division in late 2017, the report "Black Identity Extremists Likely Motivated to Target Law Enforcement Officers" describes an illusory "extremist" movement characterized by a few highly publicized, though wholly unrelated, attacks on police. From the report: "The FBI assesses it is very likely Black Identity Extremist (BIE) perceptions of police brutality against African Americans spurred an increase in premeditated, retaliatory lethal violence against law enforcement and will very likely serve as justification for such violence."[89] In a year when police killed 1,147 people—more than half of them people of color—the FBI not only troublingly conjured BIE from thin air but did so while dismissing "police brutality" as a mere "perception." While it only mentions "Moorish sovereign citizens" by name, the report makes clear that the FBI views any form of Black political collectivity a threat. In a *New York Times* interview one former FBI agent admitted as much, suggesting the BIE designation resulted from fear, adding plainly, "Basically, it's black people who scare them."[90]

The fear of Black political collectivity bubbles to the surface of the zombie's rotting flesh, beginning with George Romero's *Night of the Living Dead*, which initiated the postwar zombie genre and offered unvarnished criticism of American racism and Cold War xenophobia. Placed within the context of the postcrash, post-Ferguson era, the racist fears of Black political collectivity exemplified by the FBI's warning about "Black Identity Extremists" transforms the shambling herds of mindless zombies into a *zombie riot*,[91] a threatening mob of insurgent, but nevertheless surplus, *cheap life*. Not just an overwhelming force of pure numbers, the zombie riot also portends contagion, a mutating form of political solidarity and a challenge to the police notion of what it means to be a proper liberal and, hence, a *living* political subject. Here, the police face a truly terrifying enemy: a motivated collectivity—already rendered surplus, hence dead, by the social and political order—with nothing to lose. We can, as such, place the necropolitical horde of the zombie riot alongside the "creative anthropomorphism" of Jack Halberstam's bees, Michael Hardt and Antonio Negri's multitudinous swarm, Peter Linebaugh and Marcus Rediker's Many-Headed Hydra, and any number of other beasts, living or dead, that challenge the supremacy of the state and its police with the multiplicity of the mob.[92]

Portents of the zombie riot are precisely what Johanna Isaacson finds in Romero's follow-up, *Dawn of the Dead* (1978).[93] While the standard critique of *Dawn* is that its women—like those in so many other mainstream action/horror films[94]—are one-dimensional receptacles for sex and violence and that its critical potentials inevitably dissolve into a predictable critique of consumerism,[95] Isaacson instead reads the film's obligatory swarming riot of excess, cheap life as explicitly revolutionary. In her inverted reading, the zombie riot, in all of its fractured chaos, moves as a feminized, irrational, oversized human body laying waste to the "orderly, rationalized, masculinized, sublimated symbolic order" of the shopping mall. It is our perpetual temptation, she argues, to place our hopes for social progress in heroic individuals, but it's only when aligned against the hubristic, clownish male action figures of *Dawn* (many of which are SWAT cops, I might add) that we realize that it's not the charismatic individual but solidarity and "collective action that will star in our hoped-for future."[96] To put it plainly, if they stand in for racialized, exploited labor, as so many cultural analyses insist, shouldn't we be on the side of the zombies? After all, against the cast-off excess mass of the zombie riot stand the police, in Josh Clover's words, "the violence of the commodity made [*living*] flesh."[97]

There are a number of texts that offer a glimpse of the zombie riot from the fearful and imperiled position of police. In *The Walking Dead*, as we have discussed, an ex-cop leads a band of survivors from one siege to another, season after undead season. Also recall how prominently the imaginary of the siege (wall and garrison) featured in *Game of Thrones* and how it was picked up by nativist reactionaries and the official labor union of the U.S. Border Patrol. In the film adaptation of Brooks's *World War Z*, its hero, a UN security specialist, travels to Jerusalem in hopes of locating patient zero and halting the outbreak. While Jerusalem, the most militarized and policed city on the planet, is initially secure, as survivors begin to sing together in a gesture of solidarity, the gathering horde outside the walls is enraged and quickly overruns the city.

The Settler and the Siege

While the siege is a defining characteristic of zombie horror, or "riot horror," as Isaacson calls it, two films, John Carpenter's *Assault on*

Precinct 13 (1976) and Daniel Petrie's *Fort Apache, the Bronx* (1981), play out policing's fearful stand against enraged subproletarian hordes with uncanny prescience. Set in late-'70s Los Angeles, *Assault* features a clumsy rendering of the threat posed by armed revolutionaries like the Panthers and SLA, while *Fort Apache* transposes the settler-colonial western onto a more general representation of urban blight and racialized "street crime." The former film, as Jeff Chang argues in *Can't Stop, Won't Stop,* "ushered in a new genre—the urban horror flick." Rather than "Indian braves, Zulu warriors or graveyard zombies, *Assault on Precinct 13*'s heroes defended themselves in a desolate police station against marauding waves of dark, heavily armed gang members seeking revenge for their cop-killed brothers."[98] Contra Chang, however, Carpenter himself admitted that he sought to zombify the gang members as much as possible, taking inspiration for their single-minded siege on the police station directly from Romero's zombie opus.[99] Describing the film as part *Night of the Living Dead* and part *Rio Bravo,* Carpenter also made direct overtures to his hero Howard Hawks. Mirroring *Rio Bravo*'s clean us-versus-them arrangement, after the LAPD kills several members of "Street Thunder," the gang swears a revenge pact and relentlessly attacks a deserted South-Central police station defended by a motley collection of police, prisoners, and secretaries. The film pits the police against the monstrous bringers of revolutionary terror, conspicuously armed with military-grade assault weapons and led by two men who look a whole lot like Huey P. Newton and Che Guevara. While in his own defense, Carpenter pointed to the "multiracial" composition of his imagined gang, it is hard to dismiss the resemblance as mere coincidence, particularly when considering some of Carpenter's other villains.[100] In *Escape from New York* (1981), Isaac Hayes's "the Duke" is a lampooned Blaxploitation drug dealer and pimp. Even more on the nose, in the sequel, *Escape from LA* (1996), the antagonist is again a beret-sporting Che-lookalike revolutionary named "Cuervo Jones." Against charges of conservatism, Carpenter insisted that *Assault* was simply a tale of "good guys versus the bad guys" and any semblance of a political or social statement was nothing but an unconscious expression.[101] As if "good guys versus the bad guys" is ever empty of political expression.

The fear of political collectivity and swarms of excess cheap life evident in *Assault on Precinct 13* is not merely a matter of cinematic representation, however. In an interview a few weeks after the '92 LA uprising, Mike Davis referred to leaked LAPD intelligence reports that blamed a united Bloods and Crips under "the direction and leadership of Muslims" for the "riots" and warned of planned assaults on police stations and "ambushes of individual cops on their way home from work." Foreshadowing the language of the universal adversary, Davis suggested the reports revealed an "all-embracing conspiracy scenario that links gangs, urban unrest, Farrakhan, and perhaps even certain Colombians and Iraqis."[102] Making obvious connections to COINTELPRO disinformation campaigns, he further suggested the anonymously sourced bulletins were likely the work of agents provocateurs, intended to incite an already fearful police force to violence with warnings of being ambushed, assassinated, and overrun. "This is right off that movie *Assault on Precinct 13*," Davis quipped, and "it's just fantasy."[103]

Again, paraphrasing Marx, we might say that for police, the fear of the zombie riot is the fear of having produced one's own gravediggers.[104] Weighing in on the '92 LA riots, Ice-T said similarly, calling it a consequence issued by the city's overpoliced residents:

> The people cannot issue a consequence against the government. When they do wrong, what do we do? How many people have filed civil suits against the police and won? So what L.A. did was say, "You all been bad, check this out," and we issued a consequence. In New York just the other night they shot somebody, people issued a consequence . . . And every time when the LAPD whup on somebody now, they take their chance on starring another riot. Maybe it'll make them think. I totally predict that if we don't listen, people are going to move to bloodshed.[105]

Fears of Black Identity Extremism, "antipolice activism," and the so-called "war on cops" do, perhaps, reflect a deep recognition that police have sown the seeds of their undoing. Even as I write in late 2019—and no doubt as you read, whenever that is—police continue to fear and plan for revolt. In early June 2019, residents of Memphis, Tennessee, threw rocks and bottles at police and damaged patrol cars after U.S. Marshals shot and killed a twenty-year-old man named Brandon Webber. Wanted by police for several violent crimes,

Webber posted a video on social media in which he purportedly made threats against police. True to his word, he did not go willingly and was later shot and killed by police attempting to arrest him. In the ensuing days of unrest, Memphis police issued an "officer safety bulletin" citing "credible intelligence" that the Gangster Disciples planned to kill cops in retaliation.[106]

The police know all too well that every city holds within it the specter of revolt, waiting as a vengeful wraith to return yet again.[107] Arguably, no city bears out this assertion more fully and in more stunning detail than New York City. "It is almost as if social peace is the exception," writes Don Mitchell, "a small island of calm in an always churning sea."[108] As suggested by the heroic tagline "No Cowboys, No Indians, No Cavalry to the Rescue, Only a Cop," *Fort Apache, the Bronx* places the police on this small island amid the ever-churning sea of racialized crime and violence. Indeed, as Stefano Harney and Fred Moten write in their book, *The Undercommons: Fugitive Planning and Black Study*, we would do well to recognize the whole world from the "upside-down" vantage of the colonizer, surrounded as he often is by relentless swarms of uncivilized natives.[109] *The Bronx* advances the upside-down settler-colonial fantasy of its 1948 forbearer, *Fort Apache*, which was inspired by Custer's "last stand," and fuses it with the conservative tough-on-crime trope initiated by the Dirty Harry films and the heroic tales of two veteran NYPD cops "walking a beat in a war zone."

Set in the Forty-First Precinct—home of "Street Warrior" Ralph Friedman—*Fort Apache, the Bronx* can, of course, be read as another chapter in the big book of the thin blue line, depicting an unruly world brought to heel by heroic cops. This was a point not lost on many of the South Bronx residents who protested the film's anti–Puerto Rican and anti-Black sentiments. As one resident complained, "Fort Apache was a racist name, it evokes images of savage people, uncontrollable people, people society gives up on."[110] *The Bronx* is indefensible on these grounds, depicting, as did its predecessor, invading hordes of nonwhite "savages" held at bay by the sharp shooting of a few courageous white men. Repugnant as it is, however, such a narrative would find little dramatic purchase if it did not tap into and replay some elements of policing's fearful settler-colonial imaginary. The "make-believe national narrative" in which

Gathering to commemorate "walking the beat in a war zone," NYPD cops display their "Fort Apache Reunion" banner, depicting the station house besieged by Native attackers.

the aggressor takes the role of victim began, as Nick Estes writes, when settlers first invaded Indigenous lands and persists as a heroic and fearful reminder of the settler's precarious claims to land and belonging.[111] The upside-down or reversed narrative of the besieged rather than invading settler is not confined to the imaginary terrain of the United States. As Didier Fassin's *Enforcing Order* likewise documents, the view of the racialized poor as "savages" who inhabit a "jungle," widely held by French police, justifies, in Paris as it does in New York, an endless war for civilization, hiding the settler-colonial project of conquest, occupation, and defense of "threatened territories," in policing's language of law and order.[112] Always placing themselves on the right side of the gun and of history, real-life cops of the "4-1" still perform this ideological work, gathering with some frequency to trade stories of their time defending "Fort Apache."[113]

Perhaps because it remains a point of embarrassment, seldom discussed is the NYPD station house actually overrun by angry New Yorkers in late December 1978. Three years before the release of *Fort Apache, the Bronx*, Brooklynites fed up with the actions and inactions of the NYPD marshaled the power of revolt and swarmed the

Sixty-Sixth Precinct, pushed aside attending officers, and trashed the building's interior, tossing files and equipment from windows onto the street. Headlines reported, "Killing Leads to NYC Melee"; "3,000 Hasidic Jews Wreck Cop Station"; "Irate Jews Storm NY Cops; 70 Hurt." On this day, the NYPD witnessed first-hand its tenuous grip on social order. Enraged by the murder of a sixty-five-year-old plumber named Irving Sussman—who had been stabbed to death in a botched robbery and left on the street for nearly an hour before police arrived—hundreds, perhaps thousands, of Brooklyn's Hasidic community converged on the Crown Heights precinct. As reported by *Times* columnist Robert McFadden:

> Hundreds of angry Hasidic Jews, outraged over the fatal stabbing of an elderly Jewish man in a predawn street robbery and demanding greater police protection, besieged and briefly took over a police station house in Brooklyn yesterday. They were ejected in a bloody, 30[-]minute melee of screams, punches, swinging clubs and hurtling rocks. The violence—one of the worst clashes of civilians and police officers in New York since the riots of the 1960's—erupted shortly before noon at the 66th Precinct station, at 5822 16th Avenue in Borough Park. The clash left at least 70 people injured, 62 of them police officers and the rest civilians. About 100 police reinforcements and [a] dozen ambulances and other emergency vehicles rushed to the scene, where as many as 2,000 protesters clad in black coats, fedoras and fur caps milled around outside, with 150 to 200 more inside the station.[114]

Another local columnist reminded that the "Hasid's riot" was not unprecedented, citing at least two previous protests following violent crime. Indeed, Sussman himself had complained about his "deteriorating" neighborhood in a series of letters to his congregation in which he urged them to petition Mayor Ed Koch and "demand more police."[115] It was around this time that the community instituted its own armed street patrols, which continue today.[116] Given the NYPD's long-standing unwillingness to bend to the public's demands, it is quite instructive that the lopsided skirmish, which sent more than sixty cops to the hospital, did not produce a single arrest.

An NYPD challenge coin commemorates the 1978 sacking of the Sixty-Sixth Precinct, otherwise known as Fort Surrender. From "NYPD Challenge Coins: Members Only."

Henceforth known among the NYPD as "Fort Surrender," the Sixty-Sixth Precinct holds the illustrious distinction of being the only station house in the city overtaken by a crowd since the Civil War.[117]

The Specter of Revolt

Recall that under the counterinsurgency (COIN) model, police aim to produce order by means that include, but are not limited to, outright violence. This is the ideological "war by other means" championed by U.S. military leaders and waged by U.S. police for decades. Emerging in its modern form from colonization efforts in "French Indochina" and, later, the Vietnam War, counterinsurgency theory conceives of a subject population in terms of three parts: a small group of hostile insurgents, a small group of allies opposed to the insurgency, and a large majority with no particular allegiance. As Bernard Harcourt writes in *The Counterrevolution*, "the principal objective of counterinsurgency is to gain the allegiance of that passive majority."[118] This, of course, is not done only to win a war but to assume control of a population and territory so that its productive capacities remain intact. Always underlying the colonial and anti-revolutionary aims of COIN, then, are the ends of pacification—the formation of obedient subjects committed to, or at least not disruptive of, the reproduction of capitalist social relations. While U.S. police departments have long adhered to elements of COIN, they have done so under the guise of community policing, which, unsurprisingly, emerged as a buzzword and official doctrine from the tumult of the '60s and '70s. Harkening to a mythic time when "Officer Friendly" lived in the same community where he walked the beat, community policing advocates emphasize trust building and outreach to win the cooperation of unruly or unaligned subjects. Some variant of community policing is typically offered by police administrators and sometimes demanded by aggrieved community members following a "critical incident," such as the killing of an unarmed citizen. Ranging from efforts to increase the proportion of racial minorities or women among a particular department's ranks to midnight basketball and "coffee with a cop," the underlying aim of community policing is to give the appearance of reflexivity and democratic accountability. Because it has been a key tactic of COIN and a concession of liberal reform for decades, by tracing its application, community policing usefully identifies those subjects identified by police as enemy (from the position of absolute enmity, any noncop is enemy).

Returning to New York City of the late 1960s, consider the Stonewall riots from the vantage of counterinsurgency and pacification. Long a target for extortion rackets, undercover "vice" operations, and full-scale police raids, the Stonewall Inn, the only open gay bar in the city, became a key battleground in the struggle for queer liberation when a late-night attempt by police to "take the place!" met violent opposition.[119] Like for preceding uprisings at Cooper Do-nuts in Los Angeles and Gene Compton's Cafeteria in San Francisco, consistent police pressure, harassment, and violence set the conditions for Stonewall. The raid, which occurred just after midnight June 27–28, 1969, ignited a tinderbox when patrons and a gathering crowd pushed back against the invading cops. Outnumbered and quickly overwhelmed, police holed up inside the bar and tried to defend themselves with a fire hose until they were rescued by a phalanx of the NYPD Tactical Patrol Force (riot squad). Over the next couple of days, the Greenwich Village queer community, including, notably, two trans women of color, Sylvia Rivera and Marsha P. Johnson, duked it out with the NYPD, throwing rocks and bottles, resisting arrest, and defiantly chanting "Gay Power!" until the police at last relented.[120]

Due in no small part to the efforts at Stonewall, in the ensuing decades, the NYPD slowly moved from an overt policy of "homocriminality"[121] that aggressively policed nearly every facet of queer New Yorkers' lives to one of performative inclusion. Described by criminologist Emma K. Russell as "carceral pride,"[122] in recent years police departments nationwide have attempted to rebrand themselves as "gay friendly" by actively participating in Pride parades, deploying "rainbow cruiser" patrol cars, and advertising "antihomophobic" slogans, such as #NYPDout on social media. This is in no way to suggest that the years after Stonewall have been without struggle. Nor does it suggest that police do not still routinely harass, brutalize, and kill queer people, particularly trans people of color, as they did in the years leading up to Stonewall. Indeed, academic studies consistently confirm the word on the street, which is that police pose the greatest threat to the safety and well-being of queer people.[123] As Russell explains, by selectively retelling or apologizing for their misdeeds, as is the case with Stonewall, police craft a teleology of enlightened progress, hiding the shame of their "bad past" behind a "proud" and increasingly rainbow-colored institutional identity of the present.[124] Read symptomatically, this proud institutional identity cultivated and advertised by departments like the NYPD demonstrates with remarkable clarity a unique ideological regime, which, in keeping with counterinsurgency doctrine, aims to accomplish political goals by means other than the violent iron fist.

Just as corporations have responded to the tremendous market power of the queer community by commoditizing and corporatizing Pride, police no doubt recognize the political power and sheer numbers of potential adversaries in the queer community and have responded in kind. Faithful and uncritical adherents of community policing predictably advocate for formal outreach, including analogues to Russell's carceral pride, in order to build allegiances and give the appearance of solidarity.[125] More critically, then, we can read any group targeted for "community policing outreach," whether a youth gang or an ethnic group (as is the case with Muslims in NYC post-9/11), as one that has been deemed a threat to the established order.[126] In other words, community policing should not be understood as a "kinder, gentler" form of policing but rather as an ideological response to a political rival—*an enemy*. Recall that the Obama administration's Task Force on Twenty First Century Policing emphasized that the police must be seen "as allies rather than as an occupying force."[127] With their rainbow-colored uniform patches, cars, hashtag slogans, participation in Pride parades, and ceremonial inclusion of queer people among their ranks, police are doing precisely this, wheeling out a multicolored "Officer Friendly" yet again in hopes of assuming the position of "ally" and, ultimately, making their violence appear more legitimate. This is, as Correia and Wall put it, occupation masking as cooperation.[128]

Fortunately, police attempts to win the favor of, or simply intrude upon, the activities of target communities have not gone unnoticed. In the aftermath of the Pulse nightclub shooting in Orlando, Florida, police departments offered solidarity with the queer community, notably appearing as a show of force and as participants at Pride parades in the following weeks. Yet the security offered by police was quickly recognized as a Faustian bargain, as Toby Beauchamp writes, functioning "not to protect an already constituted community of good citizens, but to produce the very category of good citizen that is defined as deserving and important precisely because the state provides it with this benevolent oversight."[129] The disciplinary regime enacted by carceral pride and the "security" provided by openly gay cops operate as a domestic analogue to Jasbir Puar's homonationalism—a state-sanctioned queerness from "above" that polices and defines the boundaries of its oppositional and alter forms "below."[130] Just as the

NYPD worked to forge relationships and, thus, better avenues to observe Muslim communities following 9/11, "antihomophobic" outreach enhances proximity to suspect communities and provides police additional avenues to gather "intel." As Russell's work shows, partnerships with community-based sex worker organizations, for instance, allowed police to more easily make criminal cases on patrons and to pursue sex workers for "reckless" HIV transmission.

From New York to San Francisco and abroad, organizers and participants in Pride events now routinely intervene in and disrupt police participation. When Black Lives Matter withdrew as organizational grand marshal of the 2016 San Francisco Pride Parade, for instance, it did so to expressly object to police involvement. Explaining the group's decision, BLM spokesperson Malkia Cyril wrote, "As queer people of color, we are disproportionately targeted by both vigilante and police violence. We know first-hand that increasing the police presence at Pride does not increase safety for all people. Militarizing these events increases the potential for harm to our communities and we hope in the future SF Pride will consider community-centered approaches to security at pride events."[131] At New York's 2017 Pride celebration, protestors marched with a banner reading "There are no queer friendly cops" spanning Fifth Avenue and others formed a human chain to interrupt the path of the NYPD's Gay Officers Action League (GOAL) just as they passed the Stonewall Inn.[132] Again in 2019, a group challenging police participation in San Francisco's Pride parade brought it to a halt for more than an hour as they scuffled, amid the irony, with cops wearing rainbow-colored uniform patches. As these and other examples attest, and as police well know, pacification is an ongoing process not easily won.

The Genius of the Crowd

The aim of this chapter was to take seriously police claims of fear. This has proven a complicated task. As self-proclaimed monster fighters, police are defined by society and define themselves in relation to their enemies. At every turn, they marshal social and political capital by naming and fighting the monster and emboldening, rather than assuaging, fear. And though they routinely claim to have "feared for their lives," they do this, almost always, in order to justify and disown their own violence. When conflict is scaled up as spontaneous protest or sustained movement, the dialectic between police and adversary nevertheless remains. Even the disorder, destruction, and spectacle of revolt allows police to "show off," in Daryl Gates's words, rising in defense of liberal order and property, once again. As its long history displays in open detail, any sort of challenge to police authority and to the security police represent permits them to dig in deeper, to secure more funding, weaponry, legal cover, and, ultimately, power. They are, as they like to remind, *all that stands between monsters and the weak.*"

In his book *Specters of Revolt*, Gilman-Opalsky puts it this way: "Those who condemn the revolts actually love them because they get to condemn a 'violence' that justifies the violence they defend, the violence they love. Critics of revolt do not, therefore, fear the violence, but rather the transformative potentialities of revolt, its abolitionist and creative content. Their wager and hope is that nothing they love will be abolished, that the present state of things will be defended against every revolt."[133] Gilman-Opalsky's claims recall a few lines of the Charles Bukowski poem "The Genius of the Crowd," which reads, "and the best at murder are those who preach against it, and the best at hate are those who preach love, and the best at war finally are those who preach peace."[134] Given what I have written thus far, perhaps the addendum "and the best at fear are those who offer security" is warranted. Police do, in fact, depend on the fear, terror, and horror of violence and crime for their own power. We should therefore cast a dubious eye and finally dismiss their claims of fear entirely. *The police protest too much, methinks.* They do not *fear* the monster, they *need* the monster. Police *are* the monster.

So, if they genuinely do not fear the criminal or the crowd, do police fear anything at all? Police fear a change to the present state of affairs; they fear a world not dependent on their own violence; they fear *a world without police.* So, in the next and final chapter, I ponder the unthinkable: social life not ordered by fear, violence, and police.

CHAPTER 5

The Unthinkable World

> The ultimate, hidden truth of this world is that it is something
> we make and could just as easily make differently.
>
> —David Graeber, *The Utopia of Rules*

This book took much longer to finish than expected. By the time I thought it was done, Covid-19 had descended on the world, wrapping it in fear, confusion, and death. Days, then weeks, then months, holed up at home, keeping a schedule, or just marking time, I sat at this table tapping out words, staring out the window at the birds and squirrels the cat and I feed. Beyond our window and the squirrels, the dead piled in refrigerated trucks turned makeshift morgues. Was this the end? Was Mike Davis's monster at our door? If the apocalypse has shown itself, it looks nothing like those imagined pages back. But the unwelcomed end never comes on our terms, does it? All of this is a bit dramatic—I hope. Suffering will continue, for sure, but this is not the world killer of millenarian fantasy. If the pandemic holds any sort of apocalypse, it is in the Ancient Greek *apokalypsis*, an unveiling of that which was unseen. Yes, this monster will die, but what else will die with its passing? And what might be born or revealed in the wreckage of bodies, tattered relations, and institutions proven wholly inadequate?

A few weeks into the stay-at-home orders in my state, I was contacted by an editor from a big online media group and asked to write an essay on the failures of U.S. police during the pandemic. Interested in my take on "bad lockdown cops," the editor envisioned a rhetorical inventory of police misdeeds and one, from my perspective, only slightly altered by the global pandemic. There was, of course, no shortage of stories of cops behaving badly. But this has always been the rule, not its exception.

As Covid-19 crept across New York City and death counts soared, "the Finest" prosecuted business as usual, running undercover "buy and bust" programs and, as they always have, using petty violations as pretense to shake down people and their cars. Though the legal architecture did not yet exist for criminal enforcement of social distancing orders, the NYPD cited people for "obstructing governmental administration," unlawful assembly, and the old standby, disorderly conduct. In the thick of a global pandemic, the NYPD dutifully carried out its mandate of racialized "order maintenance," issuing eight of every ten social distancing violations to Black and Latino people.[1] The rest of the country mostly followed suit. Ohio police issued thousands of citations—with punishments of up to ninety days' imprisonment and $750 in fines—again, mostly to nonwhite residents.[2] In early April 2020, onlookers shot and shared video of three cops violently dragging a Black man off a Philadelphia city bus for not wearing a mask.[3]

Just as U.S. police used the crisis to broaden their reach, they also began to report falling rates of various crime types, as if observing some objective natural phenomenon like air temperature. Compared to 2019, for instance, St. Louis police recorded drops in all crime categories of some 20 percent in early 2020, with burglaries and other crimes down nearly 30 percent. Most violent crimes were also down more than 25 percent in the first thirty days of shelter-in-place orders. Noting similar changes elsewhere, University of Missouri–St. Louis criminologist Richard Rosenfeld followed conventional reasoning that "as streets emptied, potential victims have disappeared."[4] In the city's outer-ring suburbs, changes in traffic enforcement and other "self-initiated activity" forced arrests for drug crimes down by more than 50 percent compared to the year prior.[5] A useful natural experiment, all of this showed in real time the self-justifying feedback loop that policing feeds. As one former cop offered, "maybe what police departments fear most during this pandemic is people realizing cops making thousands of BS arrests serves no actual purpose other than punishing already marginalized citizens and that when those arrests stop, life might actually improve."[6]

As if on cue, police and city leaders undercut their own data, insisting something was amiss. St. Louis mayor Lyda Krewson, for one, remained incredulous. "For a little while there, it looked like violent crime might be off a bit, but as you've seen in just the last few days, that is not the case . . . there are still way too many shootings . . . way too many homicides." While the nation's murder rate did climb (it is unclear at this point how much), and hidden crimes like domestic violence no doubt increased, we can counter the apocalyptic warnings of the pandemic police by recalling that even during the Great Depression—when more than a quarter of Americans were without work—no great jumps in crime were observed.[7]

Exigence and expedience nevertheless allowed police to clamp down and even wheel out a few toys kept in the waiting. In several U.S. cities, they deployed small "quadcopter" drones to surveil public spaces, initiating the slippery slope of policing by drone behind the tired line that the machines keep officers safe, in this case from disease.[8] In China and in Flint, Michigan, soon after, police donned Wi-Fi–enabled "smart helmets" equipped with RoboCop-style visors able to screen for the coronavirus by reading the body temperature of subjects at a distance of five meters. "The sorcery doesn't stop there," reads a report that describes how the helmets, beyond perpetually generating reams of data, would soon integrate automated license plate readers to scan for stolen cars and facial recognition software to round up the missing and the wanted.[9]

Letting no crisis go to waste, private security, represented here by Knightscope, stepped up its advertising, launching a series of Zoom webinars hoping to drum up investors. Under the new banner "Robots Are Immune," company spokespersons insisted that their products were demonstrating, in real time, how robots would be central to any form of future police.[10] Much to onlookers' puzzlement, even Boston Dynamics' robo-dog made an appearance. Patrolling a park in Singapore, the nimble robot trotted along bike paths and running trails broadcasting prerecorded social distancing orders meant to "shame parkgoers into compliance."[11] In New York a short time later, the NYPD introduced its own branded Spot robot, named Digidog, after it helped effect an arrest in Brooklyn.

While right-wing libertarians at the *Economist* worryingly foretold the rise of an all-seeing "coronopticon," vigilant critics of the

The official NYPD Twitter account pushes back against public outcry following field tests of its "Digidog."

distended security state eyed even more sinister developments.[12] Just as it had a decade prior, the U.S. government quietly set aside a good chunk of emergency funding meant to buoy the failing economy for police and prisons.[13] As unemployment rose, food lines lengthened, and threadbare safety nets fell away, some $850 million of the first wave of emergency funds went to local police, who used it to "tool up" and prepare for unrest—adding personnel and riot gear and paying overtime.[14] Yet outside cash injections, the novelty of drones and Digidogs, and the absurdity of violently enforcing social distancing orders, a few months into the coronavirus pandemic, little had changed.[15] U.S. police had no need to "tool up" their capacities for surveillance, coercion, or violence because these things were already extraordinarily high. This is a point that I hope, by now, to have made. In the ordinary emergency in which police operate, and which they produce, no cost is too great, no action too severe.[16] Whether cited post hoc by street cops to justify the "reasonableness" of their workaday violence or made formal by "states of emergency" declared by the highest executives, the police power *is* emergency power. The emergency does not begin or end; *it persists*.[17]

And so, where "bad lockdown cops" are concerned, any apparent change is an artifact either of relative privilege or of ignorance.[18] As the bumper-sticker cliché goes, if you aren't already outraged, you haven't been paying attention. But as police buzzed about doing their violent work in the thick of a spiraling crisis that had already claimed tens of thousands of lives, a single particularly grotesque and wholly avoidable death forced a few more of the hitherto oblivious among us to sit up straight and begin to pay attention.

Laid to Waste

In the waning daylight of May 25, 2020, a Minneapolis, Minnesota, cop named Derek Chauvin murdered a forty-six-year-old Black man named George Floyd. For nearly ten agonizing minutes—in full view of filming onlookers—Chauvin drove his knee into Floyd's neck as the prone, shackled man gasped for air, writhed in pain, begged for mercy, and cried out for his dead mother. With grim, devastating clarity, Chauvin and his three conspirators laid bare the horrors of a world that licenses brutality and open murder in the name of the security of a few. *Horrid. Horrible. Horrific. Horrifying.* The words that fell from slack mouths onto headlines and social media posts were not misplaced. "The world watched in *horror* as George Floyd's humanity was taken away from him," Minnesota's governor later confessed.[19]

Even Donald Trump, for a brief moment, seemed to admit the great crime of Floyd's murder before predictably falling back to defend the indefensible:

> The sad thing is that they are very professional but when you see an event like that with *the more than eight minutes of horror, it's eight minutes, really of horror, it's a disgrace.* Then people start saying, "Well, are all police like that?" They don't know, they don't think about it that much. The fact is, people start saying, police are like that. *Police aren't like that.*[20]

While their insincere rhetoric might include the word *horror*, for apologists like Trump, a police murder is only ever understood as the deed of a bad apple, a bad cop with bad training, or maybe even a symptom of "implicit bias."[21] Worse yet, murders such as Floyd's often become evidence of the bad behavior, bad character, even the bad biology of the dead. Infamous New York congressman Peter King, for instance, managed to blame Eric Garner for his own death, citing the man's weight, asthma, heart condition—anything but the NYPD agents who choked him—and, in doing so, joined the disgraceful ranks of Daryl Gates, who, years earlier, blamed similar choke-hold deaths on the "slow-opening arteries" of Black victims.[22] In Floyd's case, the Hennepin County medical examiner quickly reported their autopsy found "no physical findings" to support a "diagnosis of traumatic asphyxia or strangulation," pointing instead toward a heart attack hastened by "underlying health conditions including coronary heart disease and hypertensive heart disease."[23] The bullet didn't kill him; he died from loss of blood! This level of gymnastics is rarely seen outside the Olympic Games. All of it is accomplished with the help of a supple and compliant, if not wholly complicit, news media whose criminally passive language often performs the trick of disappearing the police altogether. Even when read in tandem with grotesque images of Floyd's murder, headlines could leave one to ponder the ambiguous relationship between the "death of black man" and police.[24]

As court cases ensued, Minnesota authorities leaned on the old forensic crutch "excited delirium" to excuse Chauvin's brutal criminality. Though the condition is not recognized by the American

Four Minneapolis police officers fired after death of black man

By Amy Forliti and Jeff Baenen
Associated Press

MINNEAPOLIS — Four Minneapolis officers involved in the arrest of a black man who died in police custody were fired Tuesday, hours after a bystander's video showed an officer kneeling on the handcuffed man's neck, even after he pleaded that he could not breathe and stopped moving.

Mayor Jacob Frey announced the firings on Twitter, saying "This is the

An Associated Press headline somehow disconnects the firing of "four Minneapolis police officers" and the "death of black man."

Psychiatric Association, the American Medical Association, or the World Health Organization, police equipment giant Axon Enterprise Inc. (previously TASER International) has done much to constitute it, using it to explain away the many deaths caused by its "conducted energy weapons."[25] Never mind that police contacted Floyd for allegedly passing a fake twenty-dollar bill. Never mind that Floyd was handcuffed. Never mind that Chauvin had his knee on his neck for nearly ten minutes. Had not Floyd entered this "excited" state, he would still be alive. Like asthma, hypertension, and "slow-opening arteries," excited delirium and other pseudoscience of its kind stand in for and stand in front of the violence police bring into being. And so, for indifferent partisans and the willfully ignorant, police killings—even the slow, manual suffocation of a prone, restrained, defenseless man—are simply the dirty, unavoidable consequences of this world, the bill that must be paid so that some may live comfortably in their homes and inside their own heads. "It is what it is," so the story goes and goes on.

Horror flashes as systems fail, heralding the end of world-making fictions. While the political class missed the lesson, for others, Floyd's murder marked such an end, shattering limits—imaginative, emotional, political. Visiting a family member a few days later, I caught a glimpse of this affective remaking. Not necessarily a cop hater but no conservative, either, this white midwestern woman, years into her eighth decade, remarked with slow, deliberate sadness how what she had encountered on her morning television regimen had been so much worse than "all the others" and quietly wondered after "his poor mother." To at last reckon the horrors hidden behind our cherished understandings, "to experience the malice of the made or revealed cosmos," in John Clute's eloquent phrasing.[26] *Vastation.* The atrocity of the thing itself. The horror of the Real. The frozen moment when lingering dread turns to cold horror. In an instant, the unthinkable is thinkable. This world is not as it seems.

While it has been an ongoing, perhaps inescapable, reality for Black people, as Afropessimists insist, Floyd's murder laid to waste the comforting illusions of so many others. In her accounting of the unevenness of this reckoning, writer and critic Saidiya Hartman described Floyd's death as a grim epiphany, a eureka moment for sleepwalking whites:

> What we see now is a translation of Black suffering into white pedagogy. In this extreme moment, the casual violence that can result in a loss of life—a police officer literally killing a Black man with the weight of his knees on the other's neck—becomes a flash point for a certain kind of white liberal conscience, like: "Oh my god! We're living in a racist order! How can I find out more about this?" That question is a symptom of the structure that produces Floyd's death. Then there's the other set of demands: "Educate me about the order in which we live." And it's like: "Oh, but you've been living in this order. Your security, your wealth, your good life, has depended on it."[27]

This "public lynching," as Cornel West described it, had accomplished what countless other sad, lonely deaths had not, "pulling the cover off who we really are and what our system really is."[28] Terror is about the threat to life, while horror is a threat to understanding, Evan Calder Williams reminds. In this moment, an untold many suddenly understood "they were behind the knife" or had it in their hands all along.[29]

Flash point.

A terrible unveiling.

Apocalypse.

The horror of police.

With that, protests, uprisings, riots—*anger*—spread like fire burning through California scrub. Along with Floyd, in the following weeks and months, the American public and the world learned the name of Breonna Taylor, a young Black woman shot to death earlier that year by careless Louisville cops on a drug raid. In Georgia, pressure from protestors forced the arrests of three white "vigilantes" who had murdered Ahmaud Arbery for simply being Black in the wrong neighborhood. In Colorado, insistent crowds raised the name Elijah McClain, a young man who was choked and drugged into brain and eventual body death for the crime of wearing a ski mask on a warm day.[30]

Reflecting on the 2011 England riots, yet another flash point touched off by police violence, Mark Fisher mapped the parameters of this ontological rupture with his usual aplomb:

> When the Real rushes in everything feels like a film: not a film you are watching, but a film you are in. Suddenly, the screens insulating late capitalist spectators from the Real of antagonism and violence fell away. Since the student revolts in late 2010, helicopters, sirens and loudhailers have intermittently broken the phoney peace of post-crash London. To locate the unrest spreading across the capital, you just had to follow the Walter Murch-chunter of chopper blades . . . So many times during 2011, you found yourself hooked to news reports that resembled the scene setting ambience in an apocalyptic flick: dictators falling, economies crashing, fascist serial killers murdering teenagers. The news was now more compelling than most fiction, and also more implausible: the plot was moving too quickly to be believable. But the sheen of unreality it generated was nothing more than the signature of the unscreened Real itself.[31]

Against an apocalyptic mise-en-scène of smoke, fire, and open warfare, the horrific unreality of the Real shines through. With police at the center, explosions of outrage that dotted the American geographic and cultural landscape flowed into an increasingly bizarre torrent of events, setting out a disorienting timeline that, in Fisher's words, moved too quickly to be believed. Too bizarre, too quick—that is, if we hadn't already seen it all before.

The Apocalyptic Real

The day after Floyd's death, protestors gathered at his murder scene and marched to the Minneapolis Police Department's Third Precinct headquarters, two miles away. Cops stationed on the building's roof began firing tear gas cannisters and rubber bullets into the crowd as protestors broke windows and vandalized police vehicles. While the causal arrangement is unclear, police, of course, insist that they only fired on the crowd after it became "disorderly" and to defend police vehicles still holding weapons and ammunition. By the next evening, MPD chief Medaria Arradondo made formal requests of the mayor and governor to deploy the Minnesota National Guard, pointing to a looted Target store as evidence of their inability to contain the protests. By midday Thursday, the MPD had quietly begun to "move critical operations" out of the Third Precinct building, making plans to effectively "give it up to the protestors." That evening, with temperatures rising, Donald Trump dog-whistle tweeted as if to incite violence, appropriating racist phrasing of the civil rights era: "These THUGS are dishonoring the memory of George Floyd, and I won't let that happen. Just spoke to Governor Tim Walz and told him that the Military is with him all the way. Any difficulty and we will assume control but, when the looting starts, the shooting starts. Thank you!"[32] Although National Guard personnel were by then already available in the area, city and police leadership made the decision not to attempt to defend the Third Precinct building, and by late evening protestors overran it and set it ablaze, giving the MPD its own "Fort Surrender."[33] While a few local protestors were quickly scooped up and charged, months later, it was learned that members of the so-called Boogaloo Bois had traveled to Minneapolis from all over the United States with the intention of "accelerating" violent confrontation and that one "boi" in particular had posed as a BLM protestor, instigated violence, and fired an assault weapon into the precinct.[34]

On June 1, Trump convened a press conference at the White House Rose Garden to offer his first formal comments on the protests. Regurgitating the grotesque politics of "American carnage," the self-anointed "president of law and order" zeroed in on so-called "professional anarchists, violent mobs, arsonists, looters, criminals, rioters, antifa, and others" blamed for the upheaval. Calling the protests "acts of domestic terror," Trump "strongly" recommended that governors deploy the National Guard and establish "overwhelming law enforcement presence" in order to "dominate the streets." Following the speech, a force gathered from the ranks of the DEA, Secret Service, ATF, FBI, Marshals, and other federal agencies did just that in Washington, clearing protestors gathered in Lafayette Square with tear gas, pepper spray, flash bangs, rubber bullets, shields, and batons in order to stage a wholly bizarre photo op. Walking from the Rose Garden flanked by a procession of loyalists, Trump stopped to pose for the press in front of St. John's Church, a Bible raised awkwardly in his right hand. Even if written by a ham-fisted illiterate like Trump, the preferred reading of this crass event was evident. The speech, procession, clearing, and pose were all part of a ritual cleansing of the body politic. Ceremonial magic, exorcism, a sort of religious revanchism—Trump invoked the political theology of the thin blue line to cast out his enemies and promise his acolytes *their* world's imminent return.[35]

Later that month, protestors making their way through a rarefied St. Louis enclave toward the mayor's residence crossed paths with homeowners Mark and Patricia McCloskey. Outfitted in pastel-pink and striped leisure wear and nervously fingering the triggers of firearms trained at the passing crowd, the two middle-aged personal injury attorneys and their cowardly aggression occasioned another wholly bizarre photo op, characterizing, again, the world-for-us— that is, if "us" is obscenely wealthy and white. Describing the "huge and frightening crowd" (members of which never once stepped on his property), Mark McCloskey envisioned "the storming of the Bastille," claiming he feared the "mob" would leave them dead and their house in ruins. The couple's fantasy Bastille, a nine-thousand-square-foot mansion built at the turn of the twentieth century for the daughter of Adolphus Busch, is key to deciphering their greedy, panicked response. In a glowing *St. Louis Magazine* profile a few years prior, the McCloskeys had regaled readers with their painstaking efforts to find and reclaim all of the estate's original furnishings and return it to its original glory. Describing one of only a handful of new editions permitted by the pair, Mark McCloskey pridefully described how they sought and secured a rare Louis XIII *homme debout* (standing man) armoire, allegedly so named because it made a good hiding spot for French elites during the Reign of Terror.[36] Given McCloskey's fixation on his "standing man," we should perhaps read his grandiose allusions to the Ancien Régime more literally. Looking out from their multimillion-dollar mansion, 8.4 miles from the hardscrabble street where Michael Brown fell lifeless to the ground, Mark and Patricia no doubt saw a bloodthirsty mob of "BLM" and "antifa" rioters and looters, maybe even pitchforks and torches, not fellow St. Louisans exercising their rights and demanding fairness from the city's leaders. Like other members of their class able to fall back to fortified bunkers and private security, the already armed McCloskeys took upon themselves the core police function: defense of accumulated wealth and property at the point of a gun. And with that, not unlike Trump at St. John's Church, the symbolic defense, making, and remaking of their world itself.

In Portland, a city perpetually stirred by protests of some kind, agents of the "elite" U.S. Border Patrol Tactical Unit (BORTAC) jumped on the chance to field-test their own version of the CIA's "extraordinary rendition." Called by investigative journalist Todd Miller "the U.S. Border Patrol's robocops,"[37] the unit was loosed upon the "sanctuary city" by executive order to patrol it in rented minivans and abduct suspected "violent anarchists" at will and, seemingly, at random.[38] That they released their quarry as quickly as they had abducted them proves their presence was intended to strike fear, or provoke a response from those they targeted. Wearing full battle-dress uniforms but no identification, the androidized BORTAC Frankencops marshaled the terror of cynegetic power, reminding the unruly of policing's hierarchy of violence and the fact that they alone are masters of pursuit and capture, indeed, "hunters of men." As evidence they met their aim, one of the first Portlanders snatched off the street described his encounter like it was "out of a horror/sci-fi, like a Philip K. Dick novel. It was like being preyed upon."[39]

While BORTAC was running an open intimidation campaign in Portland, elsewhere, police and their supporters continued to disown other instances of overt violence, repeating the mantra "you didn't see what you think you saw," *trust us*. Footage shot by an NPR affiliate at a protest captured Buffalo, New York, police shoving seventy-five-year-old Catholic Worker activist Martin Gugino to the ground

so violently that he hit the back of his head on the concrete sidewalk, causing blood to immediately rush from the wound. Left on
the ground in a pool of blood as police casually stepped over him,
Gugino was carted away by members of the New York National
Guard and would spend weeks in the hospital convalescing. The
video of the assault quickly went viral, forcing a response from
Buffalo mayor Byron Brown. By the end of the day, the two officers
seen to have pushed Gugino were suspended without pay, and two
days later, they were charged with felony assault. Commenting on
the assault and on footage of an NYPD vehicle plowing into a crowd
of protestors a week earlier, New York City mayor Bill de Blasio articulated the police definition of reality, insisting, "Sometimes what
we see with our own eyes is the whole story. Sometimes what we see
with our own eyes, is not the whole story, if you see a video . . . observers from City Hall saw a different reality than you were seeing."[40]
Unsurprisingly, Trump and loyal Trumpists also took the opportunity to scour the footage for a different reality, one that not only excused police for trouncing a frail old man but placed Gugino at the
center of an antifa conspiracy to discredit police.[41] Read together,
the refusal to see police violence for what it is and attempts to make
victims somehow responsible for their own suffering illustrate quite
powerfully the lengths some will go to avoid a confrontation with
the true, the real, the *Real* monstrous face of police.

In late August 2020, Kenosha, Wisconsin, police attempting to
intervene in a "domestic incident" confronted and then shot twenty-
nine-year-old Jacob Blake in the back multiple times as he attempted
to get into his vehicle and drive away. The shooting, which was captured by a bystander's cell phone, was justified by the Wisconsin Department of Justice, which argued that Blake had "actively resisted,"
been armed with a knife, and threatened the safety of the responding police.[42] Unsurprisingly, Blake's shooting localized the ongoing
Floyd protests to the Kenosha area, prompting Wisconsin's governor
to immediately declare a state of emergency, impose a curfew, and
deploy the state's National Guard to "ensure individuals can exercise
their right safely, protect state buildings and critical infrastructure,
and support first responders and fire fighters."[43]

As is increasingly common, in Kenosha, a mass of self-styled
"counterprotestors" and armed self-appointed police showed up "to

maintain order" and "defend private property." One such person was seventeen-year-old Kyle Rittenhouse, who answered the call from the right-wing "Kenosha Guard" and traveled from nearby Illinois with a semiautomatic AR-15 rifle. Interviewed on camera outside a local business, Rittenhouse explained his presence, reciting the heroic mythology of armed men who "run into harm's way":

> So people are getting injured, and our job is to protect this business, and part of my job is to also help people. If there is somebody hurt, I am running into harm's way. That's why I have my rifle, because I can protect myself, obviously, but I also have my med kit.[44]

Acting on his own accord, Rittenhouse later confronted and ultimately shot three protestors, killing two. Unable to turn himself in to uninterested police on scene, Rittenhouse returned to Illinois and turned himself in the next day. Arraigned on first-degree reckless homicide, first-degree intentional homicide, attempted first-degree intentional homicide, and other charges, he was extradited to Wisconsin and held until late November, when he was released on a $2 million bond.

A former youth "police cadet" and proponent of various online "Blue Lives Matter" groups, Rittenhouse was made a cause célèbre by the propolice Christian right. Calling the case "a stand against tyranny," one of Rittenhouse's attorneys, Lin Wood, who also represented the Trump reelection campaign, established the Fight Back Foundation, which plumbed high-profile conservative donors' pockets for his bail money. Meanwhile on GiveSendGo, the internet's "#1 Free Christian Crowdfunding Site," the Friends of the Rittenhouse Family's Kyle Rittenhouse legal defense fund had well surpassed its $500,000 goal. A data breach at the website later showed that numerous public officials and police had donated to Rittenhouse's defense. Twenty-five bucks came from Lieutenant William K. Kelly, second in charge of the Norfolk, Virginia, police department's internal affairs division, who offered words of encouragement along with his donation: "God bless. Thank you for your courage. Keep your head up. You've done nothing wrong. Every rank and file police officer supports you . . ."[45]

Raise money for Kyle Rittenhouse Legal Defense

Campaign Created by: Friends of the Rittenhouse family

The funds from this campaign will be received by Friends Of The Rittenhouse Family .

Kyle Rittenhouse just defended himself from a brutal attack by multiple members of the far-leftist group ANTIFA – the experience was undoubtedly a brutal one, as he was forced to take two lives to defend his own.

Now, Kyle is being unfairly charged with murder 1, by a DA who seems determined only to capitalize on the political angle of the situation. The situation was clearly self-defense, and Kyle and his family will undoubtedly need money to pay for the legal fees.

Let's give back to someone who bravely tried to defend his community.

Kyle Rittenhouse's Facebook profile image at the time of his arrest, and a Thin Blue Line flag affixed to the GiveSendGo legal defense campaign.

Taking up arms, killing two people in defense of the property of people he did not know, the self-deputized high school dropout became a triumphant amalgamation of gun rights activism and propolice, Christian nativism, and—like the McCloskeys, Chris Kyle, and the Punisher—a cartoonish hero figure to stand against insurgent hordes of "antifa terrorists" and Black Lives Matter "rioters and looters."

Four days after the shootings in Kenosha, a so-called "Trump Train" caravan of more than one hundred vehicles—outfitted with the now obligatory inventory of American, Gadsden, Trump, and thin blue line flags—rolled through downtown Portland, honking horns, firing paintballs, and spraying crowds of protestors with bear spray. Portland resident Aaron J. Danielson, member of the far-right group Patriot Prayer and frequent participant in similar clashes with local antifascists, showed up armed with bear spray, a collapsible baton, and a nine-millimeter handgun. Video shot that evening records someone yelling "We got one right here" as Danielson rushes in, arm outstretched, discharging a large cannister of bear spray, and then the sound of two gunshots. The shooter, another local man and self-described antifascist, Michael F. Reinoehl, escaped the scene but later admitted to killing Danielson in self-defense. On the run, Reinoehl told a journalist that he would not turn himself in because he believed police were working with right-wing vigilantes. Clearly feeling the heat of cynegetic energies, Reinoehl explained, "They're out hunting me . . . There's nightly posts of the hunt and where they're going to be hunting. They made a post saying the deer are going to feel lucky this year because it's open season on Michael right now."[46] On September 3, the state of Oregon charged Reinoehl with second-degree murder and issued an arrest warrant. By the time Trump tweeted at the Justice Department and the FBI—"Why aren't the Portland Police ARRESTING the cold blooded killer of Aaron 'Jay' Danielson. Do your job, and do it fast. Everybody knows who this thug is. No wonder Portland is going to hell!"—late that evening, Reinoehl had been shot and killed by U.S. Marshals outside an apartment in Lacey, Washington.[47] A DOJ press release issued the next day by Attorney General Bill Barr crowed, "The tracking down of Reinoehl—a dangerous fugitive, admitted Antifa member, and suspected murderer—is a significant accomplishment in the ongoing effort to restore law and order to Portland . . ."[48] And with that, Barr transformed an extralegal assassination seemingly authorized and cheered on by the president of the United States into an ambiguous and bloodless "tracking down" in the name of "law and order."

A strange parade of events, each one more bizarre than the last. A world spinning palpably faster, as Geo Maher put it, compressing entire decades into a blur of weeks.[49] How fitting that it delivered a moment when people of all persuasions would begin to think the unthinkable.

A World without Police

Faced with one of the largest protest movements in the nation's history, "backers of the blue" mobilized and dug in deeper, proving again the widespread commitment to a Hobbesian vision of human nature and social order. Writing in the *Philadelphia Inquirer*, Heritage Foundation and Manhattan Institute affiliate Christopher Rufo (who would later help manufacture controversy around critical race theory) provided an example of just this. Describing the naïve utopianism of abolitionists, he scolds:

> Police abolitionists believe that they stand at the vanguard of a new idea, but this strain of thought dates to the eighteenth-century philosopher Jean-Jacques Rousseau, who believed that stripping away the corruptions of civilization would liberate the goodness of man. What police abolitionists fail to acknowledge is the problem of evil. No matter how many "restorative" programs it administers, even a benevolent centralized state cannot extinguish the risks of illness, violence, and disorder. Contrary to the utopian vision of Rousseau and his intellectual descendants, chaos is not freedom; order is not slavery.[50]

With the incessant "What about all the bad people?" Rufo's is the same tired, inaccurate condescension both the right and left have long lobbed at abolitionists. Wherever one might stand on the empirical or metaphysical nature of evil, it is not something abolitionists casually avoid. Most also do not pretend that the right combination of technocratic tinkering and "central planning" will at last exorcise the violent drives from the social body. More modestly, abolitionists begin with the simple but somehow radical insistence that our present system of justice fails miserably at its stated aims of preventing crime and redressing harm and is party to a fair amount of evil of its own. Hardly utopian naïveté, abolitionism refuses the trap of reformism, choosing instead to speculate radically, asking, in Michelle Brown and Judah Schept's words, "What kind of community (world) do we want to live in—do we envision?"[51] Under the banner "Disarm! Defund! Disband!" the movement to end police violence has, in fact, been a bit more practical than neo-Rousseauian utopianism. From a broad coalition of activists and organizers have come an array of specific programs and policy demands, among them seeking to shift current police duties and funding onto other institutions, attacking the power of police unions, dismantling "police bills of rights," ending cash bail, and, more abstractly, creating systems of care that do not rely on police and negate the belief that police ensure security. Still, Rufo's attack contains another point worthy of response:

> In the modern world, civilization cannot be rolled back without dire consequences. If anything like police abolition ever occurred, it's easy to predict what would happen next. In the subsequent vacuum of physical power, wealthy neighborhoods would deploy private police forces and poor neighborhoods would organize around criminal gangs—deepening structural inequalities and harming the very people that the police abolitionists say they want to help.

As he would have it, this "modern world," imperfect as it is, is set in stone. Put plainly, this is the ontology of the world-for-us. Rufo is not alone in this regard; most among us see the police power as an indispensable pillar of modernity, filling the "vacuum of physical power" with life-preserving and, therefore, righteous violence. As we have seen, this sort of thinking, however common, diagnoses a dark sort of pessimism: *the evil heart of man can only be restrained by a greater, monstrous violence.* Should police ever recede, open war between the haves and have-nots would soon ensue. Ignored by pundits like Rufo, however, is that for an increasing number of people, the "dire rollback of civilization" of which they warn is hardly a departure from the present order manufactured in service of the wealthy. Paraphrasing George Jackson a half century ago, the war isn't coming—it's already here, glaring and threatening.[52] And so, for those unfortunate souls trapped at the bottom of racialized class war, where their enemy draws his pay is of secondary concern.

Rife as it is, we should not presume that this sort of critique is confined to the reactionary right. In the run-up to and aftermath of the 2020 presidential election, several high-profile Democrats and liberal pundits piled on similarly, none higher profile than Barack Obama. Dismissing the "snappy slogan" of "Defund the police," Obama reiterated that the goal for any such movement should be measured reform and warned that even the whisper of the words risked alienating a "big audience."[53] As the year closed, key Democrats blamed abolitionists for their poor showing in elections across the country. Long-standing South Carolina representative Jim Clyburn, for instance, warned that the "sloganeering" of activists ran the risk of doing to the movement to end police violence what "Burn, baby, burn" did to the civil rights movement.[54] Apparently lost on Clyburn was the irony that Marvin X wrote "Burn, Baby, Burn" following the Watts Rebellion, kicked off as it was by the brutality of the LAPD.

> *Motherfuck the police*
> *Parker's sista too. [. . .]*
> Burn, baby burn . . .[55]

The more things change . . .

That liberal politicians, even veteran civil rights activists like Clyburn who have themselves felt the sting of the baton, are equally aghast as members of the right wing at the thought of defunding the police is not in the least surprising. After all, the rule of law, liberalism itself, is brought into being, actualized, made real, by the unchecked, righteous, and altogether legal violence of police. Transforming "wolves into men" and men into monsters so that some may "sleep peaceably in their beds at night," the security promised by the violence of the police power is indispensable, godlike—indeed, "the supreme concept of bourgeois society."[56]

The laughter, panic, rage engendered by the mere suggestion of reining in police, to say nothing of abolishing them entirely, demonstrates with cold clarity the terrible, pale-knuckle grip that some have on the way things are. We make this world in our own image, or so we like to think. Any departure from it would mean a fracture, break, schism of our very being, ushering in changes so profound that their mere contemplation is a frightening—indeed, horrifying—thing. This is the insidious function of apocalyptic fantasy: it subtly reaffirms the necessity, the primacy of this world. In one of her many interviews advancing the cause of prison and police abolition, activist and organizer Mariame Kaba similarly articulates how central the police are to the reproduction of not only the world of concrete material relations but our own ontological worlds of security as well:

> I believe that living in the way we live makes it difficult for most people to seriously consider the end of policing. The idea of security, the idea that cops equal security, is difficult to dislodge. To transform this mindset, where cops equal security, means we have to actually transform our relationships to each other enough so that we can see that we can keep each other safe and ourselves safe, right? Safety means something else, because you cannot have safety without strong, empathic relationships with others. You can have security without relationships but you cannot have safety—actual safety—without healthy relationships. Without getting to really know your neighbor, figuring out when you should be intervening when you hear and see things, feeling safe enough within your community that you feel like, yeah my neighbor's punching [their partner], I'm going to knock on the door, right? . . . Part of what this necessitates is that we have to work with members of our communities to make violence unacceptable. What my friend Andy Smith has said is that this is a problem of political organizing and not one of punishment. How can we organize to make interpersonal violence unthinkable?[57]

What Kaba is getting at is the persistent challenge of ensuring a sense of security without reproducing the violence of police with the violence of some other system or institution. While the human appetite for security is insatiable, there is nevertheless ongoing work toward this goal. In the Brownsville neighborhood of Brooklyn, a coalition of antiviolence workers temporarily replaced the NYPD, who fell back but remained on call through traditional 911 services.[58] For five days in late 2020, violence interrupters and crisis management workers with Brownsville Safety Alliance staffed information booths and "watched over" a two-block patch between Pitkin and Sutter Avenues. Describing the project as "defund the police in actuality," organizers recorded no emergency calls to police after five days and insisted the experiment offered tangible evidence that the visible presence of police is inessential to safety.[59] While wresting power away from police is a crucial first step, the Brownsville group's reliance on quasi-police practices nevertheless demonstrates just how difficult it is to realize security without waiting violence.

So insatiable is this desire and so inescapable the ontological prison of a world made wholly for us that even the most radical police critic risks falling victim to the logic of police. For instance, critical criminologist Meghan McDowell's community-based research in North Carolina sought to identify alternatives to police and to establish a form of mutual aid built on play, joy, and communication she calls "insurgent safety," which does not make use of banishment, policing, or criminalization. McDowell's informants, all active members of progressive community organizations, express measured skepticism on the possibilities of a world free of police violence so long as that world remains one ordered by the precepts of racial capitalism. Documenting the difficulty even among left-leaning community members to abandon knee-jerk reliance on police and other forms of "carceral safety," McDowell suggests that language and communication hold the key to "finding ways to express, and co-hold feelings of shame, trauma, and vulnerability" and to "support community generated responses to harm that do not rely on the logic of carceral safety."[60] But even when focusing on self-identified sites of insurgent safety, such as a relatively autonomous skate park, her respondents could not escape the "hegemonic carcerality" of their conditions, reproducing, in fact relying on, the *language of police*:

It's crazy, like *the skaters police the skate park*, so like if a kid is getting in the way or something like that it's up to us, it's not up to the police, to tell people "oh, you need to watch out" or it's up to us to say "dude you need to calm down."

The suggestion is that hierarchy enforced by the police power and the attendant potential for banishment are still very much in play, even in spaces explicitly organized around mutual aid and solidarity.

In another example drawn from the left end of criminology, Stanislav Vysotsky looks to the earliest days of the punk scene and conflicts between antifascists and "Nazi punks" for alternatives to police, describing how antiracist skinheads, punks, and other "militant antifascists" planned for and used violence to defend their fellows and their prefigured spaces against intrusion and disruption.[61] For Vysotsky, what he calls the "Anarchy Police" are a means to order and protection that are autonomous and directly democratic. While this may indeed be the case, Vysotsky nevertheless demonstrates the replication of policing's reliance on violence and force within a seemingly autonomous space. All of this lines up with a well-established and long history of punk rock and hardcore adherents who violently, sometimes lethally, "police their scene."[62]

In the weeks following George Floyd's murder, Seattle protestors declared a six-block "autonomous zone" in the city's Capitol Hill neighborhood. Named at first Free Capitol Hill and later the Capitol Hill Autonomous Zone (CHAZ), the self-organized occupation demanded that the city's leadership cut and shift the Seattle Police Department's funding to services for the city's residents.[63] Initially taking on the atmosphere of a neighborhood block party, protestors organized the "no-cop" space in the spirit of mutual aid, encouraging performance and free exchange. Autonomy quickly sprouted hierarchy, however, as leaders adopted familiar tactics to maintain "order." In one violent confrontation recorded and shared on YouTube, CHAZ representative Raz Simone attacked two graffiti artists for painting a mural without permission, warning, "You forget we are the police of this community now."[64] Faced with threats from right-wing activists, participants also reportedly formed armed "open carry" patrols.[65] In just over a month, there were at least four shooting incidents in the general vicinity of CHAZ. In one particularly violent confrontation that left two teen boys shot and one dead, CHAZ's "security forces" fired on a fleeing vehicle, forcing it to strike a concrete barrier.[66] Concern over seemingly escalating fire-arm violence and pressure from adjacent businesses, many of which hired their own private security forces, ultimately led to the zone's demise. As with the previous examples, all of this is not to dismiss the attempts made to forge a police-free world but rather to demonstrate the insurmountable task of doing so in a world always conditioned by self-interest.

Even the Black Panther Party, perhaps the most important revolutionary movement to emerge in the United States over the past century, could not escape the stink of police. Famously forming it as the Black Panther Party for *Self-Defense*, founders Huey Newton and Bobby Seale and first recruit Bobby Hutton took up arms to defend their communities from police terror by actively *patrolling* the LAPD.[67] As Newton put it, "the way we finally won the brothers over was by patrolling the police with arms."[68] Not only did the Panthers openly challenge the LAPD, they often served as de facto replacements themselves, stepping in to adjudicate disputes and "cool out" conflicts between community members.[69] But as the U.S. government's efforts to sow discord and create factionalism within the party proved successful, its leaders turned the police power inward, using their own style of political policing under regional "field marshals" to root out the deceivers in their midst. Again, the point here is not to question why the Panthers turned to and reproduced the police power but simply to recognize that they did. This, after all, has been this book's underlying premise: our attempts to create—even imagine—a secure world-for-us are shackled to the coercion, threats, and violence we call the police power. After such a lengthy polemic, one might expect some concrete alternatives, a new program or strategy to security without the violence of police. Unlike Hollywood, however, I have no happy endings to offer.

The Time of Monsters

In April 2021, after just under a year, Minnesota courts convicted Derek Chauvin of the murder of George Floyd—only the second time in the state's history that a cop had been convicted of murder—and with that came a small sigh of relief from a country still on the brink from a divisive presidency, a right-wing insurgency, and a global pandemic. By late June, the court sentenced Chauvin to 22.5 years in prison, and again there was a sigh of relief from those who professed faith in the criminal justice system, or from those who simply wanted revenge.

Thanking George Floyd for "sacrificing his life for justice," House Speaker Nancy Pelosi somehow made the whole affair into a blood ritual performed so that "justice," like crops or rain, could again return. In a prepared statement, attorneys for Floyd's family called it a step in the right direction but urged for Chauvin to be tried in federal court as well. Others, like CNN's Van Jones, called it a "punch in the gut," noting that Chauvin likely would serve fifteen years or less. The new president, whose decades-long record on criminal justice is anything but progressive, likewise called it a "step in the right direction," citing the "brave young woman" who filmed the murder, the officers who testified against their colleague, and the jury that adjudicated him among the "rare convergence" of citizens that delivered the case to conclusion.[70] While promising to support the George Floyd Justice in Policing Act—itself a predictable compendium of technocratic half measures like body cams and unenforceable mandates like "banning" choke holds—Joe Biden quietly promised U.S. police a huge shot in the arm in his budget request for fiscal year 2022, designating more than $100 million in new funding for the DHS, FBI, and other federal police agencies under the guise of "countering domestic terrorism." Not to be outdone, the budget of the DOJ's Community Oriented Policing Services (COPS) office is set to more than double. A pet project of Biden's since he helped to establish it with the 1994 crime bill, the COPS office is primed to deliver more than $330 million to hire more police, and suffice it to say it will do just that, provided that new racial diversity standards in hiring are met. All of this is to restate the obvious: just as they have always done, police and their benefactors are poised to use crisis and backlash to their benefit. With *New York Times* editorials arguing for police abolition alongside ginned-up warnings of "crime waves" plucked straight from the Clinton '90s, the great Leviathan, *deus mortalis*, the police rise again, restocked and rearmed to meet the enemy of the present. As a new world struggles to replace the old, so the saying goes, "now is the time of monsters."

So, now what? Toss up our hands and plunge into Hobbesian nihilism, agreeing finally with the Rufos of the world? I don't think so. To paraphrase another Black Panther, you cannot fight fire with fire, racism with racism, capitalism with capitalism, or reactionaries with equal reaction. No system can be reproduced and transformed simultaneously. I am not certain of much, but of this I am: the system of security, law, and order we call "the police" is in every sense a dead end. Abolitionists have been clear on this; the slow, plodding trail to another future begins with mutuality, collectivity, *solidarity*.

In 1759, Adam Smith, summoning Thomas Hobbes, wrote, "Death, as we say, is the king of terrors." Centuries later, Thomas Ligotti, conjuring H. P. Lovecraft, named consciousness the parent of all horrors. Separated by continents and cultures, something binds these words: fear of death. Smith and Hobbes recognized it as the life's blood of the political. For writers like Ligotti, it is not just the certainty of death but the insignificance of human life within the vast, inhospitable reaches of space and time that births true horror. These words, old and new, meet in Eugene Thacker's ontology. All manner of atrocity, blood, and gore spills forth from our futile attempts to create a secure world-for-us and to disown the primordial, anarchic world-in-itself. All the while, the unthinkable world-without-us looms above like the Elder Gods in Lovecraft's black seas of infinity. But if human solidarity is the only path to a better future, then it perhaps begins with the recognition of no future at all. Rather than fearing death, perhaps we should "earn our deaths," as James Baldwin wrote, by accepting responsibility for life, human and nonhuman.[71] Perhaps then our grip will loosen on this world. Perhaps then we will understand that while we have no time to waste making and fighting monsters, they are, nevertheless, in our midst.

ACKNOWLEDGMENTS

First and foremost, thanks to Corina Medley, whose unconditional love and support made this book possible. Thanks to Tyler Wall, who probably more than anyone has influenced my thinking about police. For endless insight and willingness to read and comment on anything I throw at him, thanks to Bill McClanahan. I am grateful for the support and friendship of Michelle Brown, who sometime in 2015 provided just the right amount of encouragement to begin this project.

For his essential writing on police and the politics of security, I am in the debt of Mark Neocleous. Likewise for their writing on police, thanks to David Correia, Alex Vitale, Geo Maher, Emma K. Russell, Brendan McQuade, Stuart Schrader, Jarrod Shanahan, and Ben Brucato. I am also grateful for the work of Eugene Thacker, Adam Kotsko, and Mark Fisher.

In criminology and everywhere else along the way, a big thank-you to Jeff Ferrell, Keith Hayward, Yvonne Jewkes, Mark Hamm, Majid Yar, Michael Fiddler, Theo Kindynis, Katherine Biber, Sarah Armstrong, Tammy Ayres, Nigel South, Oliver Smith, Eamonn Carrabine, Steve Wakeman, David Kauzlarich, Steve Hall, Eddy Green, Phil Carney, Rob Werth, and Nicholas Walrath.

I am always grateful to my first academic family, Ruth Triplett, Randy Gainey, Mona Danner, Dawn Rothe, Scott Maggard, Randy Myers, and Allison Chappell at Old Dominion University. Much love and gratitude to my Kentucky comrades, especially Justin Turner, Kaitlyn Selman, Victoria Collins, Michael Collins, Judah Schept, Douglas Peach, Avi Brisman, and Kyra Martinez. Thanks to my current academic home at Kansas State University, in particular Don Kurtz, Sue Williams, and Kevin Steinmetz.

Finally, a special thanks to Douglas Armato, Zenyse Miller, Kathleen Battles, Madeleine Vasaly, and the staff at the University of Minnesota Press: your patience and professionalism are unmatched.

NOTES

Introduction

1. Shirley Jackson, *The Haunting of Hill House* (New York: Penguin, 2013), 1.

2. Tariq Goddard and Eugene Thacker, *The Repeater Book of the Occult* (London: Repeater, 2020), 3.

3. Bruce Golding, "Sicko's Secret Recipe: 'Cannibal' Searched Google for Ways to Cook Women," *New York Post*, March 5, 2013, https://nypost.com/2013/03/05/sickos-secret-recipe-cannibal-searched-google-for-to-cook-women.

4. Rym Momtaz, "'Cannibal Cop' Goes on Trial," ABC News, February 8, 2013, https://abcnews.go.com/Blotter/cannibal-cop-trial/story?id=18442029.

5. Stephen Rex Brown, "Meat Mom Says Son Is No Cannibal," *NY Daily News*, November 24, 20212, https://www.pressreader.com/usa/new-york-daily-news/20121124/282368331935019; Dan Amira, "Tomorrow's *Post* Cannibal Cop Headline . . . Today!," Intelligencer, October 25, 2012, https://nymag.com/intelligencer/2012/10/cannibal-cop-post-headlines.html.

6. Adam Martin, "Cannibal Cop's Favorite Fantasy Dish Revealed at Trial," *New York Magazine*, February 23, 2013, http://nymag.com/intelligencer/2013/02/cannibal-cop-trial-reveals-his-favorite-dish.html.

7. Martin, "Cannibal Cop's Favorite Fantasy Dish."

8. User "tiddle," April 16, 2015, comment on Benjamin Weiser, "Gilberto Valle, Ex-New York Police Officer, Talks about His Cannibalism Fantasies in Film," *New York Times*, April 16, 2015, https://nyti.ms/33IzhT0#permid=14727276.

9. United States v. Valle. 12 Cr. 847 (PGG) (S.D.N.Y. Jun. 30, 2014), https://casetext.com/case/united-states-v-valle-22. Emphasis mine.

10. Bruce Golding, "'Cannibal Cop' Planned to Kidnap, Eat Woman for Thanksgiving: Prosecutor," *New York Post*, November 21, 2012, http://nypost.com/2012/11/21/cannibal-cop-planned-to-kidnap-eat-woman-for-thanksgiving-prosecutor.

11. A fact confirmed by the FBI. *The Federal Role in Investigation of Serial Violent Crime, Hearings before a Subcommittee of the Committee on Government Operations*, House of Representatives, 99th Cong., 2nd Session, April 9 and May 21, 1986, vol. 4, 20. Cited in Mark Neocleous, "The Monster and the Police: Dexter to Hobbes," *Radical Philosophy* 185 (May/June 2014): 8–18, 27.

12. Julia Kristeva, *Powers of Horror*, vol. 98 (University Presses of California, Columbia, and Princeton, 1982), 4.

13. Eugene Thacker, *Horror of Philosophy*, vol. 3, *Tentacles Longer than Night* (Alresford, England: Zer0/John Hunt Publishing, 2015), 6.

14. Eugene Thacker, *Horror of Philosophy*, vol. 1, *In the Dust of This Planet* (Alresford, England: Zer0/John Hunt Publishing, 2011), 1.

15. Standing in place of the economy, in Joshua Clover's words, the police are "the violence of the commodity made flesh." Clover, *Riot. Strike. Riot: The New Era of Uprisings* (New York: Verso, 2019), 126.

16. President's Task Force on 21st Century Policing, "Final Report of the President's Task Force on 21st Century Policing," 2015, 11–12.

17. The perspective of "procedural justice" is predicated on trust in the application of legal processes in a consistent and predictable manner. See the work of Tom R. Tyler on trust and its relation to criminal justice and specifically police: Tyler, *Why People Obey the Law* (Princeton: Princeton University Press, 2006).

18. For a more complete and thorough discussion of police and racial capitalism, see Ben Brucato, "Fabricating the Color Line in a White Democracy: From Slave Catchers to Petty Sovereigns," *Theoria* 61, no. 141 (2014): 30–54; Ben Brucato, "Policing Race and Racing Police: The Origin of US Police in Slave Patrols," *Social Justice* 47, no. 3–4 (September 2021); and Robin D. G. Kelley, "Insecure: Policing under Racial Capitalism," *Spectre* 1, no. 2 (Fall 2020), 12–37, 19.

19. Mark Neocleous, *The Fabrication of Social Order: A Critical Theory of Police Power* (London: Pluto Press, 2000).

20. W. J. Chambliss, "A Sociological Account of the Law of Vagrancy," *Social Problems* 12 (1964): 46–67.

21. It is this "immense hunt for the poor, idle people and vagabonds," writes Grégoire Chamayou, that set the inaugural scene of that which was to become modern policing. Chamayou, *Manhunts: A Philosophical History* (Princeton: Princeton University Press, 2012), 78.

22. Neocleous, *Fabrication of the Social Order*, 13–14.

23. The capacities and activities of slave patrols, as Hadden shows, tended to work in concert with the perceived threat of the slave population, or the actual rate of revolts, building up in times of perceived insecurity and falling back in others. This is precisely the relationship documented by Bryan Wagner in his account of the legendary escaped slave Bras-Coupé, whose menacing shadow was used to justify the presence of police in the lives of enslaved and free people alike. Wagner, *Disturbing the Peace* (Cambridge: Harvard University Press, 2010).

24. Ruth Wilson Gilmore, "Abolition Geography and the Problem of Innocence," *Tabula Rasa* 28 (2018): 57–77.

25. Kelley, "Insecure," 18.

26. Brucato, "Policing Race and Racing Police," 5.

27. Theodore W. Allen. *The Invention of the White Race* (New York: Verso, 1994).

28. Kelley, "Insecure," 19.

29. Sally E. Hadden, *Slave Patrols: Law and Violence in Virginia and the Carolinas* (Cambridge: Harvard University Press, 2003), 17.

30. Christian Parenti, "Policing the Color Line," *Nation* 273, no. 9 (2001): 30–32.

31. Hadden, *Slave Patrols*, 22.

32. Nikhil Pal Singh, "The Whiteness of Police," *American Quarterly* 66, no. 4 (2014): 1091–1099, 1094.

33. Micol Seigel, *Violence Work: State Power and the Limits of Police* (Durham: Duke University Press, 2018), 21.

34. Or "the whiteness of police," in Nikhil Pal Singh's phrasing.

35. Walter Johnson, *The Broken Heart of America: St. Louis and the Violent History of the United States* (New York: Basic Books, 2020), 6.

36. Ann Radcliffe, "On the Supernatural in Poetry," *Gothic Horror: A Guide for Students and Readers* (1826), 60–69.

37. John Clute, *The Darkening Garden: A Short Lexicon of Horror* (London: Payseur & Schmidt, 2006), 12.

38. Jacques Derrida, "Passages—From Traumatism to Promise" (interview with Elisabeth Weber), in *Points . . . : Interviews, 1974–1994*, trans. Elisabeth Weber and Peggy Kamuf (Palo Alto, Calif.: Stanford University Press, 1995), 372–95, here 385–86.

39. Or, as Noël Carroll aptly put it, horror stories prove the existence of the monster. Carroll, *The Philosophy of Horror: Or, Paradoxes of the Heart* (Routledge, 2003), 182. Or, as Darryl Jones put it, "the central power of horror is the spectacle of the monster." Jones, *Sleeping with the Lights On: The Unsettling Story of Horror* (Oxford: Oxford University Press, 2018), 29.

40. "The Police and the Ghetto," *Time*, July 19, 1969, 16–21.

41. Matt Ruff, *Lovecraft Country* (New York: Harper Perennial. 2017), 5.

42. "A Conversation with James Baldwin," WGBH, American Archive of Public Broadcasting (GBH and the Library of Congress), Boston, Mass., and Washington, D.C., June 24, 1963, http://americanarchive.org/catalog/cpb-aacip -15-0v89g5gf5r.

43. Noël Carroll, in his highly influential *Philosophy of Horror*, uses the term *impure* to describe how the monster occupies a liminal space between categories, contradicting and evading recognition and categorization.

44. Mark Neocleous, *The Monstrous and the Dead: Burke, Marx, Fascism* (Cardiff: University of Wales Press, 2005).

45. Huey P. Newton, *Revolutionary Suicide*, Penguin Classics Deluxe Edition (New York: Penguin, 2009), 176.

46. Jim Norman, "Confidence in Police Back at Historical Average," Gallup, July 10, 2017, https://news.gallup.com/poll/213869/confidence-police-back -historical-average.aspx. However, opinion polling consistently shows that a large majority of the U.S. public prefers crime control programs that "attack social and economic problems" over simply adding more police. Gallup, *The Gallup Poll*, December 21, 2010, http://www.gallup.com/poll/1603/Crime.aspx. Reprinted by permission.

47. Even now, months after the daylight murder of George Floyd, police still claim support from the majority of Americans. "Majority of Public Favors Giving Civilians the Power to Sue Police Officers for Misconduct," July 9, 2020, Pew Research Center, https://www.pewresearch.org/politics/2020/07/09/majority-of -public-favors-giving-civilians-the-power-to-sue-police-officers-for-misconduct.

48. Howard Phillip Lovecraft, *The Call of Cthulhu and Other Weird Stories* (New York: Penguin, 1999), 1.

49. Thomas Ligotti, *The Conspiracy against the Human Race: A Contrivance of Horror* (New York: Penguin, 2018), 15.

50. In a manner reminiscent of Slavoj Žižek's fetishistic disavowal, a cognitive prop that says, "I know, but I don't want to know that I know, so I don't know." Žižek, *Violence: Six Sideways Reflections* (New York: Picador, 2008), 59.

51. Žižek, *Violence*, 42

52. Thacker, *In the Dust of This Planet*, 9.

53. China Miéville, "Theses on Monsters," *Conjunctions* 59 (2012): 142–44.

54. Georges Canguilhem and Therese Jaeger, "Monstrosity and the Monstrous," *Diogenes* 10, no. 40 (1962): 27–42.

55. Joseph Packer and Ethan Stoneman, *A Feeling of Wrongness: Pessimistic Rhetoric on the Fringes of Popular Culture* (State College, Penn.: Penn State Press, 2018), 36.

56. James Baldwin, "The Art of Fiction No. 78," interview by Jordan Elgrably, *Paris Review*, no. 91 (Spring 1984), http://www.theparisreview.org /interviews/2994/james-baldwin-the-art-of-fiction-no-78-james-baldwin.

57. Jeffrey Jerome Cohen, "Monster Culture (Seven Theses)," in *Gothic Horror: A Guide for Students and Readers*, ed. Clive Bloom (London: Macmillan, 2007), 198–217.

58. For information about interpersonal violence and police crimes more generally, see the work of Philip Stinson: https://scholar.google.com/citations?user =rxOWsY4AAAAJ&hl=en&oi=ao.

59. Molly Redden, "Daniel Holtzclaw: Former Oklahoma City Police Officer Guilty of Rape," *Guardian*, December 10, 2015, https://www.theguardian .com/us-news/2015/dec/11/daniel-holtzclaw-former-oklahoma-city-police -officer-guilty-rape.

60. Philip M. Stinson, Henry A. Wallace Police Crime Database (v. 070821.1341), https://policecrime.bgsu.edu.

61. "Clearances," Crime in the United States 2017, Federal Bureau of Investigation, September 2020, https://ucr.fbi.gov/crime-in-the-u.s/2017/crime-in-the -u.s.-2017/topic-pages/clearances.

62. George Kelling, Tony Pate, Duane Dieckman, and Charles Brown, *The Kansas City Preventive Patrol Experiment: A Technical Report* (Washington, D.C.: Police Foundation, 1974).

63. Of course, like so many other police practices, "patrol" is not intended to reduce crime but to allow police to invade the spaces of everyday life. Patrol is, as David Correia and Tyler Wall suggest in *Police: A Field Guide*, concerned first and foremost with producing a particular kind of political and spatial order. Correia and Wall, *Police: A Field Guide* (Verso Books, 2018), 128.

64. Sarah Lustbader, "What's Not to Love about the NYPD Slowdown?," the Appeal, September 3, 2019, https://theappeal.org/whats-not-to-love-about -the-nypd-slowdown.

65. Christopher M. Sullivan and Zachary P. O'Keeffe, "Evidence that Cur-

tailing Proactive Policing Can Reduce Major Crime," *Nature Human Behaviour* 1, no. 10 (2017): 730.

66. Calvin Warren, *Ontological Terror: Blackness, Nihilism, and Emancipation* (Durham: Duke University Press, 2018), 1.

67. Warren, *Ontological Terror*, 4.

68. Evan Calder Williams, *Combined and Uneven Apocalypse: Luciferian Marxism* (London: John Hunt Publishing, 2011), 226.

69. Benjamin Noys, "The Horror of the Real: Žižek's Modern Gothic," *International Journal of Žižek Studies* 4, no. 4 (2016): 3.

70. Noys, "Horror of the Real," 1

71. Ligotti, *Conspiracy against the Human Race*, 54.

72. Following Levinas, Thacker uses "there is" to describe the inaccessible thing in itself—the Kantian noumenon, Hegel's "night of the word," the Lacanian Real.

73. Christopher P. Wilson, *Cop Knowledge: Police Power and Cultural Narrative in Twentieth-Century America* (Chicago: University of Chicago Press, 2000), 1.

74. D. H. Bayley, *Police for the Future* (Oxford: Oxford University Press, 1994).

75. Michael Lipsky, *Street-Level Bureaucracy: Dilemmas of the Individual in Public Service* (New York: Russell Sage Foundation, 2000).

76. Correia and Wall, *Police: A Field Guide*, 165–66.

77. Travis Linnemann, "Proof of Death: Police Power and the Visual Economies of Seizure, Accumulation and Trophy," *Theoretical Criminology* 21, no. 1 (2017): 57–77.

78. Christine Maxouris and Margaret Shuttleworth, "LAPD Officer Charged after Allegedly Fondling a Dead Woman's Breast," CNN, December 13, 2019, https://www.cnn.com/2019/12/13/us/lapd-officer-charged-fondling-dead-woman/index.html.

79. Neal King, *Heroes in Hard Times: Cop Action Movies in the US* (Philadelphia: Temple University Press, 1999).

80. Nathan Holmes, *Welcome to Fear City: Crime Film, Crisis, and the Urban Imagination* (Albany: SUNY Press, 2018).

81. Theodore Martin, "War-on-Crime Fiction," *PMLA* 136, no. 2 (2021): 213–28.

82. Drawing on examples from well-known crime films, Jared Sexton draws attention to the "institutionalized black complicity with the structures of white supremacy." Sexton, *Black Masculinity and the Cinema of Policing* (New York, NY: Palgrave Macmillan, 2017), 4.

83. Michael Aiello, "Policing the Masculine Frontier: Cultural Criminological Analysis of the Gendered Performance of Policing," *Crime, Media, Culture* 1, no. 10 (2014), 59–79.

84. On race: "1. Police Culture," Behind the Badge, Pew Research Center, September 24, 2018, https://www.pewresearch.org/social-trends/2017/01/11/police-culture/psdt_01-11-17-police-02-12-2. On gender: "Table 74: Full-Time Law Enforcement Employees," Crime in the United States 2019, Federal Bureau of Investigation, accessed January 7, 2022, https://ucr.fbi.gov/crime-in-the-u.s/2019/crime-in-the-u.s.-2019/tables/table-74.

85. Evan Calder Williams, "Objects of Derision," *New Inquiry* 13 (2012); Markus Dirk Dubber, *The Police Power: Patriarchy and the Foundations of American Government* (New York: Columbia University Press, 2005).

86. Larry Smith, "Dirty Harry Was Bad at His Job," Medium, July 19, 2019, https://medium.com/humungus/dirty-harry-was-bad-at-his-job-f57c0a6db45e.

87. Kerry Antholis, "Episode 2: Attorney General William Barr," *The Crime Story*, August 8, 2019, https://crimestory.com/2019/08/08/episode-2-attorney-general-william-barr.

88. Mark Seltzer famously dubbed this *wound culture*. Seltzer, *Serial Killers: Death and Life in America's Wound Culture* (New York: Routledge, 2013).

89. Philip Jenkins, *Using Murder: The Social Construction of Serial Homicide* (New York: Routledge, 2017), 8.

90. Harold Schechter, *Savage Pastimes: A Cultural History of Violent Entertainment* (London: Macmillan, 2005), 159.

91. Leslie Fiedler, *What Was Literature? Class Culture and Mass Society* (New York: Simon & Schuster, 1982), 50.

92. Wilson, *Cop Knowledge*, 136.

93. Citing local surveys, Laura Browder places the readership of true crime novels at roughly 75 percent women. Browder, "Dystopian Romance: True Crime and the Female Reader," *Journal of Popular Culture* 39, no. 6 (2006), 929.

94. Anne M. Vicary and Richard Fraley, "Captured by True Crime: Why Are Women Drawn to Tales of Rape, Murder, and Serial Killers?," *Social Psychological and Personality Science* 1, no. 1 (January 2010), 81–86; Kelli S. Boling and Kevin Hull, "Undisclosed Information—Serial Is My Favorite Murder: Examining Motivations in the True Crime Podcast Audience," *Journal of Radio and Audio Media* 25, no. 1 (January 2018), 92–108.

95. Laura Browder, "Dystopian Romance," 938.

96. Kate Tuttle, "'My Favorite Murder' Podcasters Get Even More Personal in Their New Book." *Los Angeles Times*, June 7, 2019, https://www.latimes.com/books/la-ca-jc-interview-karen-kilgariff-georgia-hardstark-20190606-story.html.

97. The curated gaming service Hunt A Killer allows subscribers to step into the fantasy role of police "profilers" and bring serial killers to justice. Each month, paid subscribers receive a box containing case file information and clues with which to do the work of the police, tracking and identifying the "unsub" and solving the string of murders.

98. Elizabeth Yardley, Emma Kelly, and Shona Robinson-Edwards, "Forever Trapped in the Imaginary of Late Capitalism? The Serialized True Crime Podcast as a Wake-Up Call in Times of Criminological Slumber," *Crime, Media, Culture* 15, no. 3 (December 2019), 503–21.

99. Stephen King, *Danse Macabre* (New York: Simon and Schuster, 2011), xxiii.

100. Ligotti, *Conspiracy against the Human Race*, 31.

101. Steve Hall, *Theorizing Crime and Deviance: A New Perspective* (Los Angeles: Sage, 2012), 52.

1. Bad Cops and True Detectives

1. Desson Howe, "Bad Lieutenant," *Washington Post*, January 29, 1993, https://www.washingtonpost.com/wp-srv/style/longterm/movies/videos/badlieutenantnc17hinson_a0a7e1.htm.

2. The symbolic order provides a predictable set of rules, which allow subjects to navigate everyday life. Following philosopher Adrian Johnston (*Žižek's Ontology*), criminologists Steve Hall and Simon Winlow (*Revitalizing Criminological Theory*) assert that the symbolic order cannot be reduced to an Althusserian ideological state apparatus or Gramscian hegemony and instead must be understood as a habituated practice of subjects' everyday sense-making, accomplished to escape objectless anxiety and the horror of the Real.

3. Walter Benjamin, "Critique of Violence," *Reflections* 14, no. 3 (1978): 277–300.

4. Steve Hall and Simon Winlow, *Revitalizing Criminological Theory: Towards a New Ultra-Realism* (London: Routledge, 2015), 111.

5. Benjamin, "Critique of Violence," 286–87.

6. Adam Kotsko, *Why We Love Sociopaths: A Guide to Late Capitalist Television* (London: John Hunt Publishing, 2012).

7. *The Wire*, season 3, episode 9, "Slapstick," directed by Alex Zakrzewski, aired November 21, 2004, on HBO. Emphasis mine.

8. Neal King, "Calling Dirty Harry a Liar: A Critique of Displacement Theories of Popular Criminology," *New Review of Film and Television Studies* 11, no. 2 (2013): 171–90.

9. Nicole Rafter, *Shots in the Mirror: Crime Films and Society* (New York: Oxford University Press, 2006).

10. Neal King, *Heroes in Hard Times* (Philadelphia: Temple University Press, 1999), 2.

11. Rafter, *Shots in the Mirror*, 131.

12. Giorgio Agamben, *Means without End: Notes on Politics* (Minneapolis: University of Minnesota Press, 2000), 103.

13. Georges Bataille, *Erotism: Death and Sensuality* (San Francisco: City Lights Books, 1986), 86–88.

14. Kotsko, *Why We Love Sociopaths*, 76.

15. Jean Comaroff and John Comaroff, *The Truth about Crime: Sovereignty, Knowledge, Social Order* (Chicago: University of Chicago Press, 2016), xxii.

16. Franco Moretti, "The Dialectic of Fear," *New Left Review* 136 (182): 67–85.

17. Mark Steven, *Splatter Capital* (London: Watkins Media Limited, 2017), 40.

18. Steven, *Splatter Capital*, 40

19. Moretti, "Dialectic of Fear," 68.

20. Mark Neocleous, *The Universal Adversary: Security, Capital and "the Enemies of All Mankind"* (London: Routledge, 2016), 66.

21. Leo Braudy, *Haunted: On Ghosts, Witches, Vampires, Zombies, and Other Monsters of the Natural and Supernatural Worlds* (New Haven: Yale University Press, 2016), 141.

22. Mark Neocleous, "The Monster and the Police: Dexter to Hobbes," *Radical Philosophy* 185 (2014): 8–18.

23. Aaron Baker, "Beyond the Thin Line of Black and Blue: Movies and Police Misconduct in Los Angeles," in *Bad: Infamy, Darkness, Evil, and Slime on Screen*, ed. Murray Pomerance (Albany: SUNY Press, 2012), 55–64, 57.

24. Antoine Fuqua, dir., *Training Day* (Los Angeles: Warner Bros. Pictures, 2001). Emphasis mine.

25. John Hillcoat, *Triple 9* (Atlanta: Worldview Entertainment and Anonymous Content, 2016). Emphasis mine. Harrelson's character also warns how the "monster has gone digital" in relation to identity theft: "You should be smart enough to know that the monster has gone digital. Be careful what you instagoogletweetface."

26. Benjamin Noys, "The Horror of the Real: Žižek's Modern Gothic," *International Journal of Žižek Studies* 4, no. 4 (2016): 2.

27. In the disjuncture between these two mutually exclusive poles lies ambiguous and uncertain territory, what Tzvetan Todorov (1975) called the fantastic.

28. Sarah Schulman, *Conflict Is Not Abuse: Overstating Harm, Community Responsibility, and the Duty of Repair* (Vancouver: Arsenal Pulp Press, 2016), 86.

29. These facts, with which racial minorities and poor communities are quite familiar, mirror what Hall and Winlow have called the *abject concrete universal*, "the grim individual experiences that represent the totality of the liberal-capitalist system." Building on the work of Adrian Johnston, they suggest that any universality—or constellation, in Benjamin's language—such as the inherent violence of police is the outcome and product of the struggle for structural dominance. But as Benjamin recognized, police violence actually marks the state's waning power, the precise moment at which its dreams of law and order begin to unravel. In my view, this unraveling marks a gap in the symbolic order and offers a glimpse of the Real—*the horror of police*. Hall and Winlow, *Revitalizing Criminological Theory*, 110; Adrian Johnston, *Žižek's Ontology: A Transcendental Materialist Theory of Subjectivity* (Evanston, Ill.: Northwestern University Press, 2008), 172.

30. Mark Fisher, *Capitalist Realism: Is There No Alternative?* (London: John Hunt Publishing, 2009).

31. Mark Fisher, *Capitalist Realism*, 2.

32. Mark Fisher, *Capitalist Realism*, 4.

33. Allison Shonkwiler and Leigh Claire La Berge likewise suggest that capitalist realism's strength lies in its ability to articulate the violence produced by capitalism, the lived economic, social, and affective instabilities of a world governed by ruthless self-interest, and how these forces align to disclose imagined alternatives. Shonkwiler and La Berge, eds., *Reading Capitalist Realism* (Iowa City: University of Iowa Press, 2014), 6.

34. Noys, "Horror of the Real," 2.

35. David Russell, "Monster Roundup Reintegrating the Horror Genre," in *Refiguring American Film Genres*, ed. N. Browne (Berkeley: University of California Press, 1998), 233–54, 252.

36. In a list of thirty-one cop clichés, Drew Magery, writing for Dead-

spin, notes that "despite shooting lots of people and breaking numerous law-enforcement procedures, to say nothing of the law itself, two cops walk away from the crime scene totally absolved of everything." Drew Magery, "31 Cop-Buddy Clichés on True Detective," Deadspin, 2014, http://deadspin.com/31-buddy-cop -cliches-on-true-detective-1540310306.

37. With an overarching "philosophico-theological" thrust and a conclusion that left many questions unanswered, *True Detective* can be considered a meta-physical detective story. Patricia Merivale and Susan Elizabeth Sweeney, eds., *Detecting Texts: The Metaphysical Detective Story from Poe to Postmodernism* (Phila-delphia: University of Pennsylvania Press, 2011), 2–4.

38. Howard Phillip Lovecraft, *Supernatural Horror in Literature* (London: The Palingenesis Project/Wermod and Wermod Publishing Group, 2013).

39. Alexis Madrigal, "The Sacrificial Landscape of *True Detective*," *Atlantic*, March 7, 2014, http://www.theatlantic.com/technology/archive/2014/03/the -sacrificial-landscape-of-emtrue-detective-em/284302. Emphasis mine.

40. *True Detective*, season 1, episode 1, "The Long Bright Dark," directed by Cary Joji Fukunaga, aired January 12, 2014, on HBO.

41. Some examples: *Cobra* (1983), *The Satan Killer* (1993), *The Hideaway* (1995), *End of Days* (1999).

42. Robert Hicks, *In Pursuit of Satan: The Police and the Occult* (Amherst, N.Y.: Prometheus Books, 1991).

43. Richard Ofshe and Ethan Watters, "Making Monsters," *Society* 30, no. 3 (1993): 4–16.

44. Joseph P. Laycock, "'Time Is a Flat Circle': *True Detective* and the Specter of Moral Panic in American Pop Culture," *Journal of Religion and Popular Culture* 27, no. 3 (2015): 220–35.

45. Mary DeYoung, "Another Look at Moral Panics: The Case of Satanic Day Care Centers," *Deviant Behavior* 19, no. 3 (1998): 257–78.

46. Perhaps reflecting the ceaseless desire to locate the "real" within fantastic, Vice produced a short documentary, *The Real "True Detective"?* (2014), concern-ing a church-based child molestation case in rural Louisiana, which inspired Pizzolatto's early work on the series. While police accusations of satanism proved unfounded, the specter of ritual abuse continues to loom over the tiny town.

47. Philip Jenkins, "Weird Tales: The Story of a Delusion," in *The Last Penta-cle of the Sun: Writings in Support of the West Memphis Three*, ed. M. W. Anderson and Brett Alexander Savory (Vancouver: Arsenal Pulp Press, 2004), 35–41, 37.

48. Margaret Murray, *The Witch Cult in Western Europe* (Oxford: Oxford University Press, 1921).

49. Georges Bataille, *The Trial of Gilles de Rais* (Los Angeles: Amok Books, 1991).

50. Bataille, *Trial of Gilles de Rais*, 16.

51. Paul O'Brien, "Religion, Domination, and Serial Killing: Western Cul-ture and Murder," in *Serial Killing: A Philosophical Anthology*, ed. Connole Edna and Gary Shipley (Lexington, Ky.: Schism, 2015), 183–98, 197–98.

52. Neocleous, *Universal Adversary*, 85.

53. *True Detective*, "The Long Bright Dark."

54. Carl Schmitt, *Political Theology: Four Chapters on the Concept of Sovereignty*, trans. G. Schwab (Chicago: University of Chicago Press, 2005).

55. Schmitt, *Political Theology*, 36.

56. Grégoire Chamayou, *Manhunts: A Philosophical History* (Princeton: Princeton University Press, 2012), 91.

57. As with the serial killer, Neocleous (*Universal Adversary*, 66) makes a similar observation regarding the secularization of Christian eschatology, invoked by the politics of apocalypse and the monster/figure of the zombie.

58. *True Detective*, season 1, episode 3, "The Locked Room," directed by Cary Joji Fukunaga, aired January 26, 2014, on HBO.

59. Richard Tithecott, *Of Men and Monsters: Jeffrey Dahmer and the Construction of the Serial Killer* (Madison: University of Wisconsin Press, 1997).

60. Brian Jarvis, "Monsters Inc.: Serial Killers and Consumer Culture," *Crime, Media, Culture* 3, no. 3 (2007): 326–44.

61. Supplementary material, *True Detective*, season 1 [3 discs], HBO Home Video, 2014.

62. Hart and Cohle's foe, the killer and criminal more generally, then, powerfully demonstrates how the politics of enmity are not a matter of simple illegality. Indeed, as Žižek suggests, because the enemy is "by definition, always—up to a point, at least—invisible, he looks like one of us," a crucial task for the police power is to hunt the monster, to make it known—to give it a name. Slavoj Žižek, *Welcome to the Desert of the Real! Five Essays on September 11 and Related Dates* (London: Verso, 2002), 109.

63. "Behind the Scenes: Interview with Nic Pizzolatto," *True Detective*, season 1, January 12, 2014, HBO.

64. Chamayou, *Manhunts*, 91.

65. *True Detective*, "The Locked Room."

66. *True Detective*, "The Locked Room." Emphasis mine.

67. Alain Badiou, *Theory of the Subject* (London: A&C Black, 2009). Badiou famously diagrams a philosophical topology of five key explanations for the emergence of the subject from the tensions between the external material world and the internal thinking being: the radical "subjective metaphysical idealism" of George Berkeley, where all that exists is so through thought alone; Kantian "objective metaphysical idealism," where the thinking being exists but is forever divorced from "things-in-themselves"; Hegelian "dialectical idealism," where the interior thinking being produces its externally existing realities; a "metaphysical materialism" that insists on the existence of material reality independent of thought and perception; and lastly the Marxist "materialist dialectic," where the material world and internal thought perpetually produce and reaffirm the other. Thanks to Stephen Wakeman for a concise summary. See Stephen Wakeman, "The 'One Who Knocks' and the 'One Who Waits': Gendered Violence in *Breaking Bad*," *Crime, Media, Culture* 14, no. 2 (2018): 213–22.

68. Kevin Cimino, "True Criminal: An Analysis and Discussion of the Crimes Committed by Detective Russian Cohle in Season One of HBS's Mini-Series

True Detective," Pace *Intellectual Property, Sports & Entertainment Law Forum* 6 (2016): 52.

69. Mark Neocleous, "Securitati perpetuae," *Radical Philosophy* 2, no. 6 (Winter 2019): 31.

70. *True Detective,* season 1, episode 2, "Seeing Things," directed by Cary Joji Fukunaga, aired January 19, 2014, on HBO. Emphasis mine.

71. Hall and Winlow, *Revitalizing Criminological Theory,* 115.

72. *True Detective,* "The Locked Room."

73. Emily Nussbaum, "Cool Story, Bro: The Shallow Deep Talk of True Detective," *New Yorker,* March 3, 2014.

74. *True Detective,* "The Long Bright Dark."

75. *True Detective,* season 1, episode 8, "Form and Void," directed by Cary Joji Fukunaga, aired March 9, 2014, on HBO.

76. Erin K. Stapleton, "The Corpse Is the Territory: The Body of Dora Lange in True Detective," in *True Detection,* ed. Edna Connole, Paul Ennis, and Nicola Masciandaro (Lexington, Ky.: Schism, 2015), 164–78, 178.

77. Eugene Thacker, *Horror of Philosophy,* vol. 1, *In the Dust of this Planet* (London: John Hunt Publishing, 2011), 5.

78. Mark Fisher, *Capitalist Realism,* 9.

79. Ian Bogost, *Alien Phenomenology, or, What It's Like to Be a Thing* (Minneapolis: University of Minnesota Press, 2012), 4.

80. Graham Harman, *Weird Realism: Lovecraft and Philosophy* (London: John Hunt Publishing, 2012), 16.

81. Hall and Winlow, *Revitalizing Criminological Theory,* 107.

82. Simon Winlow, "Enlightened Catastrophism," Teesside Center for Realist Criminology, December 13, 2016, https://blogs.tees.ac.uk/tcrc/2016/12/13/enlightened-catastrophism.

83. The dystopian present is of course characterized by police in the United States who kill unarmed people, most of whom are poor and people of color, at a rate not rivaled by other like nations.

84. This aligns with the growing call for police abolition and more broadly with the politics of antisecurity.

85. Henri Lefebvre, *Critique of Everyday Life: Foundations for a Sociology of the Everyday* (London: Verso, 2014), 912.

2. The Police at the End of the World, or The Political Theology of the Thin Blue Line

1. Mike Davis, *Ecology of Fear: Los Angeles and the Imagination of Disaster* (London: Macmillan, 1998).

2. Evan Osnos, "Doomsday Prep for the Super Rich," *New Yorker,* January 22, 2017, https://www.newyorker.com/magazine/2017/01/30/doomsday-prep-for-the-super-rich.

3. Majid Yar, *Crime and the Imaginary of Disaster: Post-Apocalyptic Fictions and the Crisis of Social Order* (London: Palgrave, 2015), 23.

4. Mark Neocleous, *The Fabrication of Social Order: A Critical Theory of Police Power* (London: Pluto Press, 2000).

5. Geoff Mann and Joel Wainwright, *Climate Leviathan: A Political Theory of Our Planetary Future* (London: Verso Books, 2018), 15.

6. Mike Davis, "Who Will Build the Ark?" *New Left Review* 61 (January–February 2010): 29–46, 38.

7. In *The Worst Is Yet to Come*, Peter Fleming makes a similar point, describing a condition of *nihiliberalism*, "where our ennui intersects with commodification, voter apathy and rash individualism." Fleming, *The Worst Is Yet to Come: A Post-Apocalyptic Survival Guide* (London: Repeater, 2018), 20.

8. Carlie Brosseau and Alex Lang, "Testimony Reveals How 2 SC Women Drowned in Sheriff's Van after Hurricane Florence Floods," Greenville News, May 29, 2019, https://www.greenvilleonline.com/story/news/2019/05/29/hurricane-florence-horry-county-deputies-sc-drowning-deaths-nikki-green-and-wendy-newton/1268978001.

9. Jason W. Moore, "The Capitalocene, Part I: On the Nature and Origins of Our Ecological Crisis," *Journal of Peasant Studies* 44, no. 3 (2017): 594–630.

10. In his introduction to Hobbes's *Behemoth*, Stephen Holmes seizes upon what he sees as the book's most striking suggestion: "The power of the mighty hath no foundation but in the opinion and belief of the people," which leads him to conclude that the struggle for sovereign power is "fought on a battlefield of wholly unreal imaginings or rationally unjustifiable assumptions about the future. Whoever controls the future (or the idea people have of the future) has unstoppable power." Holmes, "Introduction," in Thomas Hobbes, *Behemoth: Or the Long Parliament* (Chicago: University of Chicago Press, 1990), xiv.

11. Neocleous, *Universal Adversary*, 2.

12. "Feare of things invisible, is the natural Seed of that, which every one in himself calleth Religion; and in them that worship, or feare that Power otherwise than they do, Superstition." Thomas Hobbes, *Thomas Hobbes: Leviathan*, Longman Library of Primary Sources in Philosophy (London: Routledge, 2016), 63.

13. Michael Paul Rogin, *"Ronald Reagan," the Movie: And Other Episodes in Political Demonology* (Berkeley: University of California Press, 1987).

14. Carl Schmitt, *The Concept of the Political: Expanded Edition* (Chicago: University of Chicago Press, 2008), 49.

15. Schmitt, *Concept of the Political*, 49.

16. "For to the enemy concept belongs the ever present possibility of combat. All peripherals must be left aside from this term, including military details and the development of weapons technology. War is armed combat between organized political entities; civil war is armed combat within an organized unit. A self-laceration endangers the survival of the latter. The essence of a weapon is that it is a means of physically killing human beings. Just as the term enemy, the word combat, too, is to be understood in its original existential sense. It does not mean competition, nor does it mean pure intellectual controversy nor symbolic wrestlings in which, after all, every human being is somehow always involved,

for it is a fact that the entire life of a human being is a struggle and every human being symbolically a combatant. The friend, enemy, and combat concepts receive their real meaning precisely because they refer to the real possibility of physical killing. War follows from enmity. War is the existential negation of the enemy. It is the most extreme consequence of enmity. It does not have to be common, normal, something ideal, or desirable. But it must nevertheless remain a real possibility for as long as the concept of the enemy remains valid." Schmitt, *Concept of the Political*, 32–33.

17. Adam Kotsko, *Neoliberalism's Demons: The Political Theology of Late Capital* (Palo Alto: Stanford University Press, 2020), 25.

18. Judith Butler, *Precarious Life: The Powers of Mourning and Violence* (London: Verso Books, 2006), 56.

19. Butler, *Precarious Life*, 56.

20. Tyler Wall, "Ordinary Emergency: Drones, Police, and Geographies of Legal Terror," *Antipode* 48, no. 4 (September 2016): 1122–39, 1132.

21. Wall, "Ordinary Emergency," 11.

22. Oren Moverman, dir., *Rampart* (Los Angeles: Millennium Entertainment, 2011).

23. National Public Radio, "Ferguson Documents: Officer Darren Wilson's Testimony," *The Two-Way* (blog), November 25, 2014, https://www.npr.org /sections/thetwo-way/2014/11/25/366519644/ferguson-docs-officer-darren -wilsons-testimony. Emphasis mine.

24. Hadden, *Slave Patrols*.

25. Zygmunt Bauman, "Modernity and Ambivalence," *Theory, Culture & Society* 7, no. 2–3 (1990): 143–69.

26. P. R. Lockhart, "A Black Security Guard Caught a Shooting Suspect— Only to Be Shot by Police Minutes Later," *Vox*, updated February 6, 2019, https://www.vox.com/identities/2018/11/12/18088874/jemel-roberson-police -shooting-security-illinois-ian-covey.

27. Khushbu Shah, "EJ Bradford Was Shot Three Times from Behind by Officer, Autopsy Reveals," *Guardian*, December 3, 2018, https://www.theguardian .com/us-news/2018/dec/03/ej-bradford-alabama-police-mall-shooting -autopsy.

28. Karen E. Fields and Barbara J. Fields, *Racecraft: The Soul of Inequality in American Life* (London: Verso Books, 2014), 89.

29. Daniel Denvir, "Beyond 'Race Relations': An Interview with Barbara Fields and Karen Fields," Jacobin, January 17, 2018, https://www.jacobinmag.com/2018 /01/racecraft-racism-barbara-karen-fields.

30. Schmitt, *Concept of the Political*, 32–33.

31. Carl Schmitt, *The Leviathan in the State Theory of Thomas Hobbes: Meaning and Failure of a Political Symbol* (Chicago: University of Chicago Press, 2008), 31.

32. As Kotsko explains in *Neoliberalism's Demons*, political theology can be understood in any combination of three ways: "theologically informed political action, treating politics in quasi-religious ways, and the general study of such

transfers between the political and theological realms." Adam Kotsko, *Neoliberalism's Demons*, 25.

33. Antonin Artaud, *Artaud Anthology* (San Francisco: City Lights Books, 1965), 114. Emphasis mine.

34. Correia and Wall, *Police: A Field Guide*, 121–22.

35. Wall finds reference to police as a thin blue line as early as 1860s London. Tyler Wall, "The Police Invention of Humanity: Notes on the 'Thin Blue Line,'" *Crime, Media, Culture* 16, no. 3 (2020): 319–36, endnote 5.

36. David Shaw, "Chief Parker Molded LAPD Image—Then Came the '60s: Police: Press Treated Officers as Heroes until Social Upheaval Prompted Skepticism and Confrontation," *Los Angeles Times*, May 25, 1992, https://www.latimes.com/archives/la-xpm-1992-05-25-mn-236-story.html.

37. Mike Davis, *City of Quartz: Excavating the Future in Los Angeles* (London: Verso, 1990), 126.

38. Edward Escobar, "Bloody Christmas and the Irony of Police Professionalism: The Los Angeles Police Department, Mexican Americans, and Police Reform in the 1950s," *Pacific Historical Review* 72, no. 2 (2003): 171–99, 190.

39. Kotsko, *Neoliberalism's Demons*, 25.

40. John Sbardellati, *J. Edgar Hoover Goes to the Movies: The FBI and the Origins of Hollywood's Cold War* (Ithaca: Cornell University Press, 2012).

41. Christopher Sharrett, "Jack Webb and the Vagaries of Right-Wing TV Entertainment," *Cinema Journal* 51, no. 4 (2012): 165–71, 167.

42. Davis, *City of Quartz*, 251.

43. Alisa Sarah Kramer, "William H. Parker and the Thin Blue Line: Politics, Public Relations and Policing in Postwar Los Angeles" (PhD diss., American University, 2007).

44. Stuart Schrader, *Badges without Borders: How Global Counterinsurgency Transformed American Policing*, vol. 56 (Berkeley: University of California Press, 2019), 217. Emphasis mine.

45. David Ayer, dir., *End of Watch* (Los Angeles: Open Road Films, 2012). Emphasis mine.

46. "About the Show," *The Green Line*, accessed January 10, 2022, http://protectingthegreenline.com/about-the-show.

47. Tim Steller, "Steller: Border Patrol Union Embraces Hard-Line Politics," Tuscon.com, May 16, 2017, https://tucson.com/news/local/columnists/steller/steller-border-patrol-union-embraces-hard-line-politics/article_1a406237-8433-5870-83f6-5cffc0c91b75.html.

48. Judith Shklar, "The Liberalism of Fear," in *Political Liberalism: Variations on a Theme*, ed. Shaun P. Young (Albany: SUNY Press, 2004), 149–66.

49. This is a sentiment shared by Freud, who wrote, "Men are not gentle creatures, who want to be loved, who at the most can defend themselves if they are attacked; they are, on the contrary, creatures among whose instinctual endowments is to be reckoned a powerful share of aggressiveness. As a result, their neighbor is for them not only a potential helper or sexual object, but also someone who tempts them to satisfy their aggressiveness on him, to exploit his ca-

pacity for work without compensation, to use him sexually without his consent, to seize his possessions, to humiliate him, to cause him pain, to torture and to kill him. Homo homini lupus [man is wolf to man]. Who in the face of all his experience of life and of history, will have the courage to dispute this assertion? As a rule this cruel aggressiveness waits for some provocation or puts itself at the service of some other purpose, whose goal might also have been reached by milder measures. In circumstances that are favorable to it, when the mental counter-forces which ordinarily inhibit it are out of action, it also manifests itself spontaneously and reveals man as a savage beast to whom consideration towards his own kind is something alien. Anyone who calls to mind the atrocities committed during the racial migrations or the invasions of the Huns, or by the people known as Mongols under Jenghiz Khan and Tamerlane, or at the capture of Jerusalem by the pious Crusaders, or even, indeed, the horrors of the recent World War—anyone who calls these things to mind will have to bow humbly before the truth of this view." Sigmund Freud, *Civilization and Its Discontents* (New York: Norton, 1961), 58–59, 92.

50. Jacques Derrida, *The Beast and the Sovereign*, vol. I, *The Seminars of Jacques Derrida*, trans. Geoffrey Bennington (Chicago: University of Chicago Press, 2009), 17.

51. Derrida, *Beast and the Sovereign*, 18.

52. William Connolly, *Political Theory and Modernity* (Ithaca: Cornell University Press, 1988), 29.

53. Ryan Meldrum, Peter Lehmann, and Jamie Flexon, "Who Would 'Purge'? Low Self-Control, Psychopathy, and Offending in the Absence of Legal Controls," *Crime & Delinquency* 67, no. 10 (2021): 1582–1613.

54. Bill Wright, "Eastern Kentucky Faces Budget Shortfall Crisis," *Lexington Herald-Leader*, February 10, 2019, 1A–8A.

55. A. Merica, "Cop: OK, I'm Done. It's Time for the Purge," Law Enforcement Today, December 27, 2018, https://www.lawenforcementtoday.com/cop -time-for-the-purge.

56. Elaine de Valle, "Our Own 'The Purge' as Miami-Dade Police Cut from Budget?," Political Cortadito, July 17, 2014, http://www.politicalcortadito.com /2014/07/17/the-purge-miami-dade-police.

57. Kim Phillips-Fein, *Fear City: New York's Fiscal Crisis and the Rise of Austerity Politics* (New York: Metropolitan Books, 2017).

58. Display Ad 97—No Title, *New York Times*, June 10, 1975, 33. ISSN 03624331.

59. Tim Elfrink, "William Barr Says 'Communities' That Protest Cops Could Lose 'the Police Protection They Need,'" *Washington Post*, December 4, 2019, https://www.washingtonpost.com/nation/2019/12/04/william-barr-police -protests-communities-race.

60. William Barr, *The Case for More Incarceration* (Washington, D.C.: U.S. Department of Justice, Office of Policy Development, 1992), v.

61. William Davies, *The Limits of Neoliberalism: Authority, Sovereignty and the Logic of Competition* (Los Angeles: Sage, 2016).

62. Kotsko, *Neoliberalism's Demons*, 73.

63. Kotsko, *Neoliberalism's Demons*, 84.

64. Rogin, *"Ronald Reagan," the Movie*, xiii.

65. William Bennett, *The De-Valuing of America: The Fight for Our Culture and Our Children* (New York: Simon and Schuster, 1994), 105. Emphasis mine.

66. William Bennett, *Body Count: Moral Poverty . . . and How to Win America's War against Crime and Drugs* (New York: Simon & Schuster, 1996), 25–26.

67. Bennett, *Body Count*, 25.

68. In 2005, when commenting on the controversial suggestion that legalized abortion was a key antecedent to the mid-1990s crime drop, Bennett would go so far as to state, "If you wanted to reduce crime, you could, if that were your sole purpose, you could abort every black baby in this country, and your crime rate would go down." Not only agreeing with the now largely discredited theory, Bennett tipped his hand by suggesting that aborting *Black youth*, specifically, would offer a path to crime control.

69. "Hillary Clinton Campaign Speech," Keene State College, C-SPAN, January 25, 1996, https://www.c-span.org/video/?69606-1/hillary-clinton-campaign-speech.

70. Jessie Hellmann, "Trump: 'How Quickly People Forget' Clinton 'Super-predator' Remark," the Hill, August 26, 2016, https://thehill.com/blogs/ballot-box/presidential-races/293477-trump-how-quickly-people-forget-clinton-super-predator.

71. "Central Park Horror: Wolf Pack's Prey, Female Jogger Near Death after Savage Attack by Roving Gang," April 21, 1989, *New York Daily News*.

72. David E. Pitt, "Jogger's Attackers Terrorized at Least 9 in 2 Hours," *New York Times*, April 22, 1989, 1.

73. Michael Welch, Eric Price, and Nana Yankey, "Youth Violence and Race in the Media: The Emergence of 'Wilding' as an Invention of the Press," *Race, Gender & Class* 11, no. 2 (2004): 36–58, 44–45.

74. "N.Y.-Style 'Wilding' Death in Boston," *New York Post*, November 21, 1990, 16.

75. Donald Trump, "BRING BACK THE DEATH PENALTY. BRING BACK OUR POLICE!," *Daily News* 1, no. 5 (1989).

76. Lee Wohlfert-Wilberg, "In the Manhattan Real-Estate Game, Billionaire Donald Trump Holds the Winning Cards," *People* 16, no. 20 (1981), https://people.com/archive/in-the-manhattan-real-estate-game-billionaire-donald-trump-holds-the-winning-cards-vol-16-no-20.

77. "Full Text: 2017 Donald Trump Inauguration Speech Transcript," Politico, January 20, 2017, https://www.politico.com/story/2017/01/full-text-donald-trump-inauguration-speech-transcript-233907. Emphasis mine.

78. Kotsko, *Neoliberalism's Demons*, 116.

79. Julia Preston. "Five Lies in Trump's Favorite Campaign Ad," Marshall Project, November 2, 2018, https://www.themarshallproject.org/2018/11/02/five-lies-in-trump-s-favorite-campaign-ad.

80. Tim Newburn and Trevor Jones, "Symbolic Politics and Penal Populism:

The Long Shadow of Willie Horton," *Crime, Media, Culture* 1, no. 1 (2005): 72–87.

81. Calder Williams, *Combined and Uneven Apocalypse*, 24.

82. Michael Dillon, "Specters of Biopolitics: Finitude, Eschaton, and Katechon," *South Atlantic Quarterly* 110, no. 3 (2011): 780–92.

83. Chris Lloyd, "Judge, Jury, Executioner: Judge Dredd, Jacques Derrida, Drones," in *Graphic Justice: Intersections of Comics and Law*, ed. Thomas Giddens (London: Routledge, 2015), 201–18.

84. Martin Barker, "Taking the Extreme Case: Understanding a Fascist Fan of Judge Dredd," in *Trash Aesthetics: Popular Culture and Its Audience*, ed. Deborah Cartmell (London: Pluto Press, 1997), 20.

85. Barker, "Taking the Extreme Case," 26.

86. Neocleous, *Universal Adversary*.

87. Hobbes, *Thomas Hobbes: Leviathan*, 174.

88. Franco Berardi, *Heroes: Mass Murder and Suicide* (London: Verso Books, 2015).

89. Craig Atkinson, dir., *Do Not Resist* (Columbia, S.C.: Vanish Films, 2017).

90. Niko Georgiades, "Bulletproof Warrior Training Manual Released," Unicorn Riot, May 25, 2018, https://unicornriot.ninja/2018/bulletproof-warrior -training-manual-released.

91. Atkinson, *Do Not Resist*.

92. "'Superhero' Parking for Veterans, First Responders," FOX 5 Atlanta, March 9, 2016, http://www.fox5atlanta.com/news/most-popular/superhero -parking-for-veterans-first-responders.

93. David Kocieniewski, "Success of Elite Police Unit Exacts a Toll on the Streets," *New York Times*, February 15, 1999, 1.

94. "NYPD Challenge Coins: Members Only," Research and Destroy New York City, accessed January 10, 2022, http://researchdestroy.com/nypd-challenge -coins.pdf.

95. Tyler Wall, "Superpredators: Police on the Hunt," Verso, March 30, 2018, https://www.versobooks.com/blogs/3715-superpredators-police-on-the-hunt.

96. Honoré-Antoine Frégier, "Histoire de l'Administration de la Police de Paris Depuis Philippe Auguste jusqu'aux États Généraux de 1789," 2 vols. (Paris: 1850). Cited in Pasquale Pasquino, "Theatrum Politicum: The Genealogy of Capital-Police and the State of Prosperity," in *The Foucault Effect*. ed. Graham Burchell et al. (Chicago: University of Chicago Press, 1991), 108; and Tyler Wall, "'For the Very Existence of Civilization': The Police Dog and Racial Terror," *American Quarterly* 68, no. 4 (2016): 861–82, 869.

97. Brad Hamilton, "Meet the Most Decorated Detective in NYPD History," *New York Post*, February 15, 2015, https://nypost.com/2015/02/15/meet -the-most-decorated-detective-in-nypd-history.

98. Edward Burks, "Burglary Victim Slain by Mistake," *New York Times*, November 2, 1972, page 1, https://www.nytimes.com/1972/11/02/archives /burglary-victim-slain-by-mistake-traded-shots-with-police-patrolman.html.

99. "NYPD Challenge Coins: Members Only."

100. Chris Kyle, Scott McEwen, and Jim DeFelice, *American Sniper* (New York: Nimrod, 2012), 232.

101. Kyle et al., *American Sniper*, 231.

102. Abraham Riesman, "Why Cops and Soldiers Love the Punisher," *Vulture*, November 16, 2017, http://www.vulture.com/2017/11/marvel-punisher -police-military-fandom.html.

103. Chris Gavaler, "The Ku Klux Klan and the Birth of the Superhero," *Journal of Graphic Novels and Comics* 4, no. 2 (2013): 191–208, 192.

104. Neal Curtis, *Sovereignty and Superheroes* (Oxford: Oxford University Press, 2016).

105. Riesman, "Why Cops and Soldiers Love the Punisher."

106. Fernando Alfonso III, "Chief Removes Punisher Emblem, 'Blue Lives Matter' from Police Cars after Public Reacts," *Lexington Herald Leader*, February 24, 2017, https://www.kentucky.com/news/state/article134722264.html.

107. Allen Wood and Derek Osbeck, statement in response to questions regarding sticker on police vehicles, Solvay Police Department, n.d., https:// www.scribd.com/document/345004760/Solvay-Police-Department-statement -on-The-Punisher-deca.

108. Steve Featherston, "Professor Carnage," *New Republic*, April 17, 2017, https://newrepublic.com/article/141675/professor-carnage-dave-grossman -police-warrior-philosophy.

109. David Grossman and Loren Christensen, *On Combat: The Psychology and Physiology of Deadly Conflict in War and Peace* (Warrior Science Publications, 2008), 351.

110. Grossman and Christensen, *On Combat*, 351.

111. Wall, "Police Invention of Humanity," 325.

112. Grossman and Christensen, *On Combat*, 351.

113. Adam Davis, *Behind the Badge: 365 Daily Devotions for Law Enforcement* (New York: Broadstreet Publishing Group, 2018), 12.

114. Alison McQueen, *Political Realism in Apocalyptic Times* (Cambridge: Cambridge University Press, 2017), 133.

115. Sgt. A. Merica, "I Am Not Your Sheepdog. I Am the Wolf. And I Hunt Evil," *Law Enforcement Today*, January 26, 2019, https://www.lawenforcementtoday .com/not-your-sheepdog. Emphasis mine.

116. Nicholas Schmidle, "Getting Bin Laden," *New Yorker* 8 (2011).

117. Hans Morgenthau, "Public Affairs: Death in the Nuclear Age," *Commentary* 32, no. 3 (1961): 231; and Slavoj Žižek, *Living in the End Times* (London: Verso Books, 2011).

118. Calder Williams, *Combined and Uneven Apocalypse*, 5.

119. Calder Williams, *Combined and Uneven Apocalypse*, 8.

120. Mark Fisher, *Ghosts of My Life: Writings on Depression, Hauntology and Lost Futures* (London: Zer0 Books, 2014), 64.

3. RoboCop, or Modern Prometheus

1. Fred Glass, "The 'New Bad Future': *Robocop* and 1980s Sci-Fi Films," *Science as Culture* 1, no. 5 (1989): 7–49, 10.

2. Steffen Hantke, "Science Fiction and Horror in the 1950s," in *A Companion to the Horror Film*, ed. Harry Benshoff (Los Angeles: John Wiley & Sons, 2017), 255–72.

3. Nick Turse, "'Terminator Planet': A Drone-Eat-Drone World," Global Research, May 31, 2012, https://www.globalresearch.ca/terminator-planet-a-drone-eat-drone-world/31168.

4. Address by General W. C. Westmoreland, chief of staff, U.S. Army, annual luncheon, Association of the United States Army, Sheraton Park Hotel, Washington, DC, October 14, 1969 (Congressional Record, U.S. Senate, October 16, 1969).

5. Noel Sharkey, "Robot Wars Are a Reality," *Guardian*, August 17, 2007, https://www.theguardian.com/commentisfree/2007/aug/18/comment.military.

6. Turse, "Terminator Planet."

7. Ian Shaw, "Policing the Future City: Robotic Being-in-the-World," *Antipode* (2017), https://antipodeonline.org/wp-content/uploads/2017/05/3-ian-shaw.pdf.

8. Dan Gettinger, "Public Safety Drones: An Update," Center for the Study of the Drone, Bard College, May 28, 2018, http://dronecenter.bard.edu/public-safety-drones-update.

9. Turse, "Terminator Planet."

10. Sam Thielman, "Use of Police Robot to Kill Dallas Shooting Suspect Believed to Be First in US History," *Guardian*, July 8, 2016, https://www.theguardian.com/technology/2016/jul/08/police-bomb-robot-explosive-killed-suspect-dallas.

11. Peter Frase, *Four Futures: Life after Capitalism* (London: Verso Books, 2016).

12. Frase, *Four Futures*, 33.

13. Frase, *Four Futures*, 129.

14. Frase, *Four Futures*, 126.

15. Christopher McMichael, "Pacification and Police: A Critique of the Police Militarization Thesis," *Capital & Class* 41, no. 1 (2017): 115–32.

16. Anna Feigenbaum, *Tear Gas: From the Battlefields of World War I to the Streets of Today* (London: Verso, 2017), 188.

17. Kristian Williams, "The Other Side of the COIN: Counterinsurgency and Community Policing," *Interface* 3, no. 1 (2011): 81–117.

18. Austin Long, *On "Other War": Lessons from Five Decades of RAND Counterinsurgency Research*, RAND Corporation, 2002.

19. David Gompert and John Gordon IV, *War by Other Means—Building Complete and Balanced Capabilities for Counterinsurgency: RAND Counterinsurgency Study—Final Report*, RAND Corporation, 2008.

20. Long, *On "Other War,"* 53.

21. Mark Neocleous, "Fundamentals in Pacification Theory: Twenty-Six Articles," in *Destroy, Build, Secure: Readings on Pacification*, ed. Tyler Wall, Parastou Saberi, and Will Jackson (Ottawa: Red Quill Books Ltd., 2017), 13–27, 20.

22. Mark Neocleous, *War Power, Police Power* (Edinburgh: Edinburgh University Press, 2014).

23. Braudy, *Haunted*, 113.

24. Stephen T. Asma, *On Monsters: An Unnatural History of Our Worst Fears* (Oxford: Oxford University Press, 2011), 151.

25. Lester D. Friedman and Allison B. Kavey, *Monstrous Progeny: A History of the Frankenstein Narratives* (New Brunswick: Rutgers University Press, 2016), 12.

26. Daniel Dinello, *Technophobia! Science Fiction Visions of Posthuman Technology* (Austin: University of Texas Press, 2005), 41.

27. Isaac Asimov, *Robot Visions* (New York: Penguin Books, 1990), 6.

28. "Boston Dynamics Releases Video Showing Humans Can't Hide in a Robot Apocalypse," ABC News, February 13, 2018, https://www.abc.net.au/news/2018-02-13/boston-dynamics-releases-video-showing-robot-opening-door/9443548.

29. "Boston Dynamics All Prototypes," BeSciencer / Know the Unknown, February 14, 2015, YouTube video, 20:40, https://www.youtube.com/watch?v=-e9QzIkP5qI.

30. James Cameron, dir., *The Terminator* (Los Angeles: Orion Pictures, October 26, 1984).

31. Slavoj Žižek, *Looking Awry: An Introduction to Jacques Lacan through Popular Culture* (Boston: MIT Press, 1992).

32. Kirk Honeycutt, "'Terminator's' Generator: James Cameron Says He Uses Violence to Make a Point," *Los Angeles Times*, July 2, 1991, http://articles.latimes.com/1991-07-02/entertainment/ca-1810_1_james-cameron.

33. Rebecca Keegan, *The Futurist: The Life and Films of James Cameron* (Los Angeles: Three Rivers Press, 2010), 122–23.

34. Philip K. Dick, "The Android and the Human," *SF Commentary* 31 (December 1972): 4–26.

35. Peter Fleming, "The Death of Homo Economicus" (Chicago: University of Chicago Press Economics Books, 2017).

36. Tony Platt, Jon Frappier, Gerda Ray, Richard Schauffler, Larry Trujillo, Lynn Cooper, Elliott Currie, and Sidney Harring, *The Iron Fist and the Velvet Glove: An Analysis of the US Police* (San Francisco: Crime and Social Justice Associates, 1975).

37. Platt et al., *Iron Fist*, 82.

38. "National Crime Information Center (NCIC)," Services, Federal Bureau of Investigation, accessed January 6, 2022, https://www.fbi.gov/services/cjis/ncic.

39. James Bridle, *New Dark Age: Technology and the End of the Future* (London: Verso Books, 2018), 144.

40. "Before the Bullet Hits the Body—Dismantling Predictive Policing in Los Angeles," Stop LAPD Spying Coalition, May 8, 2018, https://stoplapdspying.org/before-the-bullet-hits-the-body-dismantling-predictive-policing-in-los-angeles.

41. "How Cops Are Using Algorithms to Predict Crimes," *Wired*, YouTube video, May 22, 2018, 12:39, https://www.youtube.com/watch?v=7lpCWxlRFAw.

42. James Vincent, "Twitter Taught Microsoft's AI Chatbot to Be a Racist Asshole in Less than a Day," Verge, March 24, 2016, https://www.theverge.com/2016/3/24/11297050/tay-microsoft-chatbot-racist.

43. "Before the Bullet Hits the Body."

44. John Hagan, *Who Are the Criminals? The Politics of Crime Policy from the Age of Roosevelt to the Age of Reagan* (Princeton: Princeton University Press, 2012).

45. "Ernie Anderson: Narrator," *Street Hawk* (1985), IMDb, https://www.imdb.com/title/tt0088618/characters/nm0026700.

46. "MOVE Bombing at 30: 'Barbaric' 1985 Philadelphia Police Attack Killed 11 & Burned a Neighborhood," Democracy Now!, May 13, 2015, YouTube video, 14:09, https://www.youtube.com/watch?v=JBZXRK_1vAQ.

47. Hugo Gernsback, "Radio Police Automaton," *Science and Invention* (New York: Experimenter Pub. Co., May 1924), 14.

48. Gernsback, "Radio Police Automaton," 15.

49. Sunny Ramayya, "Police Safety Officer Will Be On-the-Go-Bot," *Tampa Tribune*, May 30, 1986.

50. "K3 Indoor Patrolling Robot," Security Pro USA, accessed January 11, 2022, https://www.securityprousa.com/products/k3-indoor-patrolling-robot.

51. Matt Simon, "The Tricky Ethics of Knightscope's Crime-Fighting Robots," *Wired*, December 21, 2017, https://www.wired.com/story/the-tricky-ethics-of-knightscopes-crime-fighting-robots.

52. Laura Wenus, "Robot Guards the Dogs at SF Animal Shelter and Frightens Some," Mission Local, November 29, 2017, https://missionlocal.org/2017/11/robots-guard-the-dogs-at-sf-animal-shelter-and-frighten-some.

53. "Fighting Crime with Knightscope," Knightscope, accessed January 11, 2022, https://www.knightscope.com/crime.

54. The robot was a critique of mechanization and the ways it can dehumanize people. The word itself derives from the Czech word *robota*, or forced labor, as done by serfs. Its Slavic linguistic root, *rab*, means "slave." The original word for robots more accurately defines androids, then, in that they were neither metallic nor mechanical. David J. Gunkel, *Robot Rights* (Cambridge, Mass.: MIT Press, 2018), 15.

55. Ian Shaw, "Robot Wars: US Empire and Geopolitics in the Robotic Age," *Security Dialogue* 48, no. 5 (2017): 451–70.

56. Susannah Breslin, "Meet the Terrifying New Robot Cop That's Patrolling Dubai," *Forbes*, June 3, 2017, https://www.forbes.com/sites/susannahbreslin/2017/06/03/robot-cop-dubai/#1235b0a56872.

57. Yara Hawari, "'The Skunk': Another Israeli Weapon for Collective Punishment," Al Jazeera, May 12, 2021, https://www.aljazeera.com/opinions/2021/5/12/the-skunk-another-israeli-weapon-for-collective-punishment. See also "Skunk Riot Control Copter," Desert Wolf, http://www.desert-wolf.com/dw/products/unmanned-aerial-systems/skunk-riot-control-copter.html.

58. Simon, "Tricky Ethics."

59. Glenn Greenwald, "The Militarization of U.S. Police: Finally Dragged into the Light by the Horrors of Ferguson," Intercept, August 14, 2014, https://theintercept.com/2014/08/14/militarization-u-s-police-dragged-light-horrors-ferguson.

60. Emanuella Grinberg, "The NYPD Officer Who Shot a Terror Suspect

Says He Was Just Doing His Job," CNN, November 1, 2017, https://www.cnn
.com/2017/11/01/us/ryan-nash-police-new-york-terror/index.html.

61. Herb Hupfer, "Police Are Just Doing Their Jobs," letter to the editor, *Chicago Tribune*, October 9, 2014, http://www.chicagotribune.com/news/opinion
/letters/chi-letters-police-are-just-doing-their-jobs-20141009-story.html.

62. This draws interesting parallels to the phrase "cop out," extending from
"cop a plea," meaning to plead guilty to a lesser crime in order to avoid greater
scrutiny.

63. Here we might think of code in the ways that Ruha Benjamin does, as
an underlying law or command that orders a set of behaviors. In Benjamin's
case, code underlies the racialized or racist ways that a person's name might
be understood, as it does the practices that justify California's gang database.
Benjamin, *Race after Technology: Abolitionist Tools for the New Jim Code* (Los
Angeles: John Wiley and Sons, 2019).

64. Žižek, *Looking Awry.*

65. Jeffery Schwartz, dir., *Flesh + Steel: The Making of RoboCop* (Los Angeles: Automat Pictures, 2001).

66. Greenwald, "Militarization of U.S. Police."

67. Martin Kaste, "Police Militarization Becomes a Hot Topic," *Morning
Edition*, NPR, August 19, 2014, https://www.npr.org/2014/08/19/341542537
/police-militarization-becomes-a-hot-topic.

68. Nick Turse, "Pentagon Video Warns of 'Unavoidable' Dystopian Future
for World's Biggest Cities," Intercept, October 13, 2016, https://theintercept.com
/2016/10/13/pentagon-video-warns-of-unavoidable-dystopian-future-for
-worlds-biggest-cities.

69. José Padilha, dir., *RoboCop* (Los Angeles, Metro-Goldwyn-Mayer, February 12, 2014).

70. Padilha, *RoboCop.*

71. Friedman and Kavey, *Monstrous Progeny.*

72. Jackie Wang, *Carceral Capitalism*, vol. 21 (Cambridge, Mass.: MIT Press,
2018), 255.

73. Schwartz, *Flesh + Steel.*

74. On his death and resurrection, coproducer Paul Sammon remarks that
Murphy "can never go back, he's always going to be something different. He's
not a man, he's not a machine, he's different. He's his own creature maybe."

75. Donna Haraway, "A Cyborg Manifesto: Science, Technology, and Socialist-
Feminism in the Late Twentieth Century," in *Simians, Cyborgs and Women: The
Reinvention of Nature* (New York: Routledge, 1991), 149–81.

76. Žižek, *Looking Awry.*

77. Schwartz, *Flesh + Steel.* While the film's technophobia is apparent,
Verhoeven saw it as a resurrection narrative: "I wanted to show Satan killing
Jesus," he says, explaining that the violent death of Murphy was pivotal "because
you cannot have the resurrection until you have the crucifixion."

78. Wang, *Carceral Capitalism*, 255.

79. Slavoj Žižek, *In Defense of Lost Causes* (London: Verso Books, 2009),
70–88.

80. Schwartz, *Flesh + Steel.*

81. Schwartz, *Flesh + Steel.*

82. Schwartz, *Flesh + Steel.*

83. Wang, *Carceral Capitalism,* 256.

84. Stuart Schrader, "Policing Empire," *Jacobin,* November 5, 2014, https://www.jacobinmag.com/2014/09/policing-empire.

85. Peter Kraska, "All We See Are Nails: Using Militarism as a Problem-Solving Strategy," Chautauqua Lecture Series, Eastern Kentucky University, March 25, 2015, https://www.youtube.com/watch?reload=9&v=jiE6czXyrIY.

86. Samuel Butler, *Erewhon: or, Over the Range* (London: David Bogue. 1872), 219.

87. David Paul, "Man a Machine," in *Apocalypse Culture,* ed. Adam Parfrey (Portland, Ore.: Feral House, 2012).

88. Sara Heinämaa, "Embodiment and Bodily Becoming," in *The Oxford Handbook of the History of Phenomenology,* ed. Dan Zahavi (Oxford: Oxford University Press, 2018).

89. Michael Polanyi, *Personal Knowledge: Towards a Post-critical Philosophy* (Chicago: University of Chicago Press, 2015), 59.

90. Morana Alač, "Moving Android: On Social Robots and Body-in-Interaction," *Social Studies of Science* 39, no. 4 (2009): 491–528.

91. Bruno Latour, *We Have Never Been Modern* (Cambridge: Harvard University Press, 2012).

92. Elaine L. Graham, *Representations of the Post/Human: Monsters, Aliens and Others in Popular Culture* (Manchester: Manchester University Press, 2002).

93. Donna J. Haraway, *A Manifesto for Cyborgs: Science, Technology, and Socialist Feminism in the 1980s* (San Francisco: Center for Social Research and Education, 1985), 173–204.

94. Joseph Pugliese, "Prosthetics of Law and the Anomic Violence of Drones," *Griffith Law Review* 20, no. 4 (2011): 931–61.

95. Radley Balko, *Rise of the Warrior Cop: The Militarization of America's Police Forces* (New York: PublicAffairs, 2013).

96. "The Rise of SWAT: How Cops Became Soldiers," Retro Report, March 13, 2018, https://www.youtube.com/watch?v=YE-AzeR1P-c.

97. Žižek, *Living in the End Times,* 2.

98. Dick, "The Android and the Human."

99. Paul Clinton, "Cop Slang: Our Favorite Terms from You," Editor's Notes, *Police,* August 13, 2012, http://www.policemag.com/blog/editors-notes/story/2012/08/cop-slang-our-favorite-user-terms.aspx.

100. Eric Slater, "In Detroit, Oversight of Police Is Welcomed," *Los Angeles Times,* July 5, 2003, http://articles.latimes.com/2003/jul/05/nation/na-detroitcops5.

101. Gus Burns, "Imprisoned Officer Known as 'Robocop' to Be Paroled This Week," MLive, January 23, 2017, http://www.mlive.com/news/detroit/index.ssf/2017/01/imprisoned_officer_known_as_ro.html.

102. Gus Burns, "Officer Nicknamed 'Robocop' Gets 13 Months for Beating

Motorist," MLive, February 2, 2016, http://www.mlive.com/news/detroit/index
.ssf/2016/02/robocop_sentenced_to_years_in.html.

103. Ryan Felton, "Detroit's Infamous 'RoboCop' Faces Trial for Beating
Black Man during Traffic Stop," *Guardian*, November 5, 2015, https://www
.theguardian.com/us-news/2015/nov/03/detroit-police-robocop-traffic-stop
-beating-floyd-dent-trial.

104. Jim Schaefer and Gina Kaufman, "How Problem Cops Stay on Michigan's Streets," *Detroit Free Press*, July 9, 2017, https://www.freep.com/story/news
/local/michigan/2017/07/09/how-problem-cops-stay-street/414813001.

105. Ben Schmitt, "Detroit's Robocop Allegedly Led Ring," *Detroit Free Press*,
June 20, 2003, http://www.davidileelaw.com/wp-content/uploads/2010/04
/02062003melendezfreep.pdf.

106. John Hoberman, *Dopers in Uniform: The Hidden World of Police on Steroids* (Austin: University of Texas Press, 2017).

107. Kenneth Saltman, "The Strong Arm of the Law," *Body & Society* 9, no. 4
(2003): 49–67, 58.

108. Pasi Falk, "Written in the Flesh," *Body & Society* 1, no. 1 (1995): 95–105.

109. Adrian Johnston, *Žižek's Ontology: A Transcendental Materialist Theory
of Subjectivity* (Evanston, Ill.: Northwestern University Press, 2008).

110. Steve Hall, *Theorizing Crime and Deviance: A New Perspective* (Los Angeles: Sage, 2012), 208.

111. Johnston, *Žižek's Ontology*.

112. Simon Winlow, "What Lies Beneath? Some Notes on Ultra-realism, and
the Intellectual Foundations of the 'Deviant Leisure' Perspective," in *Deviant
Leisure: Criminological Perspectives on Leisure and Harm*, ed. Thomas Raymen
and Oliver Smith (Cham, Switzerland: Springer Nature, 2019), 45–65.

113. Adam Greenfield, "Shuck the Police: Are We Done with Traditional
Law Enforcement?," *Los Angeles Review of Books*, January 2, 2018, https://
lareviewofbooks.org/article/shuck-the-police-are-we-done-with-traditional-law
-enforcement.

114. Anna Feigenbaum and Daniel Weissmann, "Vulnerable Warriors: The
Atmospheric Marketing of Military and Policing Equipment before and after
9/11," *Critical Studies on Terrorism* 9, no. 3 (2016): 482–98, 494.

115. Diane Bukowski, "'Robocop' Wm. Melendez Faces Trial Nov. 2 in Near-
Fatal Beating of Detroit Autoworker Floyd Dent," Voice of Detroit, October 31,
2015, http://voiceofdetroit.net/2015/10/31/robocop-wm-melendez-faces-trial-nov
-2-in-near-fatal-beating-of-detroit-autoworker-floyd-dent.

116. Gus Burns, "Former Cop Convicted of Assaulting Motorist Reads Poem
at Sentencing," MLive, February 3, 2016, http://www.mlive.com/news/detroit
/index.ssf/2016/02/ex-cop_convicted_of_assaulting.html.

117. Ray Bradbury, "The Pedestrian," *Reporter*, August 7, 1951, 39–40.

118. Herbert Marcuse, *An Essay on Liberation*, vol. 319 (Boston: Beacon Press,
1969), 12.

119. Walter Benjamin, "Critique of Violence," *Reflections* 14, no. 3 (1978):
277–300.

120. An interesting example arises in *True Detective* when Cohle, explaining M-theory to his interrogators, describes human subjectivity "as sentience is just cycling through our lives like carts on a track." *True Detective*, season 1, episode 5, "The Secret Fate of All Life," directed by Cary Joji Fukunaga, aired February 16, 2014, on HBO.

121. Jane Bennett, *Vibrant Matter: A Political Ecology of Things* (Durham, N.C.: Duke University Press, 2010).

122. Tom Sparrow, *End of Phenomenology: Metaphysics and the New Realism* (Edinburgh: Edinburgh University Press, 2014), 174–77.

123. Bennett, *Vibrant Matter*, 23.

124. Peter Fitting, "Futurecop: The Neutralization of Revolt in 'Blade Runner'" ["Futuroflics: La Neutralisation de la révolte dans 'Blade Runner'], *Science Fiction Studies* 14, no. 3 (1987): 340–54.

125. Philip K. Dick, *Do Androids Dream of Electric Sheep?* (New York: Del Rey, 1996).

126. Dick, "The Android and the Human."

4. Monsters Are Real

1. Ed McBain, *Cop Hater* (New York: Signet, 1973).

2. "Cop Killer," track 18 on Body Count, *Body Count*, Sire, 1992.

3. Justin Turner, "'It All Started with Eddie': Thanatopolitics, Police Power, and the Murder of Edward Byrne," *Crime, Media, Culture* 15, no. 2 (2019): 239–58.

4. Douglas Jehl, "Bush Attacks 'Sick' Anti-Police Themes," *Los Angeles Times*, June 30, 1992, https://www.latimes.com/archives/la-xpm-1992-06-30-mn-1278 -story.html.

5. Dennis R. Martin, "The Music of Murder," *ACJS Today*, November/December 1993.

6. Mark S. Hamm and Jeff Ferrell, "Rap, Cops, and Crime: Clarifying the 'Cop Killer' Controversy," in *Taking Sides: Clashing Views on Controversial Issues in Crime and Criminology*, ed. Richard C. Monk (Guilford, Conn.: Dushkin/McGraw-Hill, 1998), 23–28.

7. Alan Light, "The Rolling Stone Interview: Ice-T," *Rolling Stone*, August 20, 1992, https://www.rollingstone.com/music/music-news/the-rolling-stone -interview-ice-t-247663.

8. "Chris Dorner: Ex-LA Cop Wanted in Killing Spree," ABC News, February 8, 2013, https://www.youtube.com/watch?v=RIrdvfOX4R0.

9. People v. Mercer (1962) 210 Cal. App. 2d 153, 161.; People v. Humphrey (1996) 13 Cal.4th 1073.

10. Jackie Lacey, "Officer Involved Shooting of Margie Hernandez and Emma Carranza Los Angeles Police Department," JSID File #13–0129, January 22, 2016, http://da.lacounty.gov/sites/default/files/pdf/JSID_OIS_Carranza %2C%20Hernandez.pdf. Emphasis mine.

11. Correia and Wall, *Police: A Field Guide*, 226–29.

12. Travis Linnemann and Corina Medley, "Fear the Monster! Racialised

Violence, Sovereign Power and the Thin Blue Line," in *The Routledge International Handbook on Fear of Crime*, ed. Murray Lee and Gabe Mythen (London: Routledge, 2017), 65–81.

13. Gavin de Becker, *The Gift of Fear* (Boston: Little, Brown, 1997), 34–36.

14. Gavin de Becker, in Dave Grossman and Loren W. Christensen, *On Combat: The Psychology and Physiology of Deadly Conflict in War and Peace*, Third Edition (Warrior Science Publications, 2008), xvi.

15. Peter Overby, "NRA: 'Only Thing That Stops a Bad Guy with a Gun Is a Good Guy with a Gun,'" *All Things Considered*, NPR, December 21, 2012, https://www.npr.org/2012/12/21/167824766/nra-only-thing-that-stops-a-bad-guy-with-a-gun-is-a-good-guy-with-a-gun.

16. Larry Smith, "Police Are Trained to Fear," Medium, November 17, 2008, https://medium.com/s/story/fearing-for-our-lives-82ad7eb7d75f.

17. In 2018, 108 fatal injuries to police for a rate 13.7 per 100,000. By comparison, the most dangerous occupation, logging, produced a death rate of 111 per 100,000. See "Fact Sheet | Police Officers 2018," U.S. Bureau of Labor Statistics, April 2020, https://www.bls.gov/iif/oshwc/cfoi/police-2018.htm; "25 Most Dangerous Jobs," University of Delaware, December 14, 2020, https://www.facilities.udel.edu/safety/4689.

18. Smith, "Police Are Trained to Fear."

19. David Fleshler and Megan O'Matz, "New Video Shows School Cop Scot Peterson Hiding as Gunman Shoots Parkland Students," *South Florida Sun Sentinel*, September 5, 2018, https://www.sun-sentinel.com/local/broward/parkland/florida-school-shooting/fl-florida-school-shooting-fdle-officer-20180904-story.html.

20. See also Warren v. District of Columbia (444 A.2d. 1, D.C. Ct. of Ap. 1981); Balistreri v. Pacifica Police Department (23 August 1988); DeShaney v. Winnebago County (22 February 1989).

21. Castle Rock v. Gonzales (545 U.S. 748, 2005).

22. Jen Chung, "Two Cops Suspended for Allegedly Refusing to Enter Apartment of Ax-Attack Murder Victim," Gothamist, April 23, 2019, http://gothamist.com/2019/04/23/two_police_officers_suspended_for_a.php.

23. Howard Phillips Lovecraft, *Supernatural Horror in Literature*, the Palingenesis Project (Wermod and Wermod Publishing Group, 2013), 1.

24. Correia and Wall, *Police: A Field Guide*, 187.

25. Ligotti, *Conspiracy against the Human Race*, 15.

26. Ligotti, *Conspiracy against the Human Race*, 16.

27. Ernest Becker, *The Denial of Death* (New York: Simon and Schuster, 2007).

28. Sheldon Solomon, Jeff Greenberg, and Thomas A. Pyszczynski, *The Worm at the Core: On the Role of Death in Life* (New York: Random House Incorporated, 2015).

29. Corey Robin, "Why Do Opposites Attract? Fear and Freedom in the Modern Political Imagination," in *Fear Itself: Enemies Real and Imagined in American Culture*, ed. Anna Creadeck and Nancy L. Schultz (West Lafayette, Ind: Purdue University Press, 1999), 285.3–22.

30. Neocleous, *The Monstrous and the Dead*, 72–73.

31. "Day 9 Of Manhunt for PA Barracks Shooting Suspect Eric Frein," CBS Philly, September 21, 2014, https://philadelphia.cbslocal.com/2014/09/21/day -9-of-manhunt-for-pa-barracks-shooting-suspect-eric-frein.

32. James Comey, "The FBI and the IACP: Facing Challenges Together," FBI, October 27, 2014, www.fbi.gov/news/speeches/the-fbi-and-the-iacp-facing -challenges-together.

33. Turner, "It All Started with Eddie," 13.

34. David Clarke, "Sheriff David Clarke: It's Time to Stand Up to Black Lives Matter," Fox News, July 11, 2016, https://www.foxnews.com/opinion/sheriff-david -clarke-its-time-to-stand-up-to-black-lives-matter.

35. Heather MacDonald, *The War on Cops: How the New Attack on Law and Order Makes Everyone Less Safe* (New York: Encounter, 2016), 3.

36. MacDonald, *War on Cops*, 41.

37. Nijah Cunningham and Tiana Reid, "Blue Life," *New Inquiry*, September 24, 2018, https://thenewinquiry.com/blue-life.

38. Comey, "FBI and the IACP."

39. James Comey, *A Higher Loyalty: Truth, Lies, and Leadership* (New York: Flatiron Books, 2018), 12.

40. Patrick Blanchfield, "Prig and Pig," *Baffler*, April 24, 2018, https:// thebaffler.com/latest/prig-and-pig-blanchfield.

41. Radley Balko, "Overkill: The Rise of Paramilitary Police Raids in America," CATO Institute, 2006, 6.

42. Balko, "Overkill," 6.

43. Beth Shuster and Doug Smith, "Police Kill 2 Suspects after Foiled Bank Heist," *Los Angeles Times*, March 1, 1997, https://www.latimes.com/archives/la -xpm-1997-03-01-mn-33665-story.html.

44. Jill Leovy and Henry Chu, "In the Bank, a 'Huge Monster in Black' Yelled 'Hit the Floor!,'" *Los Angeles Times*, March 1, 1997, 1; Beth Shuster and Doug Smith, "Gunfire, Hostages and Terror," *Los Angeles Times*, March 1, 1997, 1.

45. Beth Shuster and James Rainey, "Officers Face Barrage of Bullets to Take Comrades out of Line of Fire," *Los Angeles Times*, March 1, 1997, https://www .latimes.com/archives/la-xpm-1997-03-01-mn-33662-story.html.

46. Tim Carpenter and Sherman Smith, "Kansas Law Enforcement Agencies Operate with US Surplus Firearms, Armored Vehicles, Rocket Launchers," *Kansas Reflector*, December 17, 2020, https://kansasreflector.com/2020/12/17 /kansas-law-enforcement-agencies-operate-with-u-s-surplus-firearms-armored -vehicles-rocket-launchers.

47. "Powell Shooting (Cell Phone Camera)," St. Louis Public Radio, August 20, 2014, YouTube video, 6:30, https://www.youtube.com/watch?v=j -P54MZVxMU&bpctr=1558008455.

48. Ezra Klein, "Did the St. Louis Police Have to Shoot Kajieme Powell?," Vox, August 20, 2014, https://www.vox.com/2014/8/20/6051431/did-the-st -louis-police-have-to-shoot-kajieme-powell.

49. David Klinger, "Dealing with Downed Suspects: Some Lessons from the

VALOR Project about How to Properly Manage the Immediate Aftermath of Officer-Involved Shootings," *Police Chief* 79, no. 5 (May 2012): 24–29.

50. David Klinger, "Police Responses to Officer-Involved Shootings," report submitted to the National Institute of Justice, *NIJ Journal* (2006), 253. Also cited in Correia and Wall, *Police: A Field Guide*, 185.

51. Correia and Wall, *Police: A Field Guide*, 185.

52. Neocleous, *Universal Adversary*, 44.

53. Brian Suitt, shared post, Facebook, May 24, 2016, "When it's time to get tased lmao #apd #arlington #texas #getontheground #mjssmokeshop #blazinvapors #litup #carchase #brainondrugs #zombie #liteitup #agg #aggtown #bathsalt #tweakers #holdtheblue #aggtownsfinest," video, Facebook, May 24, 2016, accessed via the Plain View Project, https://www.plainviewproject.org/data /dallas-brian.suitt.7-97.

54. Matt Rushing, "There's cursing in this picture . . . okay, you've been notified, there's just nothing else that better describes how I feel this week," image, Facebook, March 20, 2013, accessed via the Plain View Project, https://www .plainviewproject.org/data/dallas-matthew.a.rushing-253.

55. Travis Linnemann, Tyler Wall, and Edward Green, "The Walking Dead and Killing State: Zombification and the Normalization of Police Violence," *Theoretical Criminology* 18, no. 4 (2014): 506–27.

56. Frank Owen, "The Miami Zombie," *Playboy*, December 29, 2012.

57. Doris Marie Provine, *Unequal under Law: Race in the War on Drugs* (Chicago: University of Chicago Press, 2008), 77–79.

58. Travis Linnemann, *Meth Wars: Police, Media, Power* (New York: New York University Press, 2016), 27.

59. Carl Hart, "How the Myth of the 'Negro Cocaine Fiend' Helped Shape American Drug Policy," *Nation*, January 29, 2014, https://www.thenation.com /article/how-myth-negro-cocaine-fiend-helped-shape-american-drug-policy.

60. Linnemann, Wall, and Green, "Walking Dead," 509.

61. Speaking to the production of the socially dead under chattel, bell hooks writes that once "reduced to the machinery of bodily physical labor, black people learned to appear before whites as though they were zombies, cultivating the habit of casting the gaze downward so as not to appear uppity. To look directly was an assertion of subjectivity, equality. Safety resided in the pretense of invisibility." hooks, *Black Looks: Race and Representation* (Boston: South End Press, 1992), 168.

62. Warren St. John, "Market for Zombies? It's Undead (Aaahhh!)," *New York Times*, March 26, 2006, https://www.nytimes.com/2006/03/26/fashion /sundaystyles/market-for-zombies-its-undead-aaahhh.html.

63. Linnemann, Wall, and Green, "Walking Dead"; Neocleous, *Universal Adversary*.

64. Calder Williams, *Combined and Uneven Apocalypse*.

65. Political theorist Jodi Dean points to 2011 and the rise of Occupy, naming the crowd the most important social and political actor worldwide. Particularly when unauthorized by state and capital, she writes, "the crowd marshals

the forces of social contagion to create an opening and the possibility of political subjectivation." Dean, "Crowds and Publics," *Stasis* 5, no. 1 (2017), 198.

66. Neocleous, *Universal Adversary*, 61–64.

67. Sarah Anderson and Brian Wakamo, "The Year in Inequality in 10 Charts," Inequality.org, December 15, 2021, https://inequality.org/great-divide/year-in-inequality-10-charts.

68. Dennis Büscher-Ulbrich, "No Future for Nobody? Zombie Riots and the Real of Capital," in *Modernities and Modernization in North America*, ed. Ruth Mayer and Ilka Brasch (Heidelberg, Germany: Universitätsverlag Winter, 2019).

69. The Center for Strategic and International Studies estimates an annual increase in mass protest worldwide of 11.5 percent from 2009 until 2019. Christian Stirling Haig, Katherine Schmidt, and Samuel Brannen, "The Age of Mass Protests: Understanding an Escalating Global Trend," Center for Strategic International Studies, March 2, 2020, *https://www.csis.org/analysis/age-mass-protests-understanding-escalating-global-trend.*

70. Correia and Wall, *Police: A Field Guide*, 211.

71. Rodney Stark, *Police Riots: Collective Violence and Law Enforcement* (Belmont, Calif.: Wadsworth Publishing Company, 1972), 1.

72. Stark, *Police Riots*, 135.

73. Stark, *Police Riots*, 135.

74. Richard Gilman-Opalsky, *Specters of Revolt: On the Intellect of Insurrection and Philosophy from Below* (London: Watkins Media Limited, 2016), 215.

75. Mark Neocleous, *Administering Civil Society: Towards a Theory of State Power* (New York: St. Martin's Press, 1996).

76. Brucato, "Policing Race and Racing Police." 115

77. Correia and Wall, *Police: A Field Guide*, 211.

78. Frank Donner, *Protectors of Privilege: Red Squads and Police Repression in Urban America* (Berkeley: University of California Press, 1992).

79. Sam Mitrani, *The Rise of the Chicago Police Department: Class and Conflict, 1850–1894* (Champaign: University of Illinois Press, 2013).

80. Stephen R. Couch, "Selling and Reclaiming State Sovereignty: The Case of Coal and Iron Police," *Insurgent Sociologist* 11, no. 1 (1981): 85–91.

81. Report of the United States Senate Select Committee to Study Governmental Operations with Respect to Intelligence Activities, S.Rep. No. 755, 94th Congress, 2d Sess., April 26, 1976.

82. Brendan McQuade, *Pacifying the Homeland: Intelligence Fusion and Mass Supervision* (Berkeley: University of California Press, 2019), 114–20.

83. Kristian Williams, *Our Enemies in Blue: Police and Power in America* (Chico, Calif.: AK Press, 2015), 424.

84. Jeffrey Haas, *The Assassination of Fred Hampton: How the FBI and the Chicago Police Murdered a Black Panther* (Chicago: Chicago Review Press, 2011).

85. James Baldwin, *The Price of the Ticket: Collected Nonfiction, 1948–1985* (London: Macmillan, 1985), 537.

86. Kristian Williams, "The Other Side of the COIN: Counterinsurgency and Community Policing," *Interface* 3, no. 1 (2011): 81–117.

87. In the century-plus since its publication, Le Bon's *The Crowd: A Study of the Popular Mind* has influenced the state response to dissent. Benito Mussolini, for instance, took much inspiration from Le Bon, particularly his reflections on the power of a leader to instigate, agitate, and ignite the crowd. Like Hitler, who was also an admirer of Le Bon's, Mussolini clearly aimed to ignite and harness the crowd. But in doing so, both must have also feared the power of the leader and crowd. Some twenty years after Hitler and Mussolini, a manual of policies meant to govern U.S. military and police responses to "civil disturbances and disasters" took seriously "agitator" and crowd. Echoing Le Bon, it outlines the fundamentals of "group behavior" in rigid detail and zeroes in on the excited loss of reason and "respect for law" distinguishing a "mob" from a simple crowd. Warning of the "ignorant and excitable" most likely to transform a peaceful gathering into a violent mob, it diagnosis "skillful agitators" as patient zero in the outbreak of "civil disturbances." With pages upon pages detailing the agitator's use of "propaganda," "forceful harangue and fiery speech," and "irritating individuals or objects" (such as a "photograph depicting alleged police brutality") to incite emotion, rumor, and, ultimately, violence, the manual reveals a fear of political collectivity and offers a means to extinguish its revolutionary potentials. "Civil Disturbances and Disasters," U.S. Department of the Army, 1968, 1–3, *https:// www.ojp.gov/pdffiles1/Digitization/82714NCJRS.pdf*. As we have seen, such fears have long motivated those charged with maintaining the established order. Born of Hoover's fear of a so-called "black messiah," COINTELPRO reached treacherous fruition in the assassination/murder of Fred Hampton. Counterinsurgency operations in Iraq and Afghanistan also prioritized agitators and leaders, famously disseminating a hierarchy of "high-value targets" in the form of playing cards that designated Saddam Hussein the ace of spades. Even more openly, the "Kingpin" or "Decapitation" strategy employed by the Drug Enforcement Administration and various components of the Department of Homeland Security aims to dissolve "drug trafficking and foreign terrorist organizations" by taking out the "king," or cutting the head off the snake. The importance COIN places upon leaders and "agitators" helps explain the ongoing police reaction to growing antifascist collectives, increasingly mobilized to challenge the ascendency of far-right groups worldwide. In the United States, for instance, antifa groups routinely take to the streets of Portland, Oregon, to disrupt open public gatherings of far-right groups like Patriot Prayer and the white supremacist Rise Above Movement. One such violent confrontation unfolded in early July 2019, when the neofascist Proud Boys and supporters of the so-called #HimToo movement gathered to agitate under the guise of free speech. Antifa—shorthand for a broader philosophy of autonomous militant antifascism, rather than a group with a clear organizational structure—is characterized by the black bloc, in which protestors don black clothing and masks to evade identification and as a show of unity and force. Following a clash with far-right groups, Portland's then police chief, Danielle Outlaw, denounced antifa and the black bloc and called for city and state legislators to criminalize masks, insisting they enabled and emboldened lawlessness. Conservatives in Congress had beaten Outlaw to

the punch the previous summer, proposing the Unmasking Antifa Act of 2018 to make wearing masks during "civil unrest" a criminal offense punishable with fines and up to fifteen years in prison. In their notable singling out of antifa, it is clear the black bloc poses problems for police. First, with no leader to capture, COIN's decapitation strategy is useless. Secondly, with masks obscuring participants' identities, it is virtually impossible for police to round up "insurgents" en masse unless captured on scene. Not so coincidentally, around this time, the *Washington Post* reported approvingly that Portland police were serving as a test case for Amazon's "artificial intelligence tool" dubbed Rekognition. Incredibly powerful facial recognition software, Rekognition purportedly has the ability to identify "sentiment" and emotions and thus read the intent of a target. There is a saying common among graffiti artists: "no face, no case." Clearly the black bloc poses a problem for police, making identification all the more difficult.

88. Bernard E. Harcourt, *The Counterrevolution: How Our Government Went to War against Its Own Citizens* (New York: Basic Books, 2018), 5.

89. Federal Bureau of Investigation, Counterterrorism Division, *Black Identity Extremists Likely Motivated to Target Law Enforcement Officers*, August 3, 2017, https://www.documentcloud.org/documents/4067711-BIE-Redacted.html.

90. Khaled Beydoun and Justin Hansford, "The FBI's Dangerous Crackdown on 'Black Identity Extremists,'" *New York Times*, November 15, 2017, https://www.nytimes.com/2017/11/15/opinion/black-identity-extremism-fbi-trump.html.

91. Here, following Clover, the riot is the appropriate mode of resistance in the postcrash, capitalist realist moment.

92. Jack Halberstam, *The Queer Art of Failure* (Durham, N.C.: Duke University Press, 2011), 50–53.

93. Johanna Isaacson, "We Don't Need Another Zombie-Killing Hero: Political Horror in Dawn of the Dead (1978)," *Blind Field: A Journal of Cultural Inquiry*, March 18, 2019, https://blindfieldjournal.com/2019/03/18/we-dont-need-another-zombie-killing-hero-riot-horror-in-dawn-of-the-dead-1978.

94. Carol Clover, *Men, Women, and Chain Saws: Gender in the Modern Horror Film*, Updated Edition, vol. 15 (Princeton: Princeton University Press, 2015).

95. Barry K. Grant, "Taking Back the Night of the Living Dead: George Romero, Feminism, and the Horror Film," *Dread of Difference*, ed. Barry Keith Grant (Austin: University of Texas Press, 2015), 232.

96. Isaacson, "Zombie-Killing Hero."

97. Joshua Clover, *Riot. Strike. Riot: The New Era of Uprisings* (London: Verso Books, 2016), 125–26.

98. Jeff Chang, *Can't Stop, Won't Stop: A History of the Hip-Hop Generation* (New York: St. Martin's Press, 2007), 170.

99. Audio commentary, John Carpenter, *Assault on Precinct 13*, DVD, widescreen edition, Image Entertainment, March 11, 2003.

100. Peter Byrnes, "Assault on Precinct 13," *Sydney Morning Herald*, March 11, 2005, https://www.smh.com.au/entertainment/movies/assault-on-precinct-13-20050331-gdl154.html.

101. David Woods, "Us and Them: Authority and Identity in Carpenter's Films," in *The Cinema of John Carpenter: The Technique of Terror*, ed. Ian Conrich and David Woods (London: Wallflower Press, 2004): 21–34.

102. Mike Davis, "The Fire This Time," *CovertAction Information Bulletin* no. 41 (Summer 1992): 12–22, 18.

103. Mike Davis and Marcos Frommer, "An Interview with Mike Davis," *Chicago Review* 38, no. 4 (1993): 21–43.

104. Franco Moretti, *Signs Taken for Wonders: On the Sociology of Literary Forms*, vol. 7 (London: Verso, 2005), 86.

105. Light, "Rolling Stone Interview: Ice-T."

106. Holly Yan, Amanda Watts, and Jamiel Lynch, "Memphis Protesters Hurl Bricks and Rocks at Police, Injuring 36 Officers in Outrage over a Man's Death," CNN, June 13, 2019, https://www.cnn.com/2019/06/13/us/memphis-shooting-officers-injured/index.html.

107. Gilman-Opalsky, *Specters of Revolt*.

108. Neil Smith, Don Mitchell, Erin Siodmak, JenJoy Roybal, Marnie Brady, and Brendan P. O'Malley, eds., *Revolting New York: How 400 Years of Riot, Rebellion, Uprising, and Revolution Shaped a City*, vol. 38 (Athens: University of Georgia Press, 2018), 1–2.

109. Stefano Harney and Fred Moten, *The Undercommons: Fugitive Planning and Black Study* (New York: Minor Composition, 2013), 17. See also Nick Estes, *Our History Is the Future: Standing Rock versus the Dakota Access Pipeline, and the Long Tradition of Indigenous Resistance* (London: Verso Books, 2019), 247.

110. Ian Fisher, "Pulling Out of Fort Apache, the Bronx; New 41st Precinct Station House Leaves Behind Symbol of Community's Past Troubles," *New York Times*, June 23, 1993, https://www.nytimes.com/1993/06/23/nyregion/pulling-fort-apache-bronx-new-41st-precinct-station-house-leaves-behind-symbol.html.

111. Estes, *Our History Is the Future*, 247–48.

112. Didier Fassin, *Enforcing Order: An Ethnography of Urban Policing* (London: Polity, 2013), 58.

113. David Greene, "'Fort Apache' Cops Recall the Good Times," *Bronx Chronicle*, June 21, 2017, https://thebronxchronicle.com/2017/06/21/fort-apache-cops-recall-good-times.

114. Robert McFadden, "70 Are Hurt, Including 62 Officers, as Hasidim Storm a Police Station," *New York Times*, December 3, 1978, 1, https://www.nytimes.com/1978/12/03/archives/70-are-hurt-including-62-officers-as-hasidim-storm-a-police-station.html.

115. "His Letter Urged Cop Petition," *New York Daily News*, December 4, 1978, 3.

116. James Harney, "Brooklyn Hasidic Protest Is Page from a Familiar Book," *New York Daily News*, December 3, 1978, 31.

117. Time has apparently not eased tensions between the NYPD and the Hasidic communities of Borough Park and Crown Heights, with cops occasionally "run out" since. And if a 2016 criminal complaint charging three NYPD commanders with corruption was accurate, rather than challenging the authority

of Hasidic leaders, it seems high-ranking NYPD administrators entered into a relationship of patronage, serving as "errand boys" for wealthy businessmen in exchange for gifts and other considerations. While garden-variety corruption might explain the NYPD's lenience, might it be that the tit-for-tat relationship was also a crude means to appease a particularly problematic adversary? See Jim Dwyer, "Favors at Fort Surrender: New Twist in History of Police and Borough Park," *New York Times*, June 22, 2016, A16; and William Rashbaum and Joseph Goldstein," "3 N.Y.P.D. Commanders Are Arrested in Vast Corruption Case," *New York Times*, June 20, 2016, https://www.nytimes.com/2016/06/21/nyregion/nypd-arrests.html.

118. Harcourt, *The Counterrevolution*, 8.

119. Erin Siodmak, "'Homosexuals Are Revolting': Stonewall, 1969," in *Revolting New York: How 400 Years of Riot, Rebellion, Uprising, and Revolution Shaped a City*, ed. Neil Smith et al., vol. 38 (Athens: University of Georgia Press, 2018), 201.

120. David Carter, *Stonewall: The Riots That Sparked the Gay Revolution* (London: Macmillan, 2004).

121. David Dalton, "Policing Outlawed Desire: 'Homocriminality' in Beat Spaces in Australia," *Law and Critique* 18, no. 3 (January 2007): 375–405.

122. Emma K. Russell, "Carceral Pride: The Fusion of Police Imagery with LGBTI Rights," *Feminist Legal Studies* 26, no. 3 (2018): 331–50.

123. Joey L. Mogul, Andrea J. Ritchie, and Kay Whitlock, *Queer (In)Justice: The Criminalization of LGBT People in the United States*, vol. 5 (Boston: Beacon Press, 2011); International Association of Chiefs of Police, "Addressing Sexual Offenses and Misconduct by Law Enforcement Officers: An Executive Guide," 2011, https://www.theiacp.org/resources/document/addressing-sexual-offenses-and-misconduct-by-law-enforcement-executive-guide; *Stonewalled: Police Abuse and Misconduct against LGBT People in the United States* (Amnesty International, 2005), https://www.amnesty.org/en/documents/amr51/122/2005/en.

124. Russell, "Carceral Pride," 335.

125. Phillip Lyons Jr., Michael J. DeValve, and Randall L. Garner, "Texas Police Chiefs' Attitudes toward Gay and Lesbian Police Officers," *Police Quarterly* 11, no. 1 (2008): 102–17.

126. Kristian Williams, "Other Side of the COIN," 81–117.

127. President's Task Force on 21st Century Policing, "Final Report," 11–12.

128. Correia and Wall, *Police: A Field Guide*, 97.

129. Toby Beauchamp, "In Security," *GLQ: A Journal of Lesbian and Gay Studies* 24, no. 1 (2018): 13–17, 13.

130. Jasbir K. Puar, *Terrorist Assemblages: Homonationalism in Queer Times* (Durham, N.C.: Duke University Press, 2017).

131. Ileana Najarro, "Black Lives Matter Withdraws from S.F.'s Pride Parade Due to Increased Police Presence," *Los Angeles Times*, June 25, 2016, https://www.latimes.com/local/lanow/la-me-ln-black-lives-matter-sf-pride-20160624-snap-story.html.

132. Tim Fitzsimons, "Police at Pride? Gay Cops, LGBTQ Activists Struggle

to See Eye-to-Eye," NBC News, June 23, 2018, https://www.nbcnews.com /feature/nbc-out/police-pride-gay-cops-lgbtq-activists-struggle-see-eye -eye-n886031.

133. Gilman-Opalsky, *Specters of Revolt*, 221–22.

134. Charles Bukowski, *The Genius of the Crowd* ([Cleveland]: 7 Flowers Press, 1965).

5. The Unthinkable World

1. Adrian Carrasquillo, "81 Percent of NYPD's Social Distancing Summonses Were Issued to Blacks and Latinos: 'It's the New Stop and Frisk,'" *Newsweek*, May 8, 2020, https://www.newsweek.com/81-percent-nypds-social -distancing-summonses-were-issued-blacks-latinos-its-new-stop-frisk-1502841.

2. Joshua Kaplan and Benjamin Hardy, "Early Data Shows Black People Are Being Disproportionately Arrested in Ohio for Social Distancing Violations," Cleveland Scene, May 8, 2020, https://www.clevescene.com/scene-and-heard /archives/2020/05/11/early-data-shows-black-people-are-being- disproportionally-arrested-in-ohio-for-social-distancing-violations.

3. Paricia Madej, "After a Viral Video Shows a Man Being Dragged off a Bus, SEPTA Reverses Its Coronavirus Face Mask Requirement," *Philadelphia Inquirer*, April 10, 2020, https://www.inquirer.com/transportation/septa-face -masks-requirement-coronavirus-20200410.html.

4. Kim Bell, "St. Louis Reports Crime Drop in Early Weeks of Stay-at -Home Order," *St. Louis Post-Dispatch*, April 17, 2020, https://www.stltoday.com /news/local/crime-and-courts/st-louis-reports-crime-drop-in-early-weeks-of-stay -at-home-order/article_ca80c7b8-65c3-5d9b-9a95-06e6a69fdb74.html.

5. Bell, "St. Louis Reports Crime Drop."

6. Larry Smith (@ljs3663), "maybe what police departments fear most during this pandemic is people realizing cops making thousands of BS arrests serves no actual purpose other than punishing already marginalized citizens and that when those arrests stop, life might actually improve," March 26, 2020.

7. Marvin D. Krohn, "Inequality, Unemployment and Crime: A Cross-national Analysis," *Sociological Quarterly* 17, no. 3 (Summer 1976): 303–13.

8. Kristine Phillips, "Police Agencies Are Using Drones to Enforce Stay-at-Home Orders, Raising Concerns among Civil Rights Groups," *USA Today*, May 3, 2020, https://www.usatoday.com/story/news/politics/2020/05/03/coronavirus -police-use-drones-enforcement-privacy-concerns/3059073001.

9. "Flint Airport to Be First in Country to Use 'Smart Mask' for Thermal Scanning and Facial Recognition," Fox 2 Detroit, August 28, 2020, https://www .fox2detroit.com/news/flint-airport-to-be-first-in-country-to-use-smart-mask -for-thermal-scanning-and-facial-recognition.

10. William Santana Li, "Robots Are Immune," LinkedIn, March 19, 2020, https://www.linkedin.com/pulse/robots-immune-william-santana-li.

11. Shashank Bengali, "Singapore Enforces Social Distancing—with a Robot Dog," *Los Angeles Times*, May 14, 2020, https://www.latimes.com/world-nation /story/2020-05-13/coronavirus-singapores-robot-dog-enforces-social-distancing.

12. "Creating the Coronopticon: Countries Are Using Apps and Data Net-

works to Keep Tabs on the Pandemic," *Economist*, March 26, 2020, https://
www.economist.com/briefing/2020/03/26/countries-are-using-apps-and-data
-networks-to-keep-tabs-on-the-pandemic.

13. Department of Justice's Coronavirus Emergency Supplemental Funding
Program, Congressional Research Service, April 16, 2020, https://crsreports
.congress.gov/product/pdf/IF/IF11508. I made this point in *Meth Wars* regarding the stimulus to "rural law enforcement" following the 2009 crash.
Linnemann, *Meth Wars*.

14. Lee Fang, "Federal Government Buys Riot Gear, Increases Security Funding, Citing Coronavirus Pandemic," Intercept, May 17, 2020, https://theintercept
.com/2020/05/17/veterans-affairs-coronavirus-security-police.

15. While it conspicuously did not include the United States or the United
Kingdom, the United Nations issued a warning to member states against vio-
lently cracking down on dissent, even in conditions of exception or emergency.
"UN Raises Alarm about Police Brutality in COVID-19 Lockdowns," Al Jazeera,
April 28, 2020, https://www.aljazeera.com/news/2020/04/raises-alarm-police
-brutality-covid-19-lockdowns-200428070216771.html.

16. Wall, "Ordinary Emergency," 1122–39, 1132.

17. Iida Käyhkö and Laura Schack, "Policing the Pandemic: 'Security' for
Whom?" *ROAR*, April 2, 2020, https://roarmag.org/essays/policing-the-pandemic
-security-for-whomed.

18. Of course, police and emergency go hand in hand—or, rather, iron fist in
velvet glove. As it turns out, so do police and pandemic. In England in 1349, the
first vagrancy laws and their adjoining police powers were conjured in order to
raise a workforce from a population decimated by the Black Plague. William J.
Chambliss, "A Sociological Analysis of the Law of Vagrancy," *Social Problems*
12, no. 1 (Summer 1964): 67.

19. "Governor Tim Walz Orders Moment of Silence for George Floyd," Office
of Governor Tim Walz and Lt. Governor Peggy Flanagan, June 9, 2020, https://
mn.gov/governor/news/?id=1055-435187. Emphasis mine.

20. Lucas Manfredi, "Trump Says 'Horror' of George Floyd's Death Unfairly Stereotypes Police Officers," Fox Business, June 11, 2020, https://www
.foxbusiness.com/lifestyle/trump-says-horror-of-george-floyds-death-is
-unfairly-stereotyping-police-officers. Emphasis mine.

21. Amanda M. Petersen, "Beyond Bad Apples, toward Black Life: A Re-
reading of the Implicit Bias Research," *Theoretical Criminology* 23, no. 4 (2019):
491–508.

22. Nia-Malika Henderson, "Peter King Blames Asthma and Obesity for
Eric Garner's Death. That's a Problem for the GOP," *Washington Post*, December 4, 2014, https://www.washingtonpost.com/news/the-fix/wp/2014/12/04
/peter-king-blames-asthma-and-obesity-for-eric-garners-death-this-is-a
-problem-for-the-gop.

23. "Medical Examiner: No Evidence George Floyd Died of Strangulation,"
MyStateline.com, May 29, 2020, https://www.mystateline.com/news/national
/medical-examiner-no-evidence-george-floyd-died-of-strangulation.

24. Amy Forliti and Jeff Baenen, "Four Minneapolis Police Officers Fired

after Death of Black Man," Associated Press, *Record-Journal Meriden* (Connecticut), Wednesday, May 27, 2020, B3.

25. John Dickerson, "Excited Delirium: The Controversial Syndrome That Can Be Used to Protect Police from Misconduct Charges," December 13, 2020, CBS News, https://www.cbsnews.com/news/excited-delirium-police-custody-george-floyd-60-minutes-2020-12-13.

26. Clute, *Darkening Garden*, 12.

27. Catherine Damman, "Interview: Saidiya Hartman on Insurgent Histories and the Abolitionist Imaginary," *Artforum*, July 14, 2020, https://www.artforum.com/interviews/saidiya-hartman-83579.

28. Hugh Muir, "Cornel West: 'George Floyd's Public Lynching Pulled the Cover off Who We Really Are,'" *Guardian*, October 19, 2020, https://www.theguardian.com/us-news/2020/oct/19/cornel-west-george-floyds-public-lynching-pulled-the-cover-off-who-we-really-are.

29. Calder Williams, *Combined and Uneven Apocalypse*, 226.

30. It is worth noting that the cops who murdered Elijah McClain and those who managed to peaceably arrest James Holmes after he opened fire in a movie theater, killing twelve people and wounding seventy more, worked for the same department.

31. Mark Fisher, "Autonomy in the UK," in *K-Punk: The Collected and Unpublished Writings of Mark Fisher* (London: Watkins Media Limited, 2018), 385–89.

32. Jordan Culver, "Trump Says Violent Minneapolis Protests Dishonor George Floyd's Memory, Twitter Labels 'Shooting' Tweet as 'Glorifying Violence,'" *USA Today*, May 29, 2020, https://www.usatoday.com/story/news/politics/2020/05/28/george-floyd-donald-trump-twitter-jacob-frey-thugs/5281374002.

33. Liz Navratil, Anna Boone, and James Shiffer, "The Siege, Evacuation and Destruction of a Minneapolis Police Station," *Star Tribune*, August 11, 2020, https://www.startribune.com/minneapolis-third-precinct-george-floyd-emails-public-records-reveal-what-happened-before-abandoned-mayor-frey/566290701.

34. WCCO-TV Staff, "Alleged 'Boogaloo Bois' Member Who Traveled to Minneapolis during Unrest Pleads Guilty to Terrorism Charge," CBS Minnesota, December 16, 2020, https://minnesota.cbslocal.com/2020/12/16/alleged-boogaloo-bois-member-who-traveled-to-minnesota-during-unrest-pleads-guilty-to-terrorism-charge.

35. Stewart Hoover, "Myth 'Today': Reading Religion into Research on Mediated Cultural Politics," *International Journal of Communication* 14 (2020): 25.

36. Stefene Russell, "The McCloskeys' Restored Midwestern Palazzo," *St. Louis Magazine*, August 16, 2018, https://www.stlmag.com/design/a-decades-long-renovation-returns-a-midwestern-palazzo-to-it.

37. Todd Miller, *Empire of Borders: The Expansion of the US Border around the World* (London: Verso Books, 2019), 4.

38. "Statement on CBP Response in Portland, Oregon," U.S. Customs and Border Patrol, July 17, 2020, https://www.cbp.gov/newsroom/speeches-and-statements/statement-cbp-response-portland-oregon.

39. Katie Shepherd and Mark Berman, "'It Was Like Being Preyed Upon': Portland Protesters Say Federal Officials in Unmarked Vans Are Detaining Them," *Washington Post*, July 17, 2020, https://www.washingtonpost.com/nation /2020/07/17/portland-protests-federal-arrests.

40. Jason Koebler, "The Police Are Gaslighting Us," Vice, June 5, 2020, https://www.vice.com/en_us/article/n7wnkz/the-police-are-gaslighting-us.

41. Yonat Shimron, "Trump Tweeted about Martin Gugino. His Friends Say He Is a Catholic Peace Activist, Not an 'Antifa Provocateur,'" *Washington Post*, June 9, 2020, https://www.washingtonpost.com/religion/2020/06/09/trump -tweeted-about-martin-gugino-his-friends-say-he-is-catholic-peace-activist-not -an-antifa-provocateur.

42. Christina Morales, "What We Know about the Shooting of Jacob Blake," *New York Times*, November 16, 2021, https://www.nytimes.com/article/jacob -blake-shooting-kenosha.html.

43. Tony Evers (@GovEvers), "We are assessing the damage to state property and will be increasing the presence of the Wisconsin National Guard to ensure individuals can exercise their right safely, protect state buildings and critical infrastructure, and support first responders and fire fighters," Twitter, August 25, 2020, 1:22 p.m., https://twitter.com/GovEvers/status/1298324999988682752.

44. Richie McGinnis (@RichieMcGinniss), "I interviewed the alleged shooter before the violence started. Full video coming soon," Twitter, August 26, 2020, 11:25 a.m., https://twitter.com/RichieMcGinniss/status/1298657958205820928.

45. Katie Shephard, "US Police and Public Officials Donated to Kyle Rittenhouse, Data Breach Reveals," April 21, 2021, *Guardian*, https://www .theguardian.com/us-news/2021/apr/16/us-police-officers-public-officials -crowdfunding-website-data-breach.

46. Niles Niemuth, "The Killing of Michael Reinoehl: A State Murder," World Socialist Web Site, September 7, 2020, https://www.wsws.org/en/articles /2020/09/07/rein-s07.html.

47. "Suspect in Portland Shooting Killed by Police during Arrest," Al Jazeera, September 4, 2020, https://www.aljazeera.com/news/2020/9/4/suspect -in-portland-shooting-killed-by-police-during-arrest.

48. "Statement by Attorney General William P. Barr on the Tracking Down of Fugitive Michael Forrest Reinoehl," Department of Justice, Office of Public Affairs, September 4, 2020, https://www.justice.gov/opa/pr/statement-attorney -general-william-p-barr-tracking-down-fugitive-michael-forest-reinoehl.

49. Geo Maher, *A World without Police: How Strong Communities Can Make Cops Obsolete* (London: Verso Books, 2022), 9.

50. Christopher F. Rufo, "No: A Dangerous New Idea Fails to Acknowledge the Problem of Evil," *Philadelphia Inquirer*, January 2, 2020, https://www.inquirer .com/opinion/commentary/police-abolish-criminal-justice-reform-20200102 .html.

51. Michelle Brown and Judah Schept, "New Abolition, Criminology and a Critical Carceral Studies," *Punishment & Society* 19, no. 4 (October 2017), 440–62.

52. George Jackson, *Blood in my Eye* (San Francisco: Black Classic Press, 1990), 54.

53. D. Watkins, "No, Obama, We Do Mean 'Defund the Police': It's Not a Snappy Slogan, It's a Demand for Justice," Slate, December 13, 2020, https://www.salon.com/2020/12/13/no-obama-we-do-mean-defund-the-police-its-not-a-snappy-slogan-its-a-demand-for-justice.

54. Jim Clyburn, interview by Jake Tapper, *State of the Union*, CNN, November 8, 2020, http://transcripts.cnn.com/TRANSCRIPTS/2011/08/sotu.01.html.

55. Marvin X [Marvin Jackmon], "Burn, Baby, Burn," *Soulbook* 1, no. 3 (Fall 1965), 153.

56. Mark Neocleous, *Critique of Security* (Edinburgh: Edinburgh University Press, 2008), 1.

57. Mariame Kaba and John Duda, "Towards the Horizon of Abolition: A Conversation with Mariame Kaba," Next System Project, November 9, 2017, https://thenextsystem.org/learn/stories/towards-horizon-abolition-conversation-mariame-kaba.

58. Across the country, the movement to end police violence seized the moment. In Los Angeles, city administrators cut 150 million of the LAPD's $1.5 billion annual budget. San Francisco, Denver, Austin, and Minneapolis imposed cuts ranging from 5 to 20 percent. In consultation with abolitionist Alex Vitale, Harris County, Texas, which includes much of the Houston metroplex, developed plans to replace police with specialized care workers on all mental health crisis calls. States from California to Maine shuttered school resource officer programs. Where some saw enormous victories, others saw budgetary sleights of hand. Bending to the moment, or perhaps cashing in, Bill de Blasio promised, among other things, to cut upwards of $1 billion of the NYPD's astounding $88.2 billion budget. But when met with the resistance from the NYPD's powerful union, the mayor was unable to keep his promises except to move the NYPD crossing-guard program to another agency and to "cut down" on overtime.

59. Yoav Gonen and Eileen Grench, "Five Days without Cops: Could Brooklyn Policing Experiment be a 'Model for the Future'?," the City, January 3, 2021, https://www.thecity.nyc/2021/1/3/22211709/nypd-cops-brooklyn-brownsville-experiment-defund-police.

60. Meghan McDowell, "Insurgent Safety: Theorizing Alternatives to State Protection," *Theoretical Criminology* 23, no. 1 (August 2019), 43–59, 52.

61. Stanislav Vysotsky, "The Anarchy Police: Militant Anti-Fascism as Alternative Policing Practice," *Critical Criminology* 23, no. 3 (September 2015), 235–53.

62. Travis Linnemann and Bill McClanahan, "From 'Filth' and 'Insanity' to 'Peaceful Moral Watchdogs': Police, News Media, and the Gang Label," *Crime, Media, Culture* 13, no. 3 (2017): 295–313.

63. Becca Savransky, "How CHAZ Became CHOP: Seattle's Police-Free Zone," seattlepi.com, June 15, 2020, https://www.seattlepi.com/seattlenews/article/What-is-CHOP-the-zone-in-Seattle-formed-by-15341281.php.

64. "Raz Simone Ejects Protestors by Force for Graffiti on Wall's [sic]," Vigi-

lance Media, June 11, 2020, YouTube video, 3:34, https://www.youtube.com/watch?v=7o7Dx1RGN20.

65. Mikael Thalen, "Seattle Protesters Set Up a Barricaded 'Cop-Free Zone,'" *Daily Dot*, June 9, 2020, https://www.dailydot.com/debug/seattle-autonomous-zone-protests.

66. Angela King, Case Martin, and Gil Aegerter, "1 Teen Dead, 1 Wounded in Shooting at Seattle's CHOP," KUOW Public Radio, June 29, 2020, https://www.kuow.org/stories/shooting-in-seattle-s-chop-leaves-one-man-dead-one-wounded.

67. Joshuah Bloom and Waldo E. Martin, *Black against Empire: The History and Politics of the Black Panther Party* (Oakland: University of California Press, 2016), 46–50.

68. Curtis Austin, *Up against the Wall: Violence in the Making and Unmaking of the Black Panther Party* (Fayetteville: University of Arkansas Press, 2006), 53.

69. Cle Sloan, dir., *Bastards of the Party* (Venice, Calif.: Fuqua Films, 2005).

70. Abby Goodnough, "Biden Calls Long Prison Sentence for Derek Chauvin 'Appropriate,'" *New York Times*, June 25, 2021, https://www.nytimes.com/2021/06/25/us/biden-calls-long-prison-sentence-for-derek-chauvin-appropriate.html.

71. James Baldwin, *The Fire Next Time* (New York: Vintage, 2013), 91.

INDEX

Page numbers in italic refer to illustrations.

ABC News, 158
abolitionists, 211, 212, 219
Abu-Jamal, Mumia, 122, 123
Academy of Criminal Justice Sciences
    (ACJS), 157
Act for Better Ordering Slaves (1690),
    12
activism: antipolice, 184; gun rights, 210
Adkins, Lou, 142
Adorno, Theodor, 46
Affleck, Casey, 39
Afropessimists, 202
Agamben, Giorgio, 36, 37, 176
Ailes, Roger, 88
Airwolf (TV series), 121, 122
Alien (O'Bannon), 121
All Cops Are Bastards (ACAB), 19
All Cops Are Monsters, 19–24
Allen, Chris, 39
Allen, Jeffrey, 39, 40
Amazing Spiderman, The (film), 96
American Medical Association, 201
American Psychiatric Association,
    200–201
American Sniper (film), 96
"Android and the Human, The" (Dick),
    116, 149, 153
androidization, 116, 117, 127, 128,
    140, 142, 150
androids, 140, 144, 150, 243n54
Anker, Elisabeth, 77
annihilation, as condition, 103–7
Anthropocene, 66
anti-Blackness, 12, 23, 185

Antifa, 206, 210, 252n87
antihomophobia, 190, 192
antiviolence workers, 215
anxiety, 59, 62, 163–65
apocalypse, 23–24, 57, 82, 106, 107,
    195, 232n57
apocalypticism, 57, 103, 105, 106–7
Arbery, Ahmaud, 203
Aristotle, 164
Arradondo, Medaria, 204
Artaud, Antonin, 71
artificial intelligence, 109, 122, 136,
    253n87
Asimov, Isaac, 114, 130
ASPCA, 125
Assault on Precinct 13 (film), 182–84
Association of the United States
    Army, 110
Atwater, Lee, 88
automated license plate readers
    (ALPRs), 120
automaton, 123, *124*, 163
Axon Enterprise, Inc., 201
Ayer, David, 75, 92

Bacon, Francis, 71
bad cops, 33, 34–42, 58, 199
Badges without Borders (Schrader), 74
Badiou, Alain, 232n67
Bad Lieutenant (film), 33, 36
Bailey, F. Lee, 29
Baldwin, James, 16, 17, 118, 219;
    interview of, 19–20; storm of fire
    and blood and, 180

Balko, Radley, 139
Baltimore, 17, 96, 167, 168, 179
Bank of America, 171
Barker, Martin, 90
Barr, Bill, 27, 81, 82, 210, 211
Bataille, Georges, 36, 37, 45
Battle of Balaclava, 72
Battle of Thermopylae, 101
Bauman, Zygmunt, 69
Beame, Abraham, 80
Beast and the Sovereign, The (Derrida), 77
Beauchamp, Tony, 191
Becker, Ernest, 164
Behemoth (Hobbes), 38, 53, 165
Benjamin, Ruha, 244n63
Benjamin, Walter, 35, 151, 230n29; police power and, 34; violence and, 90
Bennett, Jane, 151, 152
Bennett, William, 83, 84, 238n68
Benson, Olivia, 26
Berardi, Franco "Bifo," 91
Berkeley, George, 232n67
Berkeley School of Criminology, 153
Bezos, Jeff, 177
Biden, Joe: COPS and, 218
BIE. *See* Black Identity Extremism
Bierce, Ambrose, 8
big data, analysis of, 119
BigDog, 115
bin Laden, Osama, 105
Bittner, Egon, 38
Black children, pacification of, 15
Black Identity Extremism (BIE), 181, 184
Black Lives Matter (BLM), 22–23, 84, 192, 204, 206; countering, 167, 168; criticism of, 169–70; rise of, 167–68
Black Mirror (TV series), 127, 152
Blackness, 12, 70
Black Panthers, 17, 19, 82, 129, 171, 172, 173, 179, 180, 183, 217, 219
Blacks, 15; stopping/questioning, 12
Blade Runner (film), 110, 128
Blake, Jacob, 207
Blanchfield, Patrick, 170

BLM. *See* Black Lives Matter
Bloody Register (anonymous), 28
Bloom, Beth, 162
Blue Lives Matter, 99, 167, 169; Rittenhouse and, 208; Twitter account of, *21*
Blue Thunder, 121–22, 132
bobbies, 12
Body Count (band), 156, 157
Boogaloo Bois, 204
Borough Park, 187, 254n117
BORTAC. *See* U.S. Border Patrol Tactical Unit
Boston Dynamics, 115, 127, 197
Bracamontes, Luis, 87–88
Bradbury, Ray, 149, 150, 151
Bradford, Emantic "EJ," Jr., 69, 70
Bras-Coupé, 224n23
Braudy, Leo, 38
Bright (TV series), 75
Brinsley, Ismaaiyl, 167, 169, 172
Bronson, Charles, 27
Brooks, Max, 177, 182
Broward Sheriff's Office, 162
Browder, Laura, 29, 228n93
Brown, Byron, 207
Brown, Charles Brockden, 28
Brown, Dave, 68
Brown, Michael, *21*, 206; death of, 9, 13, 69, 173
Brown, Michelle, 212
Brownsville Safety Alliance, 215
Brucato, Ben, 11
Buffett, Warren, 187
Bukowski, Charles, 193
"Bulletproof Mind" seminars, 92
"Bulletproof Warrior" seminars, 92, 93, 100, 160
Bundy, Ted, 6
Bureau of Labor Statistics, 161
Burke, Edmund, 165
Burns, Ed, 35
Busch, Adolphus, 205
Büscher-Ulbrich, Dennis, 178
Bush, George H. W., 27, 82, 119, 167; campaign of, 88; "Cop Killer" and, 157

Bush, George W., 110
Butler, Judith, 67
Butler, Samuel, 135
Byrne, Edward, 157, 167

Calder Williams, Evan, 23, 62, 106, 114; on *Mad Max* universe, 89; terror/horror and, 202
Calibre Press, 92, 93, 100
Callahan, "Dirty Harry," 27, 35, 91, 98, 128, 185; as white middle class protector, 26
Call of Cthulhu, The (Lovecraft), 18
Cameron, James, 110, 116, 127
Cannibal Cop, 5, 6, 7
Can't Stop, Won't Stop (Chang), 183
Cape Fear (film), 158
Čapek, Karel, 123, 126, 130
caper/capere, term, 26
capital: political, 192; self-valorization of, 178; social, 192; violence of, 107
capitalism, 11, 38, 57, 65, 132, 219; end of, 41; industrial, 10; racial, 12, 13, 127, 146, 224n18
Capitalocene, 66
Capitol Hill Autonomous Zone (CHAZ), 216–17
Captain America, 99
Carceral Capitalism (Wang), 131
Carlin, George, 62
Carpenter, John, 2, 3, 89, 182–84
Carranza, Margie, 158, 159
Carroll, Noël, 225n39, 225n43
Case for More Incarceration, The (Barr), 72
Castile, Philando, 17, 92, 161
Castle, Frank, 96
Center for Strategic and International Studies, 251n69
Center for the Study of Law and Society (UC Berkeley), 178
Centers for Disease Control, 177
Central Park jogger case, 84–85
Centurion Law Enforcement Ministry, 102
Cesnik, Sister Catherine, 30
challenge coins, 93, 96, *188*

Chamayou, Grégoire, 47, 48, 49, 224n21
Chambers, Robert W., 42
Chandler, Nahum, 23
Chandler, Raymond, 38
Chang, Jeff, 183
Chauvin, Derek, 199, 217, 218; criminality of, 200–201
Chicago Police Department, 179, 180
Childress, Erroll, 50, 56
Childs, Gary, 35
Cho, Seung-Hui, 91
Christensen, Loren, 100, 101, 160
Christianity, 45–46, 73, 210; dialectic of, 46, 47, 82
CIA, 206
City College of New York, 180
City of Quartz (Davis), 73
"City Wide Anti-Crime" unit, 93–94
civil disturbances, 119, 121, 133, 134, 171, 252n87
civil liberties, 86
civil peace, 40
civil rights movement, 16, 129, 173, 213
civilization, 14, 62, 63, 64, 72, 81, 95, 186, 212; battle for, 103; demise of, 76; rollback of, 213; savagery and, 105, 156; violence and, 95
civil war, 12, 95, 188
Clansman, The (Dixon), 98–99
Clapton, Eric, 157
Clarke, Arthur C., 151
Clarke, David, 168, 169
Cleary, Steve, 35
climate change, 64, 65, 112, 177
Climate Leviathan (Mann and Wainwright), 64
Clinton, Bill, 83, 86, 119, 157–58, 218
Clinton, Hillary: on predation, 84
Clover, Josh, 177, 182, 224n15, 253n91
Clute, John, 14, 23, 202
Clyburn, Jim, 213
Coal and Iron Police, 179
Cohle, Rustin, 42, 43, 46, 47, 50, 91, 96; Hart and, 48, 49, 54–55, 56; life trap of, 53; self and, 55–56;

subjectivity and, 51–52, 56; world-for-us and, 56

COIN, 189, 252n87; decapitation and, 253n87

COINTELPRO, 119, 180, 184, 252n87

Colangelo, Robert, 85

Coleman, Ronnie, 144

colonization, 128, 189

Comaroff, Jean and John, 37

Combined and Uneven Apocalypse (Calder Williams), 106

Comey, James, 165, 166, 167, 169–70, 171

Community Oriented Policing Services (COPS), 218

Concept of Mind, The (Ryle), 150

Concept of the Political, The (Schmitt), 67

Conflict Is Not Abuse (Schulman), 40

Connolly, William, 78

Connor, Bull, 12

Conspiracy against the Human Race, The (Ligotti), 18

Conway, Gerry, 98

Cooper Do-nuts, 190

Cop Hater (McBain), 155

cop haters, 155, 201

"Cop Killer" (Body Count), 156, 157, 158

cop killers, 156, 158

cops: Black, 26; conviction of, 217; female, 26; gay, 191; mechanical, 124; queer friendly, 192; riot, 140; robot, 126; street, 199; term, 25–26, 33; warrior, 147. *See also* bad cops; good cops

Cornelius, 101

Correia, David, 72, 163, 175, 191, 226n63; cop and, 25–26

Council for Public Safety, 80

counterinsurgency, 113, 131, 133, 134, 188, 190, 252n87; theory, 189

Counter Intelligence Program. *See* COINTELPRO

counterprotestors, 207–8

Counterrevolution, The (Harcourt), 189

Counterterrorism Division, 181

Covid-19, 195, 196

Crawford, 17

crime, 22, 24, 25, 157, 185, 193, 218; bills, 83–84; disorder and, 133; drug, 196; preventing, 41, 113, 122; property, 69; sex, 26, 41; true, 29–30; urban, 121; violent, 184–85, 196

Crime and the Imaginary of Disaster (Yar), 63

Crimean War, 72

CrimeCon, 29

Criminal (podcast), 29

criminal justice, 28, 83, 98, 149, 218, 224n17

Critical Response Command, 180

crowd, genius of, 192–93

Crowd, The (Le Bon), 252n87

Crutcher, Terrence, 17

Crutchfield, Ernest, II, 142

Cruz, Nikolas, 162

culture, 27, 28, 145, 160; consumer, 150; country and, 26; industries, 25; police, 31; pop, 75, 121, 133, 177

Cunningham, Nijah, 169

Curtis, Neal, 99

Custer, George Armstrong, 185

Customs and Border Protection, 111

cyberpunks, 128

"Cyborg Manifesto" (Haraway), 136

Cyril, Malkia, 192

Dahmer, Jeffrey, 6

Dallas Police Department, robots and, 111, 112

Danielson, Aaron J., 210

Darkfetishnet.com, 4

Dateline, 29

Davies, Will, 82

Davis, Mike, 61, 73, 112, 184, 195

Davison, Jon, 131–32

Dawn of the Dead (film), 88, 182

DEA. *See* Drug Enforcement Administration

Dean, Jodi: Occupy and, 250n65

DeAngelo, Joseph James, 6

death, 66; fear of, 161, 164; violent, 87
Death Wish (film), 27, 88, 98
de Becker, Gavin, 160–61
de Blasio, Bill, 207, 260n58
decapitation strategy, 252n87
Defense Advanced Research Projects
    Agency (DARPA), 115
dehumanization, 67, 116, 150, 177,
    243n54
Deleuze, Gilles, 151
demilitarization, police, 113, 134
Democrats, 87, 88, 213
demons, 8, 67, 69, 82
de Montaigne, Michel, 164
Denial of Death, The (Becker), 164
Dent, Floyd, 142, 147
de Rais, Gilles, 45, 46
Derrida, Jacques, 14, 77–78
destroyers, makers and, 13–15
determinism, 31, 133; technological,
    118, 134, 135
Detroit Free Press, headline from, *143*
Detroit Police Department, 142
deus mortalis, 71, 88, 102, 218
De-Valuing of America, The (Bennett),
    83
devil: as Enemy of All Mankind, 46;
    war on, 46
Dexter (TV series), 38
DHS. *See* U.S. Department of
    Homeland Security
Dialectic of Enlightenment (Adorno), 46
Diallo, Amadou, 94
Dick, Philip K., 116–17, 119, 120, 127,
    152–53, 206; androidization and,
    117, 128, 140, 142, 149; Bradbury
    and, 150; on human as instrument,
    141; language of, 149
Dickson, Byron, 166
Digidog, 197, *198*, 199
DiIulio, John, 83, 84
Dinello, Daniel, 114
Dirty Harry (film), 35, 36
disorder: barbarism of, 31; crime and,
    133; war on, 82
Divergent, 109, 129
Dixon, Thomas, Jr., 98–99

Do Androids Dream of Electric Sheep?,
    153
DOJ. *See* U.S. Department of Justice
Do Not Resist (film), 91, 93
Dopers in Uniform (Hoberman), 144
Dorner, Christopher, 158, 159
Doyle, Arthur Conan, 37
Dracula (film), 37
Dragnet (TV series), 35, 73, 74, 155
Dredd, Joseph: social ills and, 90–91
drones, 68, 112, 137, 199; policing,
    197; public safety, 111
Drug Enforcement Administration
    (DEA), 111, 157, 205, 252n87
Du Bois, W. E. B., 11
Dubber, Markus Dirk, 26
dystopia, 57, 59, 107, 109, 110, 111,
    114, 128

E. and M. Viney (publisher), 28
Eastwood, Clint, 26, 35, 96
Ecology of Fear (Davis), 61
economic problems, 41, 132, 178,
    225n46
Economist, 197
Edwards, Omar, 70
87th Precinct series, 155, 156
Elder Gods, 16, 219
Elysium (film), 112, 132, 178
emergencies, 215; ordinary, 68; per-
    petual, 93; police and, 257n18
Emergency Service Unit, 171, 198
End of Watch (film), 74
enemy, 66, 67, 72, 123, 191; imagina-
    tion of, 49
Enforcing Order (Fassin), 186
Engels, Friedrich, 95
English Civil War, 103
enmity, 66–71, 235n16
Epidemic Type Aftershock Sequences
    (ETAS), 120
Erewhon (Butler), 135
Escape from LA (film), 183
Escape from New York (Carpenter), 89,
    129, 183
Estes, Nick, 186
Eugene, Rudy, 175, 176

Everdeen, Katniss, 110

evil, 30, 37, 41, 44, 48, 74, 87, 89, 104, 116, 132, 141, 162, 177, 211, 212; battle with, 46; good and, 20, 34, 40, 54, 56, 67, 71, 93, 100, 103, 105

Executioner, The: Punisher and, 96

Facebook, 30, 62, 92

Fahrenheit 451 (Bradbury), 57, 150

Farrakhan, Louis, 184

fascism, 178; for liberals, 132–41

Fassin, Didier, 186

FBI, 4, 165, 179–80, 181, 205, 218; COINTELPRO and, 119; image of, 73

fear, 89, 165, 170, 171, 178, 193; dialectic of, 46; freedom from, 77; gift of, 160–63; total, 159, 160

Federal Aviation Administration, 111

Feigenbaum, Anna, 113, 146

Ferguson, 9, 13, 17, 96, 122, 127, 128, 129, 134, 174, 179

Ferguson, Andrew, 120

Ferrell, Jeff, 157

feudalism, 10, 179

Fiedler, Leslie, 28

Fields, Barbara, 70

Fields, Karen, 70

"Final Inspection, The" (poem), text of, 147–48

Fisher, Mark, 41, 65, 114; on annihilation, 106; capitalist realism and, 57, 132; on the Real, 203

fleeing felon rule, 68

Fleming, Peter, 109, 234n7

Flesh + Steel (documentary), 128

Floyd, George, 203, 207, 217, 218; murder of, 199, 200, 201, 202, 204, 216, 225n47

Floyd, Pretty Boy, 157

Forrest, Nathan Bedford, 12

"Fort Apache Reunion" banner, *186*

Fort Apache, the Bronx (film), 95, 183, 185, 186

Fort Surrender, 188, 204

Forty-First Precinct Station House, 95, 185

Four Futures (Frase), 112

Fox News, 168

Frankencops, 130, 146, 206

Frankenstein, 37, 132

Frankenstein (Shelley), 37, 114

Frase, Peter, 112, 113, 114, 126

Free Capitol Hill, 216

Frégier, Honoré-Antoine, 95

Frein, Eric, 166, 172

Freud, Sigmund, 236n49

Friday, Joe, 73

Friday the 13th (film), 115

Friedman, Ralph, 95, 185

Friends of the Rittenhouse Family, 208

Game of Thrones (TV series), 75, 88, 182

Gangster Disciples, 185

Garner, Eric, 22, 69, 200

Gates, Bill, 177

Gates, Daryl, 171, 193, 200

Gates, Rupert, 62

Gatto, Julia, 5

Gavaler, Chris, 98–99

Gay Officers Action League (GOAL), 192

Gene Compton's Cafeteria, 190

"Genius of the Crowd, The" (Bukowski), 193

George Floyd Justice in Policing Act, 218

Ghost in the Shell, 151

Gibson, Mel, 89

Gift of Fear, The (de Becker), 160

Gilman-Opalsky, Richard, 179, 193

Giuliani, Rudy, 167

Glass, Fred, 110, 114, 128

God, 30, 66–71; understanding of, 47; warriors and, 101

Goddard, Tariq, 1

Gonzales, Dominic, 142

good cops, 33, 36

Gorman, Herbert S., 44

Grace, Nancy, 29

Graeber, David, 195

Great Depression, 76, 197

Greenfield, Adam, 146
Green Line, The (podcast), 75
Greenwald, Glenn, 128
Grimes, Rick, 13–14, 88, 89
Grossman, David, 91, 93, 100, 160; on
    God/warriors, 101; Killology and,
    161
Guardian, 110, 112
Guattari, Félix, 151
Guevara, Ernesto Che, 118, 183
Gugino, Martin, 206–7

Hadden, Salley, 11, 224n23
Halberstam, Jack, 181
Hall, Steve, 58, 145, 229n2, 230n29
Halloween (film), 115
Hamm, Mark, 157
Hammer, Mike, 128
Hammett, Dashiell, 38
Hampton, Fred, 180, 252n87
Handmaid's Tale, The, 109
Hansberry, Lorraine, 16
Hantke, Steffen, 110
Haraway, Donna, 131, 136–37
Harcourt, Bernard, 189
Hardstark, Georgia, 30
Hardt, Michael, 181
Harman, Graham, 58
Harney, Stefano, 185
Harrelson, Woody, 39, 42, 68, 230n25
Harris, Alonzo, 39, 49
Harris, Eric, 91
Hart, Martin, 42, 43, 46, 232n62;
    Cohle and, 48, 49, 54–55, 56
Hartman, Saidiya, 202
Haunting of Hill House, The
    (Jackson), 1
Hawke, Ethan, 39
Hawks, Howard, 183
Hayes, Isaac, 183
Haymarket Square, 179
Hearst, Patty, 172
Heat (film), 171–72
Hegel, Georg W. F., 145, 146, 227n72
Heidegger, Martin, 135, 137, 140
helicopters, 119, 121, 122, 126
Hemingway, Ernest, 95

Henry A. Wallace Police Crime
    Database, 20
Heritage Foundation, 211
Hernandez, Emma, 158, 159
Heroes (Berardi), 91
Higher Loyalty, A (Comey), 170
High Plains Drifter (film), 89
#Him Too movement, 252n87
Hitler, Adolf, 120, 165, 252n87
Hobbes, Thomas, 31, 38, 59, 67, 71,
    77, 83, 164, 165; darkness and, 52;
    on death, 219; deus mortalis of, 88;
    Leviathan and, 39; on security, 91;
    social upheaval and, 103
Hoberman, John, 144
Holder, Eric, 68
Holliday, George, 116
Holmes, James, 258n30
Holmes, Stephen, 234n9
Holtzclaw, Daniel, 19
homo economicus, 117
homo homini lupus, 77, 89, 237n49
hooks, bell, 250n61
Hoover, J. Edgar, 73, 179–81, 252n87
Horkheimer, Max, 46
horror, 4, 165, 200, 201; central power
    of, 225n39; drama and, 42; terror
    and, 14, 202
horror films, 76, 88, 182
Horror of Philosophy (Thacker), 7
horror stories, 8; police, 24–32
Horton, Willie, 88
Hoyt, Jake, 39
humankind, evolution and, 55
human nature, Hobbesian vision of,
    211
human reason, limits of, 8
Hunger Games, 109, 110
Hunter, Evan, 155
Hussein, Saddam, 252n87
Husserl, Edmund, 135
Hutton, Bobby, 217

I Am Legend (Matheson), 89
"I Am Not Your Sheepdog. I Am the
    Wolf. And I Hunt Evil." (anony-
    mous), 103

Ice-T, 156, 158, 184
Ideal, Real and, 145
identification, 118, 119, 206, 253n87;
    evading, 252n87
identity, 169, 253n87; institutional,
    190; theft, 230n25
I'll Be Gone in the Dark (TV series), 29
inequality, 2, 59, 63, 132, 169, 212
Institute for New Economics, 63
International Association of Chiefs of
    Police, 165
In the Dust of This Planet (Thacker), 8
In the Heat of the Night (TV series), 43
Into the Kill Zone (Klinger), 175
Invisible Committee, The, 155
iron fist, 113, 118–23, 125–28
Iron Fist and the Velvet Glove, The
    (Platt et al.), 118, 119, 121, 133, 153;
    title page of, 153
Irving, Washington, 28
Isaacson, Johanna, 182
"I Shot the Sheriff" (Marley), 157–58

Jackson, George, 118, 213
Jackson, Samuel L., 130
Jackson, Shirley, 1, 3, 19, 23–24
Jameson, Fredric, 41
Jarvis, Brian, 49
Jaws (film), 121
Jenkins, Philip, 44, 45
Jim Crow, 12, 70
Jinx, The (TV series), 29
John Birch Society, 26, 168
Johnson, Adrian, 230n29
Johnson, Lyndon B., 178
Johnson, Marsha P., 190
Johnson, Micah, 111, 168
Johnson, Robert, 63
Johnson, Walter, 13
Johnston, Adrian, 145, 146, 229n2
Jones, Aphrodite, 29
Jones, Cuervo, 183
Jones, Darryl, 225n39
Jones, Dick, 132
Jones, James, 72
Jones, Van, 218
Judge Dredd, 90

justice: cosmic, 25; ideals/norms of, 67;
    street, 33. See also criminal justice

Kaba, Marianne, 214
Kansas City Police Department, 22
Kaplan, Robert, 129
Keaton, Michael, 138
Keepers, The (web series), 30
Keitel, Harvey, 33, 34
Kelley, Robin D. G., 11
Kelly, William K., 208
Kennedy, Robert, 16, 178
Kenosha, counterprotestors in, 207–8
Kenosha Guard, 208
Kersey, Paul, 98
Kidd, Captain, 28
killing machines, 122, 127, 138, 147
Killology Research Group, 92, 160,
    161
King, Martin Luther, Jr., 178
King, Neal, 26, 35
King, Peter: on Garner's death, 200
King, Rodney, 116, 156, 172
King, Stephen, 30, 151
King Kong, 39
Kipling, Rudyard, 72, 92
Kirk, John, 79
KKK. See Ku Klux Klan
Klebold, Dylan, 91
Klein, Ezra, 174
Klinger, David, 174, 175
Knight Rider (TV series), 122
Knightscope, 123, 125–26, 149, 197
"K-9" units, development of, 95
Koch, Ed, 187
Kotsko, Adam, 34, 36, 67, 73, 82, 87,
    91, 102, 235n32
Kraska, Peter, 134, 139
Krewson, Lyda, 197
Kristeva, Julia, 7
Ku Klux Klan (KKK), 12, 16, 70, 98,
    180
Kyle, Chris, 96, 99, 210; Punisher
    symbol and, 97–98

La Berge, Leigh Claire, 230n33
LA Confidential (film), 158

Lafayette Square, protest at, 205
LAPD. *See* Los Angeles Police
  Department
LASER. *See* Los Angeles Strategic
  Extraction and Restoration
Latour, Bruno, 136, 151
law enforcement, 25, 79, 80, 132, 134,
  137, 157; attack on, 168–69; future
  of, 131, 133; respect/support for, 82;
  trust and, 9–13; violence of, 87
law and order, 24, 133, 156, 186; liber-
  alism and, 116; restoring, 211
Law and Order (TV series), 26
Law and Order: Special Victims Unit
  (TV series), 41
Law Enforcement Today (website), 79,
  103
Laycock, Joseph, 44
LeBon, Gustave, 179, 252n87
Lefebvre, Henri, 59
Leonidas, Battle of Thermopylae and,
  101
Levchin, Max, 63
Leviathan, 39, 53, 218
Leviathan (Hobbes), 38, 70
Levitz, Eric, 65
liberalism, 6, 116, 165; freedom from
  fear and, 77; myths of, 78–79; state
  of nature and, 78
"Liberalism of Fear, The" (Shklar), 77
"Liberalism of Horror, The" (Anker),
  77
liberals, fascism for, 132–41
Ligotti, Thomas, 18, 19, 24, 42, 54,
  164, 219
Linebaugh, Peter, 181
Liu, Wenjian: death of, 167, 169
Lloyd, Chris: *Judge Dredd* and, 90
Locke, John, 68, 165
"Locked Room, The," 47–48
Loehmann, Timothy, 152
London Metropolitan Police Service,
  10
Lord of the Rings (Tolkien), 120
Los Angeles Police Department
  (LAPD), 15, 16, 26, 39, 116, 117,
  121, 151, 156, 158, 159, 172, 174,
184; Black Panther Party and, 171;
  brutality of, 213; drones and, 112;
  encounter with, 149–50; patrolling,
  217; predpol and, 119, 120; public
  image of, 73, 74; television dramas
  of, 73–75; thin blue line and, 72–73
Los Angeles riots, 72, 184
Los Angeles Strategic Extraction and
  Restoration (LASER), 120, 125
Los Angeles Times, 30, 72, 172
Lovecraft, Howard Phillips, 8, 17, 18,
  19, 24, 42, 44, 51, 57, 163, 219
Lovecraft Country (Ruff), 16
Lynch, Patrick, 22

MacDonald, Heather, 168–69
Mach, Jesse, 121
Machiavelli, 164
"Machine Gun Squad," 171
machines, 151; criminal justice and,
  149; rise of, 111–18
Mack, David, 39
Mad Max (film), 88, 89
Maher, Geo, 211
makers, destroyers and, 13–15
Making a Murderer, 29, 30
Manhattan Institute, 168, 211
Mankiewicz, John, 29
Mann, Geoff, 64
Manny's Blue Room, 69
Many-Headed Hydra, 181
Marcuse, Herbert, 150
Marjory Stoneman Douglas High
  School, shooting at, 162
Marley, Bob, 157–58
Marrow, Tracy Lauren. *See* Ice-T
Martin, Dennis R.: "Cop Killer" and,
  157
Marvel Comics, 96
Marvin X, 213
Marx, Karl, 95, 184
Mătăsăreanu, Emil, 171, 172
materialism, 57; metaphysical, 232n67;
  transcendental, 31, 118, 145, 147;
  vital, 118, 152
Matheson, Richard, 89
Mayberry RFD (TV series), 35

Maze Runner, The (film), 109
McBain, Ed, 155, 156, 166
McCarthy, Cormac, 13
McClain, Elijah, 203, 258n30
McCloskey, Mark, 205, 206, 210
McCloskey, Patricia, 205, 206, 210
McConaughey, Matthew, 42
McDonald, 17
McDowell, Meghan, 215
McFadden, Robert, 187
McGruff the Crime Dog, 131
McMartin preschool case, 44
McNulty, Jimmy, 34–35, 91, 99
McQueen, Alison, 103
Mead, Leonard, 149
media, 5, 167; consumption/effects of,
    74; online, 195
Megacities (video), 129
Mega-City One, 90
Mein Kampf (Hitler), 165
Melendez, William "Robocop," 142,
    143, 147, 148–49; moniker for, 144,
    149; police power and, 144; trans-
    formation of, 145, 146; violence/
    corruption of, 152
Melville, Herman, 28
Merica, Sgt. A., 79, 103
Merleau-Ponty, Maurice, 135
Mesoamerican Long Count (Mayan)
    calendar, 62
"Metalhead," 127
Miami-Dade County, 80
Miami-Dade Police Department,
    parody by, 80, *81*
Miami Zombie, 175, 176
Miéville, China, 19
militarization, 31, 138; police, 113,
    114, 117, 118, 127, 128, 129, 134,
    139, 144, 167
Miller, Todd: robocops and, 206
Miner, Michael, 131, 132
Minneapolis Police Department, 203
Minnesota National Guard, 204, 205
Minority Report, The (Dick), 120
misery, impact of, 141–42, 144–49
Mitchell, Don, 185
modernity, 24, 31, 38, 61, 212

Modern War Institute, 177
monsters, 16, 31–32, 40, 175, 192, 193,
    213; at the end, 50–54; detectives
    and, 38; fear of, 59; fighting, 20, 38,
    192; horror cinema, 19; hunt for, 49;
    police and, 38, 105, 122, 173, 207;
    real, 165–73; robotic, 116; time of,
    217–19
"Monsters, Inc.," 49
monsters with badges, 15–19, 154
Monstrous and the Dead, The
    (Neocleous), 165
Montoya, Malaquias: illustration by,
    153
morality, 16, 19, 28, 82, 157, 170
Moretti, Franco, 37, 38, 46
Moten, Fred, 185
MOVE, 122–23, 133
murder, 30, 40, 199, 201, 202, 204,
    216; convictions for, 217; mass, 125;
    police, 200
Murdoch, Rupert, 62
Murphy, Alex, 128, 130, 131, 132, 138,
    139, 140, 244n74; behavior of, 141;
    death of, 244n77
Murray, Charles, 83
Murray, Margaret, 44
music, popular, 158, 163
Muslims, 87, 180, 184, 191
Mussolini, Benito, 252n87
My Favorite Murder (podcast), 30

Nada, John, 2–3
nanorobotics, 151
National Association of Chiefs of
    Police, 157
National Border Patrol Council
    (NBPC), 75–76
National Commission on the Causes
    and Prevention of Violence, 178
National Crime Information Center
    (NCIC), 4, 118
nationalism, 37, 73, 161; ethno, 178;
    homo, 191
Native Americans, stopping/
    questioning, 12
Navy SEALs, 96, 105

NBC, 29, 122

NCIC. *See* National Crime Information Center

Negri, Antonio, 181

Neocleous, Mark, 33, 38, 46, 66, 67, 82, 91, 165, 170, 172, 177; on community policing, 113

neoliberalism, 82, 83, 87

Neoliberalism's Demons (Kotsko), 82, 235n32

Netflix, 29, 75, 127

Neumeier, Edward, 128, 133

Neville, Robert, 89

New Founding Fathers, 76

New York City, 80, 85, 189, 192; Covid-19 in, 196

New York Daily News, 5

New Yorker, 62, 89

New York National Guard, 207

New York/New Jersey Regional Fugitive Task Force, 96

New York Police Department (NYPD), 4, 22, 33, 70, 95, 127, 157, 162, 167, 171, 180, 185, 186, 188, 200, 207, 215; challenge coins and, 93, 96, *188*; commandos of, 93; crossing-guard program of, 260n58; Digidog and, 197, *198*; electronic war room of, 119; GOAL and, 192; Hasidic community and, 254n117; ideological regime of, 190; order maintenance and, 196; social order and, 187; Stonewall and, 190; Tactical Patrol Force, 190

New York Post, 5, 95

New York Southern District Court, 4

New York Times, 65, 80, 94, 118, 176, 187, 218

Newton, Huey P., 17, 183, 217

Night of the Living Dead (Romero), 181, 183

Nightsuns, 119

nihilism, 55, 56; capitalist, 65; Hobbesian, 219

1984 (Orwell), 57, 109

Norton, Dennett, 138, 139, 140

Now (The Invisible Committee), 155

Noys, Benjamin, 23–24, 40, 42

NWA, 156

NYPD. *See* New York Police Department

Obama, Barack, 9, 65, 83, 111, 191, 213; criticism of, 168; drone program and, 68; police and, 167

O'Bannon, Dan, 121

O'Brien, Paul, 46

Occupy, rise of, 250n65

OCP. *See* Omni Consumer Products

Officer Friendly, 138, 189, 191

Oldman, Gary, 138

Olympic Games, 200

Omni Consumer Products (OCP), 128, 130, 131, 132, 139

OmniCorp, 137, 138, 139, 140

On Combat (Grossman and Christensen), 100, 160

O'Neil, John, 35

order, 196; barbarism of, 31, 57; chaos and, 14

Orwell, George, 96, 153, 154

Osnos, Evan, 62, 63, 89

Other-Thing, 140

Outlaw, Danielle, 252n87

pacification, 113, 130, 134, 189, 192

Palantir Technologies, 120

pandemic, 61, 195, 196, 199, 257n18

Pantaleo, Daniel, 22

Paradise Lost (documentary), 45

Paris Commune, 179

Paris Review, Baldwin and, 19–20

Parker, William H., 61, 92, 171; influence of, 74; thin blue line and, 72–73

Parkland, shooting in, 162, 163

Patrick, Robert, *117*

Patriot Prayer, 210, 252n87

"Pedestrian, The" (Bradbury), 149, 150

Peel, Sir Robert, 10, 133

Pelosi, Nancy, 218

Pentagon, 129, 130; 1033 program of, 127, 167

Pérez, Rafael, 39

Peterson, Scot, 162

Petrie, Daniel, 183
Philadelphia Inquirer, 211
Philadelphia Police Department, 122, 133
Phillips, Larry, Jr., 171, 172
Philosophy of Horror (Carroll), 225n43
Pitt, Brad, 57
Pizzolatto, Nic, 42–43, 49, 58, 231n46
Place Called Dagon, The (Gorman), 44
Platt, Tony, 118, 153
Poe, Edgar Allan, 8, 28, 37
Polanyi, Michael, 136
police: absence/impotence of, 76; automated, 150; benevolence of, 105, 149; enemy of, 72; horrified, 154, 165; horror of, 53, 59, 163; humanizing, 166; limits/failings of, 66; misdeeds of, 195–96; monsters and, 38, 105, 122, 173, 207; natural, 34–35; on-duty deaths of, 161–62, 175; reform of, 15, 94, 134; security, 193; social order and, 80; trusting, 9; war and, 133; world without, 32, 211–17
Police: A Field Guide (Correia), 72
"Police and Ghetto, The" (Reddin), 15
police bill of rights, 212
"Police Bill" program, 15
Police Chief, Klinger and, 174
"Policeman Bill" program, 15
Police1 website, 142
Police Riots (Stark), 178
police story, 25, 29, 59, 68; ideology of, 54
police unions, 22, 75, 182, 212, 260n58
policing: aggressive, 142; benevolent/good, 149; community, 84, 113, 131, 191; dangers of, 166–67; martial drift of, 113, 150; predictive, 119, 120, 125; professional, 74; smart, 119
political collectivity, 177, 181
Political Realism in Apocalyptic Times (McQueen), 103
politics, 16, 19, 73, 110, 145, 164, 183; antisecurity, 233n84; of carnage,

86–87, 204; partisan, 83; reactionary, 74; retrenchment, 178; Schmittian, 170
Poppo, Ronald, 175–76
populism, 86; authoritarian, 29, 35
posthumanism, 57, 135
poverty, 86, 156; feminization of, 87; moral, 83
Powell, Kajieme, 173, 174
power, 67, 206, 212; emergency, 68, 199; police, 10, 11, 13, 25, 34, 70, 91, 114, 138, 144, 151, 152, 172, 213, 216; sovereign, 64, 109; state, 34; war, 113, 114
Powers of Horror (Kristeva), 7
Predator drones, 111, 137
predpol. *See* policing: predictive
President's Task Force on Twenty-First Century Policing, 9, 191
Pride parades, 190, 191, 192
private property, 10, 125, 157, 208
Professional Police Warriors, 101
Prometheus, postmodern, 128–32
Proud Boys, 252n87
Psychiatric Center for Research on Regressive Tendencies, 149
Puar, Jasbir: homonationalism and, 191
Public Information Division, 73
Pugliese, Joseph, 137
Pulse nightclub, 191
Punisher, 96, 105, 210; political correctness and, 98; vigilantism of, 99
Punisher skull, 97–98, 97, 99, 100
Purge, The (film), 78, 79, 80; law and order/police and, 76; liberalism and, 77
Purge Night, 76–77

quadcopters, 111, 197
queer people, 190; Pride and, 191; violence and, 192

racecraft, power of, 70
Racecraft (Fields and Fields), 70
racism, 37, 70, 84, 88, 156, 157, 161, 181, 219

Radcliffe, Ann, 14
Rader, Dennis, 6
Radio Police Automaton, 123, *124*
Rafael Ramos and Wenjian Liu National Blue Alert Act (2015), 167
Rafter, Nicole, 35, 36
Ramos, Rafael: death of, 167, 169
Rampart, 68
Rampart scandal, 39, 68
RAND Corporation, 113
Randolph, Edward, 175
rappers, 156, 158
Reagan, Ronald, 3, 74, 82, 110, 119, 128
Reaganomics, 128, 133
"Reagan Revolution," 82
Real, 42, 203, 230n29; apocalyptic, 204–8, 210–11; horror of, 202, 229n2; Ideal and, 145; Lacanian, 23, 227n72
realism, capitalist, 41, 57, 58, 132
Reaper, 137
Reddin, William, 15
Rediker, Marcus, 181
Red Squads, 179
Register of Voters, 16
Reid, Tiana, 169
Reign of Terror, 206
Reinoehl, Michael F., 210
Rekognition, 253n87
Remotec ANDROS Mark V-A1 bomb disposal robot, 111, 126
Return of the Living Dead, The (film), 121
revolt, 184, 193; power of, 186–87; specter of, 188–92
Revolutionary Suicide (Newton), 17
"Revolving Door" ads, 88
Rice, Tamir, 17, 123, 152
Rio Bravo (film), 183
riots, 169, 182, 184, 190, 203
Rise Above Movement, 252n87
Rise of Big Data Policing, The (Ferguson), 120
Rise of the Warrior Cop (Balko), 139
Rittenhouse, Kyle, 208, *209*
Rivera, Sylvia, 190

Road, The (McCarthy), 13
Roberson, Jemel, 69, 70
Robin, Corey, 164
RoboCop, 128, 129, 130, 131, 132, 133, 137, 138, 142, 151; depicting, 139, 141; weapons of, 144
RoboCop (film), 118, 123, 129, 132, 144; law and order and, 133; as satire, 128; social science fiction of, 138
robocops, 123, 129, 136, 140, 146
robo-dogs, 127, 197
robota, 126, 130, 243n54
robot adjuncts, 126
robots, 115, 197, *198*; autonomous security, 123; hand of, 118–23, 125–28; killer, 111, 112, 152; security, 126, 127, 149; term, 123; tools and, 136
Rockatansky, Max, 89
Rogin, Michael, 67, 82
Rojas, David, 26
Rolling Stone, 158
Romero, George, 181, 182
Roombas, 125, 126
Rose, Antwon, 152
Rosenfeld, Richard, 196
Rosfeld, Michael, 152
Rousseau, Jean-Jacques, 211
Rowlandson, Mary, 28
Ruff, Matt, 16
Rufo, Christopher, 211, 212–13, 219
rule of law, 63, 170, 213
R.U.R. (Čapek), 123
Russell, David, 42
Russell, Emma K., 190, 191, 192
Ryle, Gilbert, 150

Sabotage (TV series), 75
safety, 18, 81, 86, 144, 162, 163, 178, 179, 190, 192, 207, 214, 215
Saipov, Sayfullo, 127
Saltman, Kenneth, 144
Sammon, Paul, 244n74
Sanders, Bernie, 84
Sandy Hook Elementary, 125
San Francisco Pride Parade, 192
Satanic Panic, 44

satanism, 44, 45, 46, 47, 231n46
Savage Pastimes (Schechter), 28
savagery, 89, 185, 186; civilization and, 105, 156
Schachter, Max, 162
Schaefer, Gerard John, 6, 19
Schechter, Harold, 28
Scheider, Roy, 121
Schept, Judah, 212
Schmitt, Carl, 31, 47, 67, 77, 80; *deus mortalis* of, 88, 102; on state of nature/slaying, 70–71
Schrader, Stuart, 74, 134
Schulman, Sarah, 40
Schwarzenegger, Arnold, 115, 116, 144
Science and Invention, 123; mechanical cop from, *124*
science fiction, 114, 116; films, 110, 123; social, 112, 113, 126, 137, 138
Scott, Walter, 17, 159, 160
Seale, Bobby, 217
Seattle, protests in, 216
Seattle Police Department, 216
Second Amendment, 101
security, 24, 25, 71, 88, 91, 113, 180, 193, 198; appetite for, 214–15; liberalism and, 115; multinational, 128; national, 68; police and, 40; robotic, 126; security forces, 62, 69, 216–17
Seigel, Micol, 12
September 11th, 104, 164, 180
Serial (podcast), 29, 30
serial killers, 48–49
settler, siege and, 182–88
Sexton, Jared, 26, 227n82
SF Pride, 192
Sharkey, Noel, 110, 111
Sharrett, Christopher, 73
Shaw, David, 72
Shaw, Ian, 111
Sheepdog, 103, 104, 105
Shelley, Mary, 37, 114, 115, 118, 130, 132, 148
Shklar, Judith, 77, 164
Shonkwiler, Allison, 230n33
Shots in the Mirror (Rafter), 35
siege, settler and, 182–88

Silicon Valley, 63, 123
Simone, Raz, 216
Simpson, O. J., 119
Singh, Nikhil Pal, 225n34
Sister Souljah, 157
Sixty-Sixth Precinct, 187, 188; challenge coin for, *188*
Skolnick, Jerome, 178
Skunk Riot Control Copter, 126
Sky Knight program, 119
SLA. *See* Symbionese Liberation Army
Slager, Michael, 159–60
slave patrols, 12, 179, 224n23
slavery, 11, 69, 126, 211, 243n54
Smith, Adam, 219
Smith, Andy, 214
Smith, Larry, 161, 162
"Smoked Pork" (skit), 156
social body, 177; violence from, 212
social change, 107
social circumstances, 78, 86
social distancing, 196, 197, 199
Socialist Workers Party, 180
social life, 25, 69, 193
social media, 20, 185, 190, 199
social order, 7, 14, 19, 22, 24, 27, 30, 37, 46, 64, 77, 112, 132, 169, 177, 187; breakdown of, 85; capitalist, 189; Hobbesian vision of, 50, 211; liberal capitalist, 157; police and, 80; violence of, 109
social upheaval, 103, 110, 132
South Carolina Department of Corrections, 66
sovereign: anomic, 99; authority, 88–103; beast and, 77–78; violence of, 64
Sovereignty and Superheroes (Curtis), 99
Spanish–American War, 134
"Special Weapons Attack Team." *See* SWAT teams
Specters of Revolt (Gilman-Opalsky), 193
Spot (robot), 115, 197
Stapleton, Erin K., 56
Stark, Rodney, 178, 179
State of Grace (film), 36

state of nature, 70–71, 78, 89
Stay Sexy and Don't Get Murdered (Hardstark), 30
Stephens, Stacy, 125
Steven, Mark: vampire/monster dialectic and, 37
Stewart, Martha: prosecution of, 170
Stinson, Philip, 20
St. John's Church, Trump at, 205, 206
St. Louis Magazine, McCloskeys and, 205–6
St. Louis Police, 196
Stoker, Bram, 37
Stone, Roger, 88
Stonewall riots, 189, 190
Stop LAPD Spying Coalition, 112
S-Town (podcast), 29, 30
Street Crime Unit, 93, 94; coin of, 95
Street Hawk, 121, 122
Street Kings (film), 75
Street Survival Calibre seminars, 92
"Street Thunder," 183
Student Nonviolent Coordinating Committee, 180
Students for a Democratic Society, 180
subjectivity, 24, 56, 145, 146, 149, 150, 154, 165, 247n120; Cartesian, 14, 53; theory of, 51–52
supercops, 37
Superman, 99
superpredators, 84, 85
surveillance, 11, 12, 118, 119, 120, 121, 125, 199
Sussman, Irving, 187
SWAT teams, 96, 112, 129, 139, 140, 171, 173, 182
Symbionese Liberation Army (SLA), 171, 172, 173, 183

tactics, 29, 63, 129, 134, 216
Tamerlane, 237n49
TASER International, 201
Taylor, Andy, 131
Taylor, Breonna, 203
Team Knight Rider (TV series), 122
technology, 114, 122, 125, 129, 134,

136–37, 150; corruption and, 135; police, 31, 118; weapons, 234n16
Tennessee v. Garner, 68
"Termination Planet," 110
Terminator, 115–16, 127, 131, 147, 152
Terminator, The (film), 110, 115, 128
Terminator Planet, 111, 112, 114
Terminator 2 (film), 116, 151; still from, *117*
terror, 111, 134, 165, 173, 179, 205; horror and, 14, 202; international, 82, 96; police, 123
terror management theory, 164
Thacker, Eugene, 1, 7, 18, 19, 40, 43, 57, 65, 106, 114, 227n72; horror and, 8; ontology of, 219; world-for-us and, 13
theology, 73; political, 47, 71, 81, 103, 170, 235n32
Theriot, Joel, 50, 51
They Live (film), 2; still from, *3*
Thiel, Peter, 63, 120
thin blue line, 31, 47, 48, 71, 75, 97, 100, 105, 205; mythology of, 72; political theology of, 81, 103; protection of, 74, 158; rhetoric of, 72
Thin Blue Line, The (TV program), 73–74
Thin Blue Line flag, *209*, 210
thin green line, 75, 76
thin red line, 72
Third Precinct headquarters, march on, 204
Thompson, Shaneka, 167
Three Laws, 130
"365 Daily Devotions for Law Enforcement," 102
Thucydides, 164
Tiger King (film), 29
Time, 15
Todorov, Tzvetan, 230n27
To Live and Die in L.A. (film), 36
Tolkien, J. R. R., 120
"Tommy" (Kipling), 72
T-1000 Terminator, *117*, 151, 152
Total Recall (film), 121
Training Day (film), 39, 75

Triple 9 (film), 39
True Detective (TV series), 31, 42–45, 46, 48, 50, 54, 58, 231n37, 247n120
Trump, Donald, 27, 64, 65, 84, 207, 210; border wall and, 88; campaign advertisements of, 87–88; on Floyd's murder, 200; Hobbesian world-view of, 86–87; incitement by, 204; military/law enforcement and, 87; press conference by, 204–5; social circumstances and, 86; sovereign authority and, 88–103; street crimi-nals and, 98; thin blue line and, 205
Turner, Justin, 167
Turse, Nick, 110, 111, 112, 114, 129
Tuttle, Billy Lee, 46
Tuttle, Norman, 121
20/20 (TV show), 43
2012 (film), 61, 62, 76
Tyler, Tom R., 224n17

Undercommons, The (Harney and Moten), 185
United Farm Workers, 129, 170
Universal Adversary (Neocleous), 33, 46, 66, 82, 177
Unmasking Antifa Act (2018), 253n87
U.S. Bank, 82
U.S. Border Patrol, 75, 76, 182
U.S. Border Patrol Tactical Unit (BORTAC), 206
U.S. Department of Defense, 177
U.S. Department of Homeland Secu-rity (DHS), 98, 111, 252n87
U.S. Department of Justice (DOJ), 210, 218
U.S. Marshals, 184, 205, 210
U.S. Supreme Court, 162
Utopia of Rules, The (Graeber), 195
utopianism, 211, 212

Valle, Gilberto, 4; as "Cannibal Cop," 5, 6, 7
Vancouver Science Fiction Conven-tion, 116
vastation, 14, 163, 202

Verhoeven, Paul, 128, 244n77
Vibrant Matter (Bennett), 151
Vietnam War, 113, 121, 189
vigilantism, 96, 99, 203
violence, 12, 15, 25, 29, 30, 40, 59, 64, 67, 72, 79, 92, 96, 157, 164, 167, 173, 181, 182, 185, 188, 196, 199, 204, 216; administering, 63; admonish-ment against, 100; casual, 148, 202; cheap, 128; civilization and, 95; domestic, 41, 197; indiscriminate, 14, 89; inhuman/superhuman, 176; instigating, 204; knee-jerk, 159; legitimate, 10; lethal, 181; mecha-nistic, 146; monstrous, 212; police, 53, 69, 78, 90, 102, 107, 113, 151, 158, 175, 176–77, 179, 190, 193, 201, 212, 213, 214, 215, 217; racist, 146; righteous, 25, 93; sexual, 20; war and, 68
Violent Crime Control and Law En-forcement Act (1994), 83–84
Vitale, Alex, 260n58
Vollmer, August, 134
Vysotsky, Stanislav, 216

Wagner, Bryan, 224n23
Wagner, John, 90
Wainwright, Joel, 64
walking dead, fear of, 173–82
Walking Dead, The (TV series), 13, 88, 175
Wall, Tyler, 68, 72, 92, 163, 175, 191, 226n63; civilization/violence and, 95; cop and, 25–26; ordinary emer-gency and, 68; on thin blue line, 101, 236n35
Walters, John, 83, 84
Walz, Tim, 204
Wang, Jackie, 131, 132, 133
war, 66–71, 130, 178; Hobbesian, 83; ideological, 188; mythology of, 73; ontology of, 69, 71, 161; police and, 133; unconventional/asymmetrical, 158; violence and, 68
war on cops, 168–69

War on Cops, The (MacDonald), 168, 169
war on crime, 72
war on drugs, 72, 114, 129, 139
war on gangs, 114
War on Terror, 68, 72, 113
Warren, Calvin, 22, 23
warrior cops, 138, 146, 147
Warriors (film), 129
Washington, Denzel, 39
Washington Post, 253n87
Watts Rebellion, 61, 171, 179, 213
Webb, Jack, 73, 92
Webber, Brandon, 184–85
"We Can Remember It for You Wholesale" (Dick), 152–53
Weissman, Daniel, 146
Welcome to Fear City, 80
welfare queens, 82
welfare reform, 83
Weller, Peter, 131
West, Cornel, 202
West, Dominic, 34
West, Kanye, 62
West, Kim Kardashian, 62
Westmoreland, William, 110, 111
Whigham, Shea, 50
white supremacy, 13, 73
Williams, Kristian, 180
Wilson, Christopher P., 25, 29
Wilson, Darren, 9, 69, 173
Wilson, James Q., 77, 83

Winlow, Simon, 58, 146, 229n2, 230n29
Wisconsin Department of Justice, 207
Wisconsin National Guard, 259n43
Witch-Cult in Western Europe, The (Murray), 44
without the rule of law (WROL), 62
Wood, Allen, 100, 240n107
Wood, Lin, 208
Worden, Don, 35
world-for-us, 13, 14, 56, 57
world-in-itself, 13
World Health Organization, 201
World War Z (Brooks), 57, 182
world-without-police, 59
Worst Is Yet to Come, The (Fleming), 109

Yanez, Jeronimo, 92
Yar, Majid, 63–64
Yardley, Elizabeth, 30

Zapffe, Peter Wessel, 18, 54
Žižek, Slavoj, 40, 115, 128, 145, 232n62; burka bans and, 139–40; disavowal of, 226n50
zombie genre, 181, 182
zombie riot, 181, 182
zombies, 61, 75, 76–77, 88, 175, 177, 181, 250n61
zombification, 176, 177

TRAVIS LINNEMANN is associate professor of sociology at Kansas State University. He is the author of *Meth Wars: Police, Media, Power* and a coeditor of the journal *Crime, Media, Culture*.